The EDGAR ALLAN POE SCRAPBOOK

The EDGAR ALLAN POE SCRAPBOOK

Articles, essays, letters, anecdotes, illustrations, photographs and memorabilia about the legendary American genius

EDITED BY
PETER HAINING

Foreword by
ROBERT BLOCH

SCHOCKEN BOOKS • NEW YORK

For
VINCENT PRICE
who has helped
keep Poe
alive

Sir John Tenniel's illustration for 'The Raven' (1858)

ACKNOWLEDGEMENTS

The Editor and publishers are grateful to the following for providing material for this book: Robert Bloch, Edgar Allan Poe Museum and Miss Denise B. Bethel, National Film Archive, Ken Chapman, British Museum, London Library, New York Public Library, Irvine Development Corporation, Dick Institute, Kilmarnock, I. O. Evans, *Time* magazine, Ron Haydock, Ray Bradbury, *Radio Times* Hulton Picture Library, Scott Meredith Literary Agency for Ellery Queen and H. P. Lovecraft, Doubleday & Co Inc, Denis Gifford, Mystery Writers of America Inc, National Periodical Publications Inc, Warren Publishing Co, Marvel Comics and D.C. Comics.

First published by Schocken Books 1978

Copyright © 1977 by Peter Haining

Library of Congress Cataloging in Publication Data

Main entry under title:
The Edgar Allan Poe scrapbook.

1. Poe, Edgar Allan, 1809-1849—Miscellanea.
2. Authors, American—19th century—Biography—
Addresses, essays, lectures. I. Haining, Peter.

PS2631.E33 1978   818'.3'09 [B]   77-87863

Manufactured in the United States of America

You speak of 'an estimate of my life' – and, from what
I have already said, you will see that I have none to give.
I have been too deeply conscious of the mutability and
evanescence of temporal things to give any continuous
effort to anything – to be consistent in anything. My life has
been *whim* – impulse – passion – a longing for solitude – a
scorn of all things present, in an earnest desire for the
future –

EDGAR ALLAN POE, 1809–49

Robert Bloch (WALTER J. DAUGHERTY)

ROBERT BLOCH perhaps more than any other modern writer in the field of macabre fiction has inherited the mantle of Edgar Allan Poe for his consistently ingenious and entertainingly horrifying stories and novels. His most famous work remains *Psycho*, which Alfred Hitchcock made into a classic film, but his novels and short stories are also constantly being reprinted, translated and anthologised, and he has scripted numerous very successful horror films. He lives in Los Angeles.

FOREWORD

EVERY READER of fantasy or mystery fiction owes a debt of gratitude to Edgar Allan Poe. In my case that obligation is doubled, for I am both a reader and a writer of what Poe called *Tales of the Grotesque and Arabesque*.

From earliest childhood I was aware of the blackbound volumes of his work on my parents' bookshelves, and it was there that I made my first acquaintance with his poetry and prose.

At the age of eight, much of what I read was beyond my interest or comprehension. The essays on poetry, architecture and criticism seemed dull and filled with terminology which sent me scurrying to the dictionary; the point of many of his humorous efforts escaped me; I was bored by poems entitled 'To . . .'

But the cadences of 'The Raven' and 'The Bells' echoed endlessly in my ears, and 'The Conqueror Worm' burrowed into my brain – where it remains, feasting, until this very day.

Ladies named Berenice and Ligeia introduced me to the mysteries of love-in-death and death-in-love; I found a new home in the 'House of Usher', and in the geography of my mind the principal thoroughfare of Paris was always the rue Morgue. Poe opened a new window on the world: and through that window came chilling yet colourful glimpses of Red Death and Black Cats, Gold Bugs bearing a design of doom, and White Birds screaming *'Tekeli-li!'* in Antarctic seas. And there were sounds, too – the hissing of a descending pendulum, the beating of a hideous heart, the whispers of the dead M Valdemar and the shriek of the unfortunate Fortunato – *'For the love of God, Montresor!'*

Glimpses and sounds turned dreams to nightmares; nightmares which beckoned and guided my own faltering fancies when first I ventured into the realms of writing where Poe reigned.

Dr Tarr and Prof Fether provided the system which led me eventually to my story, 'A Home Away from Home', a film called *Asylum,* and a novel, *Night-World*. William Wilson undoubtedly peered over my shoulder as I wrote *Psycho*. And most certainly and consciously, Roderick Usher assisted at the birth of 'The Man Who Collected Poe' in which I deliberately incorporated paraphrases of his story as a pastiche tribute to a literary mentor. 'The Man Who Collected Poe' eventually served as the *finale* of one of my films, *Torture Garden* – a title not of my selection, inasmuch as it dealt with neither sadism nor horticulture.

'The Man Who Collected Poe' led, in turn, to an even closer linkage between us, for a Poe scholar, Thomas O. Mabbott, chanced to read my tale. In the course of research he had unearthed an unfinished manuscript of Poe's story, 'The Lighthouse'. He wrote to me about his discovery and asked if I might care to complete it. The challenge was irresistible. And thus it was that I became not only an *aficionado* of Poe, but his actual collaborator.

A strange feeling, this; to find myself *impersonating* the master of fantasy over a hundred years after his own capitulation to the Conqueror Worm. The task was not an easy one. Emulating Poe's style required intensive effort, and attempts to conform with his archaic and individualistic habits of punctuation complicated the endeavour. But the completed story apparently succeeded on at least one level – without my assistance no one seemed able to guess the exact point where Poe left off writing and I began. (A letter by Professor Mabbott about the story – reprinting what Poe wrote – and how it was discovered again appears on page 111. The reader interested in the completed story by Mr Bloch is referred to Sam Moskowitz's *The Man Who Called Himself Poe* (New York, 1969).)

In a curious way, the composition of this story discharged my personal debt to the work of Edgar Allan Poe: but it did not end my interest in the man himself. Over the years I continued to read the biographies and critiques dealing with this unique figure in the literature of the fantastic.

Elsewhere, in an essay dealing with another great fantasiste, H. P. Lovecraft, I commented on some of the contradictions in the concept of Poe's *persona*. Like Lovecraft, he seemed to have consciously contrived an eccentric image of himself; in effect, Edgar Allan Poe was a character of his own creation.

But the more I pondered, the more I realised that the public Poe had little in common with the man behind the myth and the life behind the legend. And it is the private Poe with whom I concern myself here.

The child, they say, is father to the man. In Poe's case the belief gains added credibility. For he never knew his own father, a bibulous actor who disappeared when Poe was scarcely nine months old. Moreover, Poe was only three when his actress mother died, and although the little orphan was adopted by the merchant John Allan he was never entirely comfortable in their father-son relationship, never completely at ease or at home.

He did not feel at home in England where he was sent to boarding school at the age of six, nor did he subsequently

THE EDGAR ALLAN POE SCRAPBOOK

Peter Cushing as 'The Man Who Collected Poe' from the film Torture Garden *based on Robert Bloch's story*

enjoy a sense of security upon returning to America. The growing estrangement with his stepfather marred and scarred his adolescence and he found no permanent refuge in the University of Virginia, the United States Army, or West Point.

What he did find was the solitary solace of scholarship, the boon companionship of books. In a world of rootless relationships and transient friendships, of economic instability occasioned by the vagaries of his stepfather's fortunes and personal attitudes, young Poe became his own man.

There is ample evidence that he was not a misanthrope by nature; he was a prepossessing youth, attractive to women, gregarious among his fellows. But his personal relationships seemed inevitably doomed to end in disaster. Drinking and gambling were the common pastimes of young gentlemen of his acquaintance, and he wasn't equipped to handle either.

But the hand that fumbled for a glass or trembled at the turning of a card became steady when it grasped a pen. Poe made the transition from reader to writer while still a schoolboy, and in early manhood he had already embarked on what was to prove a lifelong career.

Poet, essayist, short-story writer, journalist, critic, editor, publisher – he ran the gamut, although, in his case, running the gauntlet was a more apt description of his literary life. Acclaimed prize-winner one day, critically castigated the next; one month the proud author of a published book, and in the following a rejected contributor to obscure papers; this year the envied editor of a prestigious publication, then cast back into the ranks of penniless freelance scribblers; such is his sorry history.

Nor was his personal existence enduringly rewarding. His marriage to a thirteen-year-old girl ended in the agony of her long illness and early death; his abortive flirtations with a succession of older women brought no more success than his flirtation with fame.

These matters, together with the mystery of his still-disputed death – was he the victim of alcoholism or of organic illness? – combine to make of him a tragic figure.

But the private Poe was not a *figure*; he was a human being. A child who felt unwanted, who yearned for love and acceptance. A young man awkward and ill-at-ease in shabby clothing, whose courtly speech and manner could not disguise the genteel poverty which alienated him from his peers. A writer who had no niche in contemporary literature, who was grudgingly granted a fleeting notoriety but who never attained the critical acceptance and economic security he so desperately sought.

The private Edgar Allan Poe was just plain 'Eddie' to his wife and mother-in-law: a man who played the flute; who turned up his frayed cuffs when calling upon a publisher with a manuscript; a chronic worrier bedevilled by debt and domestic responsibilities. A man who, above all, lived in the shadow of death.

The death of his mother; of 'Helen', his maternal surrogate as a youth; the death of his stepmother and of his own wife: these were the mortal tragedies which haunted his days and drove into his poetry and prose.

It was the private Poe who poured his frustration and his fear into fictional form; the private Poe whose work formed a confession of failure and futility. At times he attempted to place a comic disguise upon the mask of tragedy, on occasion he succumbed to fantasies of revenge. Most frequently he sought to appear the objective narrator, the dispassionate critic, or the keen and coldly analytical observer embodied in his M Dupin – the first great cerebral detective.

It was the private man who became the conscious poseur, embroidering his conversation with pretentious erudition and dramatising his dreary days with fabrications concerning his antecedents, achievements and adventures. Drama played an important role throughout his life; the child of actors himself, he became an actor in manhood. His striking mannerisms and romantic melancholy of appearance were consciously contrived. Like his great contemporary, Charles Dickens, he turned eagerly to the public platform as an 'elocutionist', reading his own works.

It is in the private man that we can recognise our own human frailties: the personal vanities, the rankling sense of injustice, the hidden jealousies. All of us show a measure of these traits as common mortals, and Poe – an uncommon mortal we call genius – surely had more than his share.

How he must have envied Dickens his growing fame and fortune, even while acknowledging his right to such rewards! And surely he brooded over the triumphs of American rivals already established – Washington Irving, the socially prominent gentleman author, elevated to the post of an ambassador of the United States; James Fenimore Cooper, the commercially successful equivalent of today's best-selling novelist; even the critically celebrated horde of 'lady poetesses' whose names are now forgotten. How he must have dreamed, during all of his brief, unhappy lifetime – dreamed of recognition and renown and rich rewards!

Today reality has surpassed the dream. The name and fame of Edgar Allan Poe are secure at last.

But it is the public Poe whose work we praise, while our debt to the real man must now and forever remain unpaid – the sad and lonely man who, out of mortal misery, created immortal mystery.

Robert Bloch

THE EDGAR ALLAN POE SCRAPBOOK

From that mansion I fled aghast, into the storm
that was still abroad in all its wrath. . . .

Stephen Lawrence's superb illustration for Bloch's 'The Man Who Collected Poe' from *Famous Fantastic Mysteries,* **October 1951**

INTRODUCTION

ONE HUNDRED and fifty years ago – in June 1827 – a struggling, impoverished young American writer succeeded in getting his first book published. The edition consisted of less than fifty copies, of which only a handful were sold, yet that book and, more particularly, its author were to change the course of world literature in just over twenty years.

The book was a collection of poetry with the unprepossessing title *Tamerlane and Other Poems* and was stated simply on the title page to be the work of 'A Bostonian'. The eighteen-year-old author who concealed himself unsurely behind that pseudonym was to become the dark colossus of literature, the genius called Edgar Allan Poe.

Tamerlane was published by another young man named Calvin Thomas, a jobbing printer in Boston, and it may have been that he printed the book out of friendship for Poe – although it has been suggested that Poe himself financed the work. What is beyond dispute is that it had no distribution, no sales beyond those which Poe instigated among his friends, and that it received no attention whatever in the press.

Yet, in this slim volume which sold for $12\frac{1}{2}$ cents (and of which only seven copies are known to survive – one in the Library of Congress insured for $50,000) was the germ of Poe's genius. As one of his most important biographers, Arthur Hobson Quinn, has written in *Edgar Allan Poe: A Critical Biography* (Appleton-Century-Crofts, New York, 1941):

> Throughout his career, Poe was to develop in many forms the four themes of pride, love, beauty and death. They are all in his first poem, and to any student of his life, they are natural selections. He was a worshipper of beauty, his capacity for love was unusual, his pride was intense, and his preoccupation with death was constant.

Poe's was indeed a multiple talent, and the laurels which now rest on his memory are these:

> *He was perhaps the first true literary critic in America and a pioneer of 'exposure' journalism.*
>
> *He was 'The Father of Detective Fiction' and arguably 'The Father of Science Fiction'.*
>
> *And, most famously of all, he was a major influence on the short story form and the creator of the modern horror story.*

Poe's life and legend tower over literature, his fame assured and his work immortal. Yet he lived and died in penury, struggling against his own tortured soul and the indifference of the literary world in which he tried to make a modest living. Even after his death, his memory was heartlessly attacked by the man he had appointed his literary executor, and it took years of dedicated work on the part of admirers far from his homeland to ensure him his rightful place in world esteem.

Even today Poe remains something of an enigma. Despite many biographies, endless discussions about his work, and the most painstaking research, not a small proportion of his life and motivation lies

The only known full-length photograph of Poe – from a daguerreotype in the Lilly Library, Indiana University

shaded in mystery. That is perhaps appropriate, for Poe lived his forty short years of life in the shadows, known by few, cared for by even less. Yet he is now one of the very few classic authors whose work remains constantly in print in almost every language, and has proved the source of material for almost any medium of communication you care to mention.

These days, critics from one generation to the next heap praise on his name. Take Edmund Wilson, for example, on his critical faculties (writing in *New Republic* in 1926):

> Perhaps more than any other writer, French or English, of the first half of the century, he had thought seriously and written clearly about the methods and aims of literature. He had formulated a critical theory, and he had supplied brilliant specimens of its practice.

Or Professor C. A. Smith of the University of Virginia on Poe's effect on the short story (writing in 1916):

> The short story came from Poe's hands a new art form, not changed with a new content, but effectively equipped for a new service. In his equal exercise of executive, legislative and judicial authority, Poe standardised the short story.

And we need only turn to any of the leading authorities on detective fiction, science fiction and the macabre to find confirmation of his paramount importance in those genres too. Nor must we forget that he was also a brilliant poet, superb reviewer, masterful cryptographer and hoaxer *par excellence!*

Poe, then, is a man of many facets – as many facets, indeed, as his work. What the voluminous literature on this man still seems to lack (at least to my mind) is an examination of him, not from only one viewpoint, but from the many opinions, good, bad and indifferent, that have been taken towards him over the years. Hence *The Edgar Allan Poe Scrapbook* now in your hands, in which I have attempted to present this star of literature through a unique kaleidoscope of words and pictures. It could not be completely exhaustive, of course, but in its pages you will find not only the details of his life and work, but the opinions which coloured his thinking, the influences that shaped his work, and the forces which have helped make his legend.

The book, as you will see, is a collection of articles, essays, newspaper reports, commentaries, reviews, souvenirs, and engravings, pictures, drawings, photographs and even comic strips, all part of one hundred and fifty years of obsession with Poe. Taken from many and diverse sources, American, British, European – even Russian – the material augments rather than repeats the numerous biographies and studies about him which already exist. Here you will find essays by his friends and contemporaries reprinted for the first time in generations, commentaries by famous admirers over the years, and articles on his importance by men revered as *the* experts in their particular fields. Added to all this is a rich selection of rare and unusual illustrations.

It is all much more than poor Edgar might have expected to be accorded to his work when he died in 1849. Perhaps, though, he had suspected his destiny all along when he wrote in his first published story, 'Ms Found in a Bottle' (October 1833): 'It is evident that we are hurrying onwards to some exciting knowledge – some never-to-be-imparted secret, whose attainment is destruction.'

Poe certainly attained his self-destruction, but what a legacy he has left us! As his great admirer Walt Whitman has said in his essay 'Polarity' – and we can only echo:

> Edgar Poe is the furnace of self-knowledge. He is our elder brother, the beloved Solitary One, and we sorely grieve that we are not able to sail up the river of years and join him, all of us, a faithful band, now so numerous, him, our king, who at that time was deserted, in the dreadful moment of his great struggle. Peace, peace be with him, our fair angel of sorrow. He lives among us, in our most delicate sensations, in the mad outcries of our sorrow, in the sonorous rhythms of our songs, in rhythms final and initial...

Peter Haining
Birch Green, Essex
1977

Two admirers of Poe's work: Peter Cushing and Jack Palance in *Torture Garden*

MY AUTOBIOGRAPHY

EDGAR ALLAN POE

POE WROTE the following brief autobiography in 1841 for his literary 'agent' and executor, Rufus Griswold, for use in connection with the publication of his work. It shows a number of deliberate errors and inventions, no doubt employed in the great literary tradition of painting an intriguing portrait of the author for his public. A truer and more accurate picture of Poe's life will emerge through the pages of this book.

MEMO. Born January, 1811. Family one of the oldest and most respectable in Baltimore. Gen David Poe, my paternal grandfather, was a quartermaster-general, in the Maryland line, during the Revolution, and the intimate friend of Lafayette, who, during his visit to the US, called personally upon the Gen's widow, and tendered her his warmest acknowledgements for the services rendered him by her husband. His father, John Poe, married, in England, Jane, a daughter of Admiral James McBride, noted in British naval history, and claiming kindred with many of the most illustrious houses of Great Britain. My father and mother died within a few weeks of each other, of consumption, leaving me an orphan at two years of age. Mr John Allan, a very wealthy gentleman of Richmond, Va, took a fancy to me, and persuaded my grandfather, Gen Poe, to suffer him to adopt me. Was brought up in Mr A's family, and regarded always as his son and heir – he having no other children. In 1816 went with Mr A's family to G Britain – visited every portion of it – went to school for 5 years to the Rev Doctor Bransby, at Stoke Newington, then 4 miles from London. Returned to America in 1822. In 1825 went to the Jefferson University at Charlottesville, Va, where for 3 years I led a very dissipated life – the college at that period being shamefully dissolute. Dr Dunglison of Philadelphia, President. Took the first honours, however, and came home greatly in debt. Mr A refused to pay some of the debts of *honour*, and I ran away from home, without a dollar on a quixotic expedition to join the Greeks, then struggling for liberty. Failed in reaching Greece, but made my way to St Petersburg, in Russia. Got into many difficulties, but was extricated by the kindness of Mr H. Middleton, the American consul at St P. Came home safe in 1829, found Mrs A dead, and immediately went to West Point as a Cadet. In about 18 months afterwards Mr A married a second time (a Miss Patterson, a near relative of Gen Winfield Scott) – he being then 65 years of age. Mrs A and myself quarrelled, and he, siding with her, wrote me an angry letter, to which I replied in the same spirit. Soon

Illustration by unknown artist for 'The Black Cat'. From the first edition of Poe's works to contain pictures, published by Clarke Beeton, London, 1851

Portrait of Poe by unknown German artist, 1971

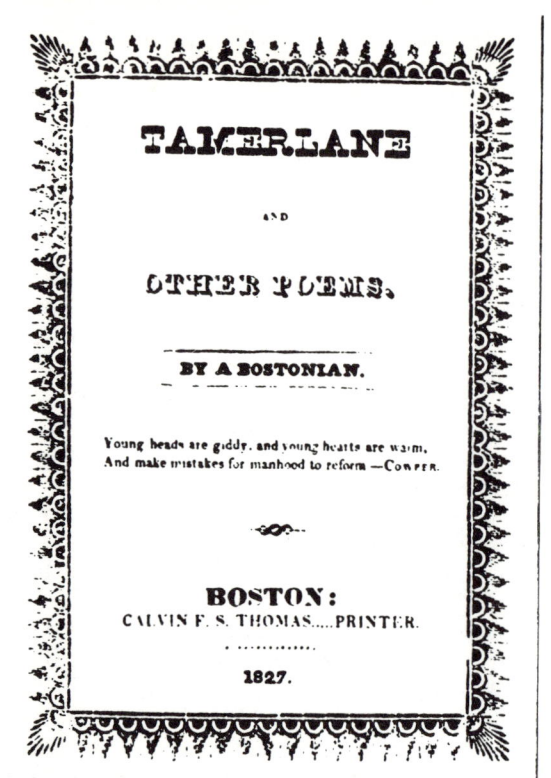

THE EDGAR ALLAN POE SCRAPBOOK

Front and back covers of Poe's first published book

A striking portrait of Poe by David Levine, 1967 (OPERA MUNDI)

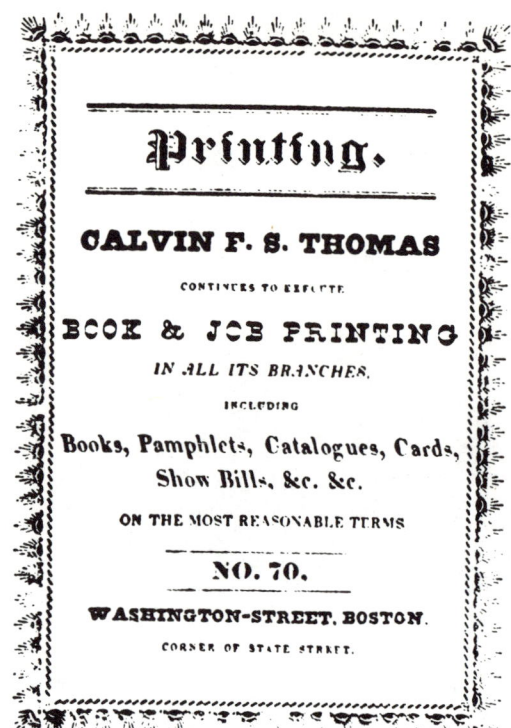

afterwards he died, having had a son by Mrs A, and, although leaving a vast property, bequeathed me nothing. The army does not suit a poor man – so I left W Point abruptly, and threw myself upon literature as a resource. I became first known to the literary world thus. A Baltimore weekly paper (*The Visiter*) offered two premiums – one for best prose story, one for best poem. The Committee awarded both to me, and took occasion to insert in the journal a card, signed by themselves, in which I was very highly flattered. The Committee were John P. Kennedy (author of *Horse-Shoe Robinson*), J. H. B. Latrobe and Dr I. H. Miller. Soon after this I was invited by Mr T. W. White, proprietor of the *South Lit Messenger*, to edit it. Afterwards wrote for *New York Review* at the invitation of Dr Hawks and Professor Henry, its proprietors. Lately have written articles continuously for two British journals whose names I am not permitted to mention. In my engagement with Burton, it was not my design to let my name appear – but he tricked me into it.

POE'S OWN SCRAPBOOK

LIKE SO many other literary and curious persons of his epoch, Poe kept a commonplace book. Into it went from time to time cullings from a thousand books, magazines and newspapers, copies of which came under his editorial eye. Nor was he by any means blind to the dusty shelves and remote alcoves of libraries public and private. He made the most of, and he improved such opportunities for browsing as *Pinakidia* and the later *Marginalia* show. These grains of gold sifted out of dust and refuse were not so valuable in themselves, but they provided an inexhaustible source upon which he drew for items of curious knowledge, for a parade of learning, and for quotations that temporarily lulled or alarmed even the learned. Above all, here was the store of ammunition for charges of plagiarism which he loved to ram home. From his careful gleaning over wide fields, there was scarcely any figure in poetry, or any idea, which Poe could not show had been used before. Often the charge was true; always it was plausible. In the great shallow

Engraving by James Godwin from an early illustrated edition of Tamerlane

lakes of American crudity, the well of erudition of the young Richmond critic seemed deep – even profound.

But there was something more to it than that. This habit of clipping and noting exercised a valuable curiosity. Out of a dead book or a banal news-sheet, Poe developed the habit of culling the one living incident, the pertinent fact, or the picturesque scene. He remembered it, and when the time came the shot was there, carefully greased and labelled, in the right locker. It was later always delivered with telling effect, and in a direction that associated it with the living thought of his time. That the French of obscure titles, the original sources, or the precise wording of quotations were sometimes garbled, is of importance only in the cemetery of the scholastic mind, for, by the living use of such matter, Poe frequently conferred upon it the only gleam of vitality which it ever possessed. Even in 1836, he stood out boldly and alone as the only arresting critic of contemporary literature in the United States.

HERVEY ALLEN
Israfel: The Life and Times of Edgar Allan Poe (1927)

THE DEATH OF EDGAR A. POE

'LUDWIG'

THE LEGEND of Edgar Allan Poe, his temperament, drunkenness and general instability, true or false, was already growing towards the end of his life, but received its most formidable impetus only two days after his death. The impetus took the form of an article in the *New York Daily Tribune* of 9 October 1849. It described the death of Poe and attacked his life and work in a manner both virulent and slanderous. Because the article was considered authoritative – and was much reprinted elsewhere – it undoubtedly affected all judgements of Poe for many years thereafter and played a major part in the growth of the 'legend' about him. The piece was signed with the name 'Ludwig', but it took only the simplest detective work to reveal the writer as none other than Dr Rufus Griswold, the Baptist minister and magazine editor, to whom Poe had entrusted his literary affairs! Griswold may well have been influenced in some of his 'facts' by the memo Poe had given him about his life, but why he should have turned so hard and callously on the man who had put his life work and affairs in his hands remains a puzzle to this day.

Reverend Rufus Griswold – the notorious 'Ludwig'

EDGAR ALLAN POE is dead. He died in Baltimore the day before yesterday. This announcement will startle many, *but few will be grieved by it*. The poet was well known personally or by reputation, in all this country; he had readers in England, and in several of the states of Continental Europe; *but he had few or no friends;* and the regrets for his death will be suggested principally by the consideration that in him literary art lost one of its most brilliant, but erratic, stars.

The family of Mr Poe, we learn from Griswold's *Poets and Poetry of America*, from which a considerable portion of the facts in this notice are derived, was one of the oldest and most respectable in Baltimore. David Poe, his paternal grandfather, was a quartermaster-general in the Maryland line during the Revolution, and the intimate friend of Lafayette, who during his last visit to the United States, called personally upon the general's widow, and tendered her acknowledgements for the services rendered to him by her husband. His great-grandfather, John Poe, married in England, Jane, a daughter of Admiral James McBride, noted in British naval history, and claiming kindred with some of the most illustrious English families. His father and mother – both of whom were in some way connected with the theatre, and lived as precariously as their more gifted, and more eminent son – died within a few weeks of each other, of consumption, leaving him an orphan at two years of age. Mr John Allan, a wealthy gentleman of Richmond, took a fancy to him, and persuaded his grandfather to suffer him to adopt him. He was brought up in Mr Allan's family; and as that gentleman had no other children, he was regarded as his son and heir. In 1816 he accompanied Mr and Mrs Allan to Great Britain, visited every portion of it, and afterward passed four or five years in a school kept at [Stoke] Newington, near London, by Rev Dr Bransby. He returned to America in 1822, and in 1825 went to the Jefferson University, at Charlottesville, in Virginia, where he led a very dissipated life, the manners of the College at that time being extremely dissolute. He took the first honours, however, and went home greatly in debt. Mr Allan refused to pay some of his debts of *honour*, and he hastily quitted the country on a quixotic expedition to join the Greeks, then struggling for liberty. He did not reach his original destination, however, but made his way to St Petersburg, in Russia, when he became involved in difficulties, from which he was extricated by the late Henry Middleton, the American Minister at that capital. He returned home in 1829, and immediately afterwards entered the Military Academy at West Point. In about eighteen months from that time, Mr Allan, who had lost his wife while Mr Poe was in Russia, married again. He was sixty-five years of age, and the lady was young; Poe quarrelled with her, and the veteran husband, taking the part of his wife, addressed him an angry letter, which was answered in the same spirit. He died soon after, leaving an infant son heir to his property, and bequeathing Poe nothing.

The army, in the opinion of the young poet, was not a place for a poor man; so he left West Point abruptly, and determined to maintain himself by authorship. He printed, in 1827, a small volume of poems, most of which were written in early youth. Some of these poems are quoted in a review by Margaret Fuller, in *The Tribune* in 1846, and are justly regarded as among the most wonderful exhibitions of the precocious developments of genius. They illustrated the character of his abilities, and justified his anticipations of success. For a considerable time, however, though he wrote readily and brilliantly, his contributions to the journals attracted little attention, and his hopes of gaining a livelihood by the profession of literature was nearly ended at length in sickness, poverty and despair.

But in 1831 [1833], the proprietor of a weekly gazette, in Baltimore, offered two premiums, one for the best story in prose, and the other for the best poem.

In due time Poe sent in two articles, and he waited anxiously for the decision. One of the Committee was the accomplished author of *Horse-Shoe Robinson*, John P. Kennedy, and his associates were scarcely less eminent than he for wit and critical sagacity. Such matters were usually disposed of in a very offhand way; committees to award literary prizes drink to the payer's health, in good wines, over the unexamined MSS, which they submit to the discretion of the publisher, with permission to use their names in such a way as to promote the publisher's advantage. So it would have been in this case, but that one of the Committee, taking up a small book, in such exquisite calligraphy as to seem like one of the finest issues of the press of Putnam, was tempted to read several pages, and being interested, he summonsed the attention of the company to the half dozen compositions in the volume. It was unanimously decided that the prizes should be paid to the first of geniuses who had written legibly. Not another MS was unfolded. Immediately the confidential envelope was opened, and the successful competitor was found to bear the scarcely known name of Poe.

The next day the publisher called to see Mr Kennedy, and gave him an account of the author that excited his curiosity and sympathy, and caused him to request that he should be brought to his office. Accordingly he was introduced; the prize money had not yet been paid, and he was in the costume in which he had answered the advertisement of his good fortune. Thin, and pale even to ghastliness, his whole appearance indicated sickness and the utmost destitution. A tattered frock-coat concealed the absence of a shirt, and the ruins of boots disclosed more than the want of stockings. But the eyes of the young man were luminous

The only known portrait of Elizabeth Arnold Poe, Edgar's mother

Poe's foster-parents, John and Frances Allan

with intelligence and feeling, and his voice and conversation, and manners, all won upon the lawyer's regard. Poe told his history, and his ambitions, and it was determined that he should not want means for a suitable appearance in society, nor opportunity for a just display of his abilities in literature. Mr Kennedy accompanied him to a clothing store, and purchased for him a respectable suit, with changes of linen, and sent him to a bath, from which he returned with the suddenly regained bearing of a gentleman.

The late Mr Thomas W. White had then recently established *The Southern Literary Messenger*, at Richmond and upon the warm recommendation of Mr Kennedy, Poe was engaged at a small salary – we believe of $500 a year – to be its editor. He entered upon his duties with letters full of expression of the warmest gratitude to his friends in Baltimore, who in five or six weeks were astonished to learn that with characteristic recklessness of consequence, he was hurriedly married to a girl as *poor as himself*. Poe continued in this situation for about a year and a half, in which he wrote many brilliant articles, and raised the *Messenger* to the first rank of literary periodicals.

He next removed to Philadelphia, to assist William E. Burton in the editorship of the *Gentleman's Magazine*, a miscellany that in 1840 was merged in *Graham's Magazine*. of which Poe became one of the principal writers, particularly in criticism, in which his papers attracted much attention by their careful and skilful analysis, and general caustic severity. At this period, however, he appeared to have been more ambitious of securing distinction in romantic fiction, and a collection of his compositions in this department, published in 1841, under the title of *Tales of the Grotesque and Arabesque*, established his reputation for ingenuity, imagination, and extraordinary power in tragical narration.

Near the end of 1844 Poe removed to New York, where he conducted for several months a literary miscellany called the *Broadway Journal*. In 1845 he published a volume of Tales in Wiley and Putnam's Library of American Books; and in the same series a collection of his poems. Besides these poems he was the author of 'Arthur Gordon Pym', a romance; 'Eureka', an essay on the spiritual and material universe; a work which he wishes to have 'judged as a poem'; and several extended series of papers in the periodicals, the most noteworthy of which are 'Marginalia', embracing opinions of books and authors; 'Secret Writing', 'Autography'; and 'Sketches of the Literati of New York'.

His wife died in 1847, at Fordham, near this city, and some of our readers will remember the paragraphs in the papers of the time, upon his destitute condition. We remember that Col Webb collected in a few moments fifty or sixty dollars for him at the Metropolitan Club; Mr Lewis, of Brooklyn, sent a similar sum from one of the courts, in which he was engaged when he saw the statement of the poet's poverty; and others illustrated in the same manner the effect of such an appeal to the popular heart.

Since that time Mr Poe had lived quietly, and with an income from his literary labours sufficient for his support. A few weeks ago he proceeded to Richmond, in Virginia, where he lectured upon the poetical character, etc; and it was understood by some of his correspondents here that he was this week to be married, most advantageously, to a lady of that city, a widow, to whom he had been previously engaged while a student in the University.

The character of Mr Poe we cannot attempt to describe in this very hastily written article. We can but allude to some of the more striking phases.

William Burton, owner-publisher of *Gentleman's Magazine*

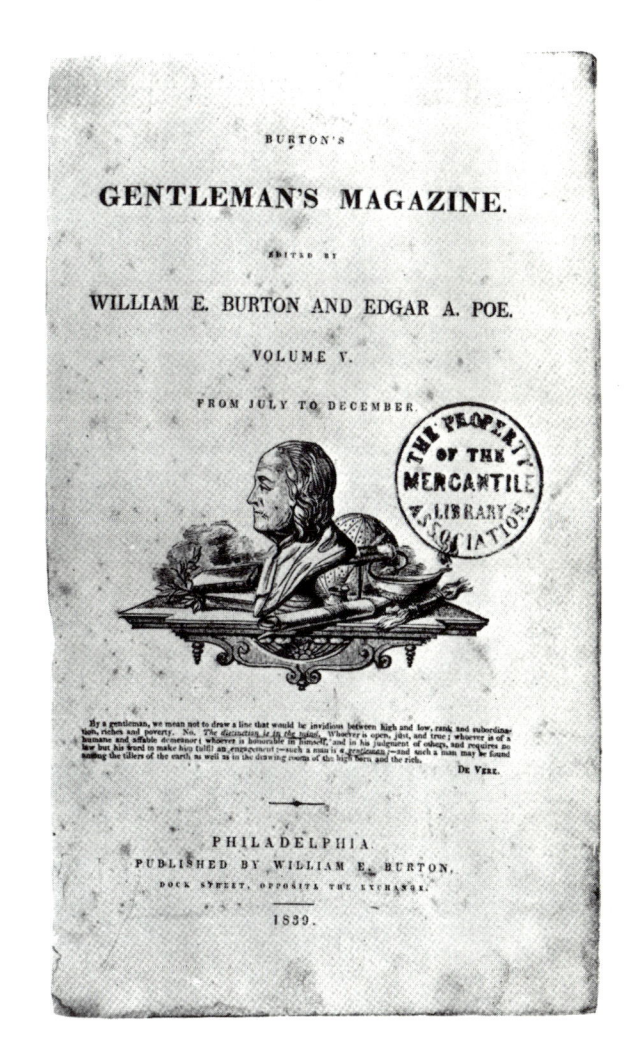

Front page of *Gentleman's Magazine* **complete with Poe by-line**

His conversation was at times almost supramortal in its eloquence. His voice was modulated with astonishing skill, and his large and variably expressive eyes looked reposed or shot fiery tumult into theirs who listened, while his own face glowed or was changeless in pallor, as his imagination quickened his blood, or drew it back frozen to his heart. His imagery was from the worlds which no mortal can see but with the vision of genius. Suddenly starting from a proposition exactly and sharply defined in terms of utmost simplicity and clearness, he rejected the forms of customary logic, and in a crystalline process of accretion, built up his ocular demonstrations in forms of gloomiest and ghostliest grandeur, or in those of the most airy and delicious beauty, so minutely, and so distinctly, yet so rapidly, that the attention which was yielded to him was chained till it stood among his wonderful creations – till he himself dissolved the spell, and brought his hearers back to common and base existence, by vulgar fancies or by exhibitions of the ignoble passions.

He was at times a dreamer – dwelling in ideal realms – in heaven or hell, peopled with creations and the accidents of his brain. He walked the streets, in madness or melancholy, with lips moving in indistinct curses, or with eyes upturned in passionate prayers (never for himself, for he felt, or professed to feel, that he was already damned), but for their happiness who at that moment were objects of his idolatry; or with his glance introverted to a heart gnawed with anguish, and with a face shrouded in gloom, he would brave the wildest storms; and all night, with drenched garments and arms wildly beating the wind and rain, he would speak as if to spirits that at such times only could be evoked by him from that Aidenn close by whose portals his disturbed soul sought to forget the ills to which his constitution subjected him – close by that Aidenn where were those he loved – the Aidenn which he might never see but in fitful glimpses, as its gates opened to receive the less fiery and more happy natures whose listing to sin did not involve the doom of death. He seemed, except when some fitful pursuit subjected his will and engrossed his faculties, always to bear the memory of some controlling sorrow. The remarkable poem of 'The Raven' was probably much more nearly than has been supposed, even by those who were very intimate with him, a reflection and an echo of his own history. He was the bird's

. . . unhappy master,
Whom unmerciful disaster
Followed fast and followed faster
Till his song the burden bore –
Melancholy burden bore
Of 'Nevermore,' of 'Nevermore'.

Every genuine author in a greater or less degree leaves in his works, whatever their design, traces of his personal character; elements of his immortal being, in which the individual survives the person. While we read the pages of 'The Fall of the House of Usher', or of 'Mesmeric Revelations', we see in the solemn and stately gloom which invests one, and in the subtle metaphysical analysis of both, indications of the idiosyncrasies – of what was most peculiar – in the author's intellectual nature. But we see here only the better phases of this nature, only the symbols of his juster action, for his harsh experience had deprived him of all faith in man or woman.

He had made up his mind upon the numberless complexities of the social world, and the whole system was with him an imposture. This conviction gave a direction to his shrewd and naturally unamiable character. Still though he regarded society as composed of villains, the sharpness of his intellect was not of that kind which enabled him to cope with villainy. He was in many respects like Francis Vivian in Bulwer's [Lytton] novel *The Caxtons*.

Passion, in him, comprehended many of the worst emotions which militate against human happiness. You could not contradict him, but you raised quick choler; you could not speak of wealth, but his cheek paled with gnawing envy. The astonishing natural advantage of this

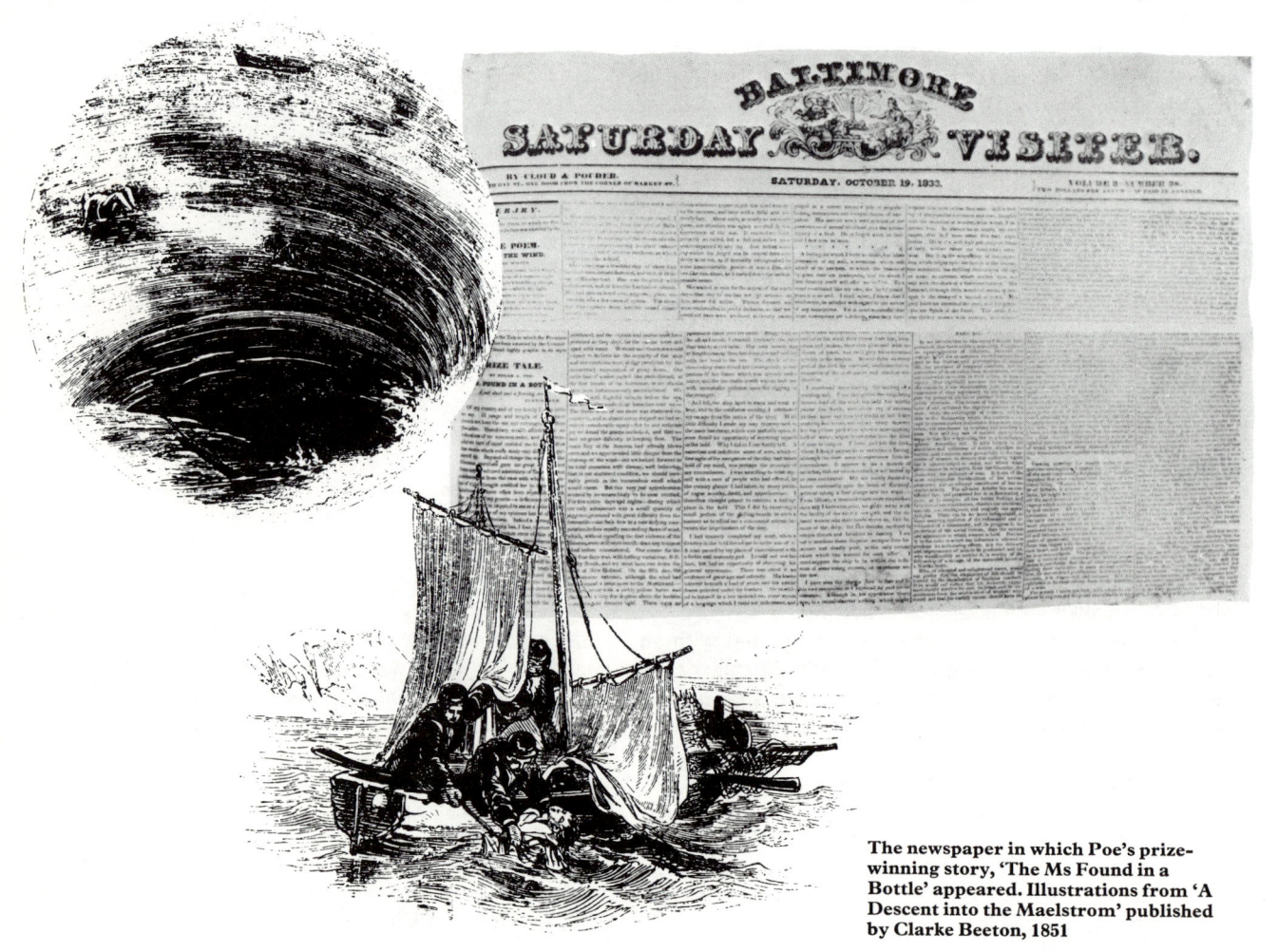

The newspaper in which Poe's prize-winning story, 'The Ms Found in a Bottle' appeared. Illustrations from 'A Descent into the Maelstrom' published by Clarke Beeton, 1851

poor boy – his beauty, his readiness, the daring spirit that breathed around him like a fiery atmosphere – had raised his constitutional self-confidence into an arrogance that turned his very claims to admiration into prejudice against him. Irascible, envious – bad enough, but not the worst, for these salient angles were all varnished over with a cold repellant cynicism while his passions vented themselves in sneers. There seemed to him no moral susceptibility; and what was more remarkable in a proud nature, little or nothing of the true point of honour. He had, to a morbid excess, that desire to rise which is vulgarly called ambition, but no wish for the esteem or the love of his species; only the hard wish to succeed – not shine, not serve – succeed, that he might have the right to despise a world which galled his self-conceit.

We have suggested the influence of his aims and vicissitudes upon his literature. It was more conspicuous in his later than his earlier writing. Nearly all that he wrote in the last two or three years – including much of his best poetry – was in some sense biographical; in draperies of his imagination, those who had taken the trouble to trace his steps, could perceive, but slightly covered, the figure of himself.

There are perhaps some of our readers who will understand the allusions of the beautiful poem 'Annabel Lee'. Mr Poe presented it in MS to the writer of these paragraphs, just before he left New York recently, remarking it was the last thing he had written.

We must omit any particular criticism of Mr Poe's works. As a writer of tales it will be admitted generally, that he was scarcely surpassed in ingenuity of construction or effective painting; as a critic, he was more remarkable as a dissector of sentences than as a commenter upon ideas. *He was little better than a carping grammarian.* As a poet, he will retain a most honourable rank. Of his 'Raven', Mr Willis observes, that in his opinion, 'it is the most effective single example of fugitive poetry ever published in this country, and is unsurpassed in English poetry for subtle conceptions, masterly ingenuity of versification, and consistent sustaining of imaginative lift'. In poetry, as in prose, he was most successful in the metaphysical treatment of the passions. His poems are constructed with wonderful ingenuity, and finished with consummate art. They illustrate a morbid sensitiveness of feeling, a shadowy and gloomy imagination, and a taste almost faultless in the apprehension of that sort of beauty most agreeable to his temper.

We have not learned the circumstance of his death. It was sudden, and from the fact that it occurred in Baltimore, it is presumed that he was on his return to New York.

'After life's fitful fever he sleeps well.'

WALT WHITMAN AT THE POE FUNERAL

Conspicuous Absence of the Popular Poets

WALT WHITMAN, the great American poet, was one of the few people to go on thinking highly of Poe in the years immediately following his death. After initially being unimpressed with Poe's work, Whitman grew to admire it and wrote in 1880, 'There is an indescribable magnetism about the poet's life and reminiscences, as well as the poems.' Whitman had, in fact, once met Poe in New York and recorded the encounter later.

I remember seeing Edgar A. Poe, and having a short interview with him (it must have been in 1845 or '6) in his office, second storey of a corner building (Duana or Pearl Street). He was editor and owner or part owner of *The Broadway Journal.* **The visit was about a piece of mine he had publish'd. Poe was very cordial, in a quiet way, appear'd well in person, dress, &c. I have a distinct and pleasing remembrance of his looks, voice, manner and matter; very kindly and human, but subdued, perhaps a little jaded.**

Whitman translated his admiration into action by being the only literary figure to attend the public reburial of Poe's remains at Baltimore, and it is believed that he was responsible for writing the section in inverted commas in the following report from the *Washington Star* **of 16 November 1875.**

Walt Whitman – a contemporary portrait

ABOUT THE most significant part of the Poe reburial ceremony yesterday – which only a crowded and remarkably magnetic audience of the very best class of young people, women preponderating, prevented from growing tedious – was the marked absence from the spot of every popular poet and author, American and foreign. Only Walt Whitman was present.

Being in Washington on a visit at the time, 'the old gray' went over to Baltimore, and though ill from paralysis, consented to hobble up and silently take a seat on the platform, but refused to make any speech, saying, 'I have felt a strong impulse to come over and be here today myself in memory of Poe, which I have obey'd, but not the slightest impulse to make a speech, which, my dear friends, must also be obeyed.' In an informal circle, however, in conversation after the ceremonies, Whitman said: 'For a long while, and until lately, I had a distaste for Poe's writings. I wanted, and still want for poetry, the clear sun shining, and fresh air blowing – the strength and power of health, not of delirium, even amid the stormiest passions – with always the background of the eternal moralities. Non-complying with these requirements, Poe's genius has yet conquer'd a special recognition for itself, and I too have come to fully admit it, and appreciate it and him.

'In a dream I once had, I saw a vessel on the sea, at midnight, in a storm. It was no great full-rigg'd ship, nor majestic steamer, steering firmly through the gale, but seem'd one of those superb little schooner yachts I had often seen lying anchor'd, rocking so jauntily, in the waters around New York, or up Long Island sound – now flying uncontroll'd with torn sails and broken spars through the wild sleet and winds and waves of the night. On the deck was a slender, slight, beautiful figure, a dim man, apparently enjoying all the terror, the murk, and the dislocation of which he was the centre and the victim. That figure of my lurid dream might stand for Edgar Poe, his spirit, his fortunes, and his poems – themselves all lurid dreams.'

The Poe Monument erected in Baltimore, November 1875

POE'S TOMB

A SLAB bearing the inscription, *Hic tandem felice conduntur Reliquiae, Edgar Allan Poe* was prepared by the order of Neilson Poe Esq, Edgar Allan Poe's cousin. But the relentless fate that pursued the unhappy poet during his lifetime, followed him after death, and a phenomenal catastrophe prevented the erection of the slab over his grave.

On the day before it was to have been erected, a freight train on the Northern Central Railroad jumped the track, and ran into the marble yard, nearby the depot, in which the slab was placed, awaiting transportation to the cemetery. The slab was directly in the course of the heavy train and was shivered to atoms.

Poe's grave, therefore, remained neglected until efforts of the Baltimore School Teacher's Association, and the munificence of George W. Childs Esq, of Philadelphia, secured the substantial monument now placed over his tomb. The dedication ceremony took place on 17 November 1875.

WILLIAM F. GILL
The Life of Edgar Allan Poe (New York, 1878)

Statue of Poe by Charles Rudy unveiled in Capitol Square, Richmond, Virginia in October 1959 (POE FOUNDATION INC)

EDGAR POE

JOHN H. INGRAM

THE FIRST man to devote himself wholeheartedly to championing the genius of Poe and making available the real facts of his life was an Englishman, John H. Ingram. Ingram, a scholar and historian, had been fascinated by the writer's life and works since his boyhood, and when he died in February 1916 his collection of Poe's letters, manuscripts and first editions was considered one of the very best in

George Graham, founder of *Graham's Magazine,* which Poe edited

John H. Ingram, the Englishman who became Poe's first biographer

existence. Apart from editing editions of Poe's works, Ingram also devoted many years to his *Edgar Allan Poe: His Life, Letters and Opinions* (1880) **which is still regarded as one of the best of the hundreds of biographies that have been published. After Ingram's death, one obituary noted:**

> **The enthusiasm for Poe which seems to have been at this time greater in England than America, was greatly augmented by Ingram's activity; he found in Swinburne, Morris and Rossetti brother enthusiasts, and not content with his exertions in England, he did all in his power to stir up the interest of France in this direction.**

Ingram had started his literary campaign to vindicate and champion Poe over thirty years previously, and here is his first article from the magazine *Temple Bar* **of June 1874.**

UNTIL THE present moment Dr Griswold's 'Memoir' of Edgar Poe has been accepted, almost unquestioned, in Europe: in America its correctness has been frequently and authoritatively impugned. Baudelaire in France, and Mr Moy Thomas in England*, it is true, have ventured to question the truth of the reverend gentleman's account of Poe's life, but, twenty-four years after the poet's decease, we still find ourselves the first in this country to appear before the public with any proofs of the thorough untrustworthiness of the said 'Memoir.' The present is not an occasion for a full and critical examination of the biography by Dr Griswold, but we confidently believe that enough evidence can be adduced here to prove that when Mr Graham styled it 'the fancy sketch of a jaundiced vision,' he was but giving utterance to the truth. Writers in search of a sensational subject are prone to resort to Poe's life for a point to their moral; but we must content ourselves with the barest and most unsophisticated narration of his career, as gathered from fresh evidence, merely pointing out on our course his biographer's more palpable deviations from the fact.

Edgar Poe could boast a gentle lineage; a fact, probably, of little value, save that it explains to some extent the delicacy of his feelings and fancies. Descended from the old Norman family of the Le Poers, the race would appear to have retained its position in society until our hero's father forsook jurisprudence to elope with an actress. After having 'donned the sock' himself for a few years, David Poe died, and within a few weeks of his youthful bride, leaving three children, Henry, Edgar, and Rosalie, utterly destitute. Mr John Allan, a wealthy merchant, and a friend of the family, having no children of his own, following a common American custom, adopted the boy Edgar and his sister Rosalie. Of this girl we learn no more, save that she is still alive and in a state of utter destitution.†

Edgar Poe was born in Baltimore, but when is still doubtful. Griswold, and other biographers copying him, say in January 1811, and this date is alleged to have been taken from a letter of the poet's, but those who have investigated the 'Memoir' will probably be inclined to question its correctness. Poe, in his wonderful story of 'William Wilson,' speaks of passing the third lustrum of his life at Dr Bransby's, and if that might be accepted as a fact

---
* *The Train Magazine,* No 16, vol iii, pp 193, &c.
† Rosalie, Edgar Poe's sister and only surviving relative, is stated to be now living at Hicks' Landing, in Virginia, in the most necessitous circumstances.

> **EDGAR ALLAN POE.**
> **A DISCLAIMER.**
>
> *From the "ATHENÆUM" of 15th January, 1876.*
>
> The "MEMORIAL VOLUME" of Edgar Poe's Poems, recently alluded to in the *Athenæum*, has now appeared in New York. It includes my vindicatory sketch of the poet, but introduced by the unwarrantable remark that "a considerable portion of Mr. Ingram's Memoir is gathered from material previously used by Mr. W. F. Gill in his lecture, 'The Romance of Edgar A. Poe,' written in September, 1873." That *I have never received a single item of information from Mr. Gill respecting Edgar Poe*, or made use of anything *written* by him on the same subject, and that the publisher of the "Memorial Volume" knew this the *following* extracts will clearly prove. Last August, Mr. Widdleton, publisher of the above book, wrote to me with reference to the proposed republication in America of my sketch,—"Mr. Gill, of Boston, asks us not to use your memoir, as it covers material *taken from his paper on Poe in 'Lotos Leaves.'* ". In reply, I not only most emphatically denied ever having made use of any information derived from Mr. Gill, but also pointed out that my sketch was published in October, 1874,* whereas "Lotos Leaves" did not appear until January, 1875. Mr. Widdleton, in acknowledgment, admitted that Mr. Gill was "evidently strangely at fault," and yet he now publishes, without previously referring to me, the above statement respecting an alleged work of September, 1873, the utter unreliability of which I can prove from Mr. Gill's own letters to me. Early in 1874, hearing that Mr. Gill was collecting material for a lecture on Poe, I wrote and asked him whether he had any reliable information about the poet, if so, whether he was willing to dispose of copies of the same to me, and whether he had any intention of writing the poet's memoir. "I do intend to write the life of Poe," he replied, "unless you should much prefer to buy out my material, which I would sell if your preference was for that. As *I have not written any minor articles*, I cannot send any portions of my materials." Responding that I was willing to purchase any reliable information about Poe other than that I already possessed, and requesting further particulars, Mr. Gill answered, but without naming any price for his collection, "Much of my material is of a peculiarly personal nature in the form of notes taken down when conversing with Mr. G. R. Graham and others, and before I could transmit it *I should be obliged to put it carefully into shape before it could be understood by another*. With all willingness to forward any material possible, I cannot, as yet, find opportunity for the necessary preliminary of arranging material." These letters from Mr. Gill are dated 6th June, and 27th August, 1874, respectively; they contained requests for copies of what I had written about Poe, requests which I complied with, and, in consequence, had the pleasure of seeing my discoveries partially reproduced, even to the extent of an uncorrected error, but without any acknowledgment, in "Lotos Leaves."
>
> This is my case: let Mr. Gill now state where his aptly styled "Romance of Edgar A. Poe" was published, and what portion of it he claims to have been reproduced in my Memoir of Edgar Poe, a work which several friends in England and America know to be the result of twelve years research.
>
> London. JOHN H. INGRAM.
>
> * Prefixed to the first volume of the complete Edition of the Works of Edgar Allan Poe. Edinburgh: A. & C. Black.

John Ingram's disclaimer as controversy grew around Poe

it would, by ante-dating his birth some few years, get rid of several singular anomalies in his biography. Griswold frequently overlooks the necessity of being accurate in his dates. On the very first page of his 'Memoir,' in order to avail himself of a ridiculous anecdote communicated to him by 'an eminent and estimable gentleman,' of Poe's conduct at a school in Richmond, Virginia, when he 'was only six or seven years of age,' he disregards the fact that, according to his own account, his hero was then and had been for two years past in England.

Accepting the date recorded by all his biographers, his adopted parents brought Poe to England in 1816, and placed him at the Manor House School, Church Street, Stoke Newington. The school was then kept by the Rev Dr Bransby, and would appear to have been situated in grounds of considerable extent, although now sadly shorn of their proportions. The poet's description of the place must be taken *cum grano salis*, and the oft quoted recollections of 'William Wilson' may well be referred to the usually exaggerated dimensions of childhood's reminiscences. In 1822, after a residence of five years in England, he returned to the United States, and, says Griswold:

> ... after passing a few months at an academy in Richmond, entered the University at Charlottesville, Virginia, where he led a very dissipated life. The manners which then prevailed there were extremely dissolute, and he was known as the wildest and most reckless student of his class; but his unusual opportunities, and the remarkable ease with which he mastered the most difficult studies, kept him all the while in the first rank for scholarship.

The 'gambling, intemperance, and other vices,' which 'induced', says this biographer, 'his expulsion from the University,' must have been the result of extraordinary precocity, because, if this authority is reliable in his dates, Poe was now in the eleventh or twelfth year of his age!

If the 'William Wilson' theory may be accepted, and the statement of Mr Powell, in his sketches of 'The Authors of America,' that Poe went to 'various academies' previous to entering the Charlottesville University, be borne in mind, the poet's age would be from fifteen to twenty during his collegiate career. Notwithstanding his alleged dissoluteness, this precocious boy, according to his more reliable biographers, actually found means to obtain the first honours of his college, and at the conclusion of his university career, instead of being expelled, as Griswold asserts, left *alma mater* with the intention of aiding the Greeks in their struggles for independence. A mere boy, Poe would appear to have joined in the various pastimes of his fellow students, but that he made himself notorious by 'his gambling, intemperance, and *other* vices,' would appear to be in direct contradiction to all unprejudiced evidence now obtainable. Griswold admits that at this period Poe was noted for feats of hardihood, strength and activity, and that 'on one occasion, in a hot day of June, he swam from Richmond to Warwick, seven miles and a half, against a tide running probably from two to three miles an hour.' Certainly a wonderful performance for a dissolute youth, and one that if not vouched for on good authority, might well have been relegated to the depths of the doctor's imagination. Apart from his athletic feats, Poe's great abilities enabled him to maintain a respectable position in the eyes of the professors. 'His time', remarks Powell, 'was divided between lectures, debating societies, rambles in the Blue Ridge mountains, and in making caricatures of his tutors and the heads of the colleges.' He was a clever draughtsman, and is stated to have had the habit of covering the walls of his dormitory with rough charcoal sketches. 'Rousing himself', adds Powell, 'from this desultory course of life, he took the first honours of the college, and returned home.'

Poe left the Charlottesville University with the intention of emulating Byron in his efforts on behalf of the Greeks. In conjunction with an acquaintance, Ebenezer Burling, the future poet purposed proceeding to Greece to take part in the struggle against the Turks, but his companion's heart failing him, Poe had to undertake the perilous journey alone. This act of chivalry on the part of the youthful adventurer was undertaken in 1827, when, according to his biographers, he had attained the prematurely mature age of sixteen! The would-be warrior got no further than St Petersburg, where he was arrested in consequence of an irregularity in his passport, and was only saved from further difficulty through the exertions of the American consul, by whose friendly assistance he was, moreover, enabled to return to his native land, the recognition of Greece by the allied powers rendering *his* aid no longer necessary. It should be noted that Griswold states his young countryman's troubles at St Petersburg arose 'from penalties incurred in a drunken debauch;' but this allegation was denied directly it appeared in print; its author never attempted to support it by evidence of any description, and every other native biographer gives the story as we have told it.

On his return home poor Poe found a sad change. Mrs Allan, who seems to have acted a mother's part to him, and whom he would appear to have regarded with deep affection, was dead. He was too late even to take a last farewell of his only friend, her funeral having taken place the day before he reached Richmond. Mrs Allan died on 27 February 1829, and from that day his biographers very justly date all his misfortunes. Mr Allan, who does not appear to have manifested much pleasure at his adopted son's return, when Poe declared his resolution of devoting himself to a military life seems to have assisted him in obtaining an appointment in West Point Military Academy. 'Here he entered upon his new studies and duties', remarks Powell, 'with characteristic energy, and an honourable career was opened to him; but the fates willed it that Mr Allan should marry a girl young enough to be her husband's granddaughter;' and this event, Poe was soon made to feel as a deathblow to his hopes of succeeding to his adopted father's property, in accordance with that person's oft-expressed intention. Here again it is necessary to revert to Dr Griswold's 'Memoir' to contradict his emphatic statement that Mr Allan, on his second marriage, so far from being sixty-five years of age, as 'stated by all Poe's biographers . . . was in his forty-eighth year.' He seems to have re-married in a twelvemonth after his first wife's death, and yet the careless recorder of the event, forgetting on the very next page his declaration of the 'forty-eighth year,' allows him to die in the spring of 1834, or barely four years later, at fifty-four instead of fifty-two years of age. The point is hardly worth quibbling over save that it is another specimen of Griswold's want of accuracy, for in his account of Poe's death, Griswold himself stated Mr Allan to have been sixty-five. Common sense would show that a man who had been so long married and so hopeless of offspring as to have adopted two non-related children in 1814-15 was more likely to be nearer sixty-five than forty-eight in 1830.

Whether the truth lies with all the other biographers or with the doctor, as regards this circumstance, matters little; it suffices to say that Poe but too speedily discovered, after Mr Allan's second marriage, that affairs had altered to his detriment at home. The birth of a son to his adopted father was made the means of completely alienating that man from his hitherto reputed heir, and poor Edgar found all his pecuniary prospects suddenly blighted. The unfortunate cadet's allowance being entirely withdrawn he was compelled to leave West Point, and resolved to proceed to

TO HELEN.*

I.

I saw thee once—once only—years ago—
I must not say *how* many, but *not* many:
It was a July midnight; and from out
A full-orbed moon, that, like thine own
        soul, soaring
Sought a precipitate pathway up through
        heaven,
There fell a silvery-silken veil of light,
With quietude, and sultriness, and slumber,

* Founded, we are told, on a real adventure.—ED.

Left: **Sarah Helen Whitman who inspired Poe's poem, 'To Helen'**

Above: **Illustrated edition of 'To Helen' by James Godwin (1880)**

THE EDGAR ALLAN POE SCRAPBOOK

The first pictorial interpretation of Poe's great story, *The Fall of the House of Usher,* 1852

Poland, to aid the patriots of that nation in their struggle to shake off the Russian yoke. Here again it is requisite to refer to a statement of Griswold's, to the effect that Poe parted in anger from Mr Allan, who refused in any way to assist him further, because, 'according to Poe's own statement, he ridiculed the marriage of his "*patron*" [the italics are ours] with Miss Paterson and had a quarrel with her; but a different story, scarcely suitable for repetition here, was told by the friends of the other party.' The different story is then referred to in a note as hinted at by the writer of an 'Eulogium' upon the life and genius of Mr Poe, in the *Southern Literary Messenger*, for March, 1850. To this 'Eulogium' and its author, we shall again refer, merely contenting ourselves now with stating that this tale can only be spoken of as unsupported by a tittle of evidence.

On 6 September 1831, the unequal conflict in Poland was ended by the fall of Warsaw. The news reached the chivalric poet in time to prevent his departure, but left him once more aimless, and almost resourceless. In 1827, in happier times, Poe had published a small volume of poems, which ran through three editions – a fact Dr Griswold forgets to mention – and which appears to have received the warm commendations of local critics. Griswold asserts that it included 'Al Aaraaf' and 'Tamerlane', pieces since republished in the collected edition; but this would not appear to have been the case; and the poet's own reference to those poems being 'reprinted verbatim from the original edition' – as if to refute his biographer's suggestion that they had been constantly revised – applies to the volume of 1830-1. Of the former work the only poem preserved would appear to be the sweet little lyric 'To Helen', embalmed by Lowell in his sympathetic sketch of its author.

Encouraged by this illusory success, Poe started for Baltimore, where he turned to literature as a means of subsistence. He quickly found that the waters of Helicon were anything but Pactolian; and although some of his finest stories were written at this time, and accepted by the magazines, they were scarcely ever paid for, and at last the unfortunate man was absolutely and literally *starving*.

At this period of the terrible tale, as frightful as the most dramatic of his own stories, Poe, according to Griswold, enlisted as a private soldier, was recognised by some officers who had known him at West Point, and who made efforts, with prospects of success, to obtain a commission for him, when it was discovered by his friends that he had deserted. About the whole of this story there is that air of improbability which the reverend doctor is so fond of. Of the many lives of the poet, by friends and foes, published in America, Griswold alone mentions the circumstance, and as his 'Memoir' has been authoritatively stigmatised by Mrs Sarah Whitman, and others, for containing anecdotes which 'are utterly fabulous,' it must be regarded with grave suspicion. There is one fact which renders it very improbable: Poe went to Baltimore in 1830, and was in that city in 1833. Griswold places the affair between those dates, stating, 'how long he remained in the service I have not been able to ascertain.' Is it likely that a man so well known as Poe was would have enlisted, deserted, and yet have remained in a place where he was so generally known? or that his friends would not have encouraged him to remain in the army to wait the result of their exertions?

In 1833, the proprietor of the *Baltimore Saturday Visiter* offered premiums for the best prose story and the best poem, and to adjudicate upon the mass of papers sent in three well-known men were obtained. The committee included the Honourable John P. Kennedy, author of the well known fiction, *Horse-Shoe Robinson*. 'The umpires,' remarks Powell, 'were men of taste and ability, and after a *careful consideration* of the productions, they decided that Poe was undoubtedly entitled to both prizes. As Poe was entirely unknown to them, this was a genuine tribute to his superior merit.' The poem sent was 'The Coliseum,' and it was accompanied by six stories for selection; 'not content with awarding the premium, they' (i.e. the committee) 'declared that the worst of the six tales referred to was better than the best of the other competitors.' Griswold, enlarging upon the 'Eulogium' already referred to, tells the story of the award in the following manner. We leave our reader to judge the value of Dr Griswold's 'Memoir' by this fact alone, if he will compare the extract we now give with the official report given below:

Such matters are usually disposed of in a very off-hand way. Committees to award literary prizes drink to the payer's health in good wines, over unexamined MSS, which they submit to the discretion of publishers, with permission to use their names in such a way as to promote the publisher's advantage. So, perhaps, it would have been in this case, but that one of the committee, taking up a little book remarkably beautiful and distinct in caligraphy, was tempted to read several pages; and becoming interested, he summoned the attention of the company to the half-dozen compositions it contained. It was unanimously decided that the prizes should be paid to 'the first of geniuses who had written legibly.' Not another MS was unfolded. Immediately the 'confidential envelope' was opened, and the successful competitor was found to bear the scarcely known name of Poe.

Thus runs the printed report of the committee, published with the award on 12 October 1833, and republished in the *Southern Literary Messenger*, previous to Poe's assuming the editorial management of that magazine:

Amongst the prose articles were many of various and distinguished merit, but the singular force and beauty of those sent by the author of 'The Tales of the Folio Club,' leave us no room for hesitation in that department. We have accordingly awarded the premium to a tale entitled the 'MS Found in a Bottle.' It would hardly be doing justice to the writer of this collection to say that the tale we have chosen is the best of the six offered by him. We cannot refrain from saying that the author owes it to his own reputation as well as to the gratification of the community, to publish the entire volume ('Tales of the Folio Club'). These tales are eminently distinguished by a wild, vigorous, and poetical imagination, a rich style, a fertile invention, and varied and curious learning.
(Signed)   JOHN P. KENNEDY,
J. H. B. LATROBE, and
JAMES H. MILLER.

Comment on this is needless.

From this time Poe's affairs mended, and his writings were not only sought after but paid for by the publishers. In the spring of the year following (1834) Mr Allan died, and of his property, to quote the elegant words of Griswold, 'not a mill was bequeathed to Poe,' and, it is alleged, the widow of his adopted father 'even refused him his own books.' Early in 1835, the poet began to contribute poems, tales and reviews to the *Southern Literary Messenger*, a newly established monthly magazine. Mr Kennedy, after a year and a half's friendship with Poe, had advised him to forward a paper to Mr White, the proprietor of the above publication. He did so; became a regular contributor, and in May 1835 he was made editor, at a salary of five hundred dollars per annum. The accession of the new editor worked wonders in the *Southern Literary Messenger*, in a short time raising its circulation from four hundred to three thousand. Its success was partially due to the originality and fascination of Poe's stories, and partially owing to the fearlessness of his trenchant critiques. He was no respecter of persons, and already began to rouse the small fry of bookmakers by his crucial dissection of their mediocrities. 'He had a scorn,' says Powell, 'of the respectable level trash which has too long brooded over American literature. Poe did not like tamely to submit to the dethronement of genius. . . . What gods and men abhor, according to Horace, a certain class of critics and readers in America adore.' Amongst the best of his productions at this period was the 'Adventure of Hans Pfaal,' which appeared in the *Literary Messenger* three weeks previous to the appearance of Mr Richard Lock's 'Moon Story,' which indeed it probably suggested, although, from the way in which Griswold alludes to 'Hans Pfaal' being 'in some respects very similar to Mr Lock's' story, one is led to believe our poet the copier instead of the copied.

In September 1835, Poe, who had hitherto performed his editorial duties at a distance, found it necessary to leave Baltimore for Richmond, where the *Messenger* was published. Again amongst his kindred, he met his cousin Virginia Clemm, a girl in years, and already manifesting signs of consumption; but undeterred by this or by their poverty, the poor poet was wedded to his kinswoman. He continued the direction of the *Messenger* until January 1837, when he left it for the more lucrative employment of assisting Professors Anthon, Hawkes, and Henry, in the management of the *New York Quarterly Review*. Griswold, it is true, states that he was dismissed from the *Messenger* on account of his irregularities, and he quotes a goody letter from its *deceased* proprietor, upbraiding him for getting drunk, but promising to allow him to 'again become an assistant in my office' on condition that he forswore the bottle. Unsupported by other evidence, we should doubt the truth of this extract. Undated, addressed to a gentleman who has raised his publication to a profitable and famous circulation, and who would appear at this time to have been married, is it probable that Poe would have been termed 'an assistant in my office', and offered 'quarters in my house', by Mr White, who, like all the authorities referred to by this biographer in corroboration of his allegations, save the writer of the aforementioned 'Eulogium,' unfortunately dies before the charge is brought?

In 1837 Poe wrote some of his slashing critiques for the *New York Review*, and by them, says Powell, 'made many enemies'. In July of the same year, he also completed and published his wonderful narrative of 'Arthur Gordon Pym'. Griswold displays his usual animus by stating that 'it received little attention', and that in England, 'being mistaken at first for a narrative of real experiences, it was advertised to be reprinted, but a discovery of its character,

With a heart of furious fancies,
   Whereof I am commander,
With a burning spear, *and a horse of air*,
   To the wilderness I wander.
Tom o' Bedlam's Song.

Another anonymous engraving from the 1852 edition of Poe's tales for 'The Unparalleled Adventures of One Hans Pfall'

I believe, prevented such a result'. In truth, it was in a short interval twice reprinted in England, and did obtain considerable notice, 'the air of truth' which, it is suggested, was only in the attempt, having excited much interest in the book.

The heavy *Review* work was not in Poe's line, and at the end of a year he left New York for Philadelphia, where he was engaged on the *Gentleman's Magazine*, since merged into *Graham's*. In May 1839 he was appointed editor of this publication, and, as usual, 'came down pretty freely with his critical axe'. At the same time he contributed tales and papers to various other magazines, so that, although obliged to labour severely, he began to get a fair livelihood. In the autumn of this year he published a collection of his best stories, in two volumes, under the title of *Tales of the Grotesque and Arabesque*.

Poe edited the *Gentleman's* until June, 1840, when it changed hands, and became known as *Graham's Magazine*. Griswold states that Mr Burton, the former proprietor of the publication, found the poet so unreliable, that he 'was never sure when he left the city that his business would be cared for,' and sometimes had to perform the editorial duties himself. Wonderful to relate, however, Poe was retained in his post until the last moment, when the following scene is alleged to have occurred (somebody, of course, had taken shorthand notes of the conversation). Mr Burton is supposed to have been absent for a fortnight, and, on his return, to have learned that his editor has not only not furnished the printers with any copy for the forthcoming number of the Magazine, but has availed himself of the time to prepare the prospectus of a new monthly, to supplant that he is now editing. Burton meets 'his associate late in the evening at one of his accustomed haunts' and says, 'Mr Poe, I am astonished! – Give me my manuscripts, so that I can attend to the duties you have so shamefully neglected, and when you are sober we will settle.' Poe interrupted him with 'Who are you that presume to address me in this manner? Burton – I am – the editor – of the *Penn Magazine* – and you are – hiccup – a fool.' Such absurd anecdotes are not worthy refutation, but an almost certain proof of their incredibility is furnished by the fact that not only did Mr George R. Graham engage Poe to continue the editorial duties of the said magazine, but he was also the first to denounce Griswold's 'Memoir' of the poet, as 'the fancy sketch of a jaundiced vision,' and as 'an immortal infamy'.

Poe retained the editorship of *Graham's Magazine* for about two years, during which period some of his finest analytical tales were produced. In 1843, not 1848, as stated by his inaccurate biographer, he obtained the one hundred dollar prize for his story of 'The Gold Bug'; a story written in connection with his theory that human ingenuity could not construct any cryptograph which human ingenuity could not decipher. Tested by several correspondents with difficult samples of their skill, the poet took the trouble to examine and solve them in triumphant proof of his theory.

In the autumn of 1844, Poe removed to New York, where, in literary circles, his fame had already preceded him. He speedily found employment on the *New York Mirror*, and Willis, who was one of the proprietors of that paper, has left us a highly interesting portraiture of the poet at this epoch in his life:

Apropos of the disparaging portion of Dr Griswold's sketch, which appeared at Poe's death [he remarks] let us truthfully say, some four or five years since Mr Poe was employed by us for several months as critic and sub-editor. He resided with his wife and mother at Fordham, a few miles out of town, but was at his desk in the office from nine in the morning till the evening paper went to press. With the highest admiration for his genius, and a willingness to let it atone for more than ordinary irregularity, we were led by common report to expect a very capricious attention to his duties. Time went on, however, and he was invariably punctual and industrious. With his pale, beautiful, and intellectual face, as a reminder of what genius was in him, it was impossible, of course, not to treat him always with deferential courtesy . . . With a prospect of taking the lead in another periodical, he, at last, voluntarily gave up his employment with us, and, through all this considerable period, we had seen but one presentment of the man – a quiet, patient, industrious, and most gentlemanly person, commanding the utmost respect and good feeling by his unvarying deportment and ability.

Residing as he did in the country, we never met Mr Poe in hours of leisure; but he frequently called on us afterwards at our place of business, and we met him often in the street – invariably the same sad-mannered, winning and refined gentleman, such as we had always known him. It was by rumour only, up to the day of his death, that we knew of any other development of manner of character . . . Such only he has invariably seemed to us in all we have happened personally to know of him through a friendship of *five or six years*. And so much easier is it to believe what we have seen and known, than what we *hear* of only, that we remember him but with admiration and respect.

Poe left the *Mirror* in order to take part in the *Broadway Journal*, and in October 1845 he was enabled to buy his partner out, and to obtain the entire possession of this periodical. Under his control it became, probably, the best work of the kind ever issued, but, from the very nature of its contents, must have appealed to too small though select a class to make it remunerative. Accordingly the poor poet had to relinquish its publication, and on 3 January 1846 the last number was issued. What he did for the next few months heaven only knows; but in the May number of the *Lady's Book* he commenced a series of articles on 'The Literati of New York City' in which, 'he professed', remarks Griswold, with the wonted sneer, 'to give some honest opinions at random respecting their authorial merits, with occasional words of personality.' The papers seem to have made the literary quacks of New York shake in their shoes. One unfortunate who came under the lash, unable to bear his castigation quietly, retorted in no measured terms; in fact, instead of waiting, as Griswold did, for Poe's death – when every ass could have its kick at the dead lion – this Dr Dunn Brown, or Dunn English, for both names are given, in a personal newspaper article, referred to the alleged infirmities of the poet. The communication being inserted in the *Evening Mirror*, on 23 June 1843, Poe instituted a libel suit, and recovered several hundred dollars for defamation of character. Let anyone who has the slightest belief in Griswold's impartiality now turn to his garbled account of this dispute. He never mentions the suit for libel or its results; indeed, his *suppressio veri* is as iniquitous as his *suggestio falsi*.

In the autumn of this year Poe was residing in a little cottage at Fordham, near New York. The household comprised the poet, his wife, a confirmed invalid, and her devoted and never-to-be-forgotten mother, Mrs Clemm,

THE EDGAR ALLAN POE SCRAPBOOK

Nathan Willis, proprietor of the *New York Mirror*, who was Poe's kindly and caring benefactor

whose name will ever be linked with that of her unfortunate son-in-law. His wife was dying of a long, lingering decline, and the poet himself was ill, and, paralysed by poverty, scarcely able to labour. 'Mr Poe wrote', says Willis, 'with fastidious difficulty, and in a style too much above the popular level to be well paid. He was always in pecuniary difficulties, and, with his sick wife, frequently in want of the merest necessaries of life.' A most interesting description of the poet's *ménage* at this bitter period of his existence is afforded by a paper which appeared in a London periodical (*The Sixpenny Magazine*, No 20. February 1863) as 'Reminiscences of Edgar Poe'. The writer gives a circumstantial account of the homely abode and its occupants, and his description of the family's poverty-stricken condition is heartrending:

The autumn came [says the writer, detailing his second visit] and Mrs Poe sank rapidly in consumption, and I saw her in her bed-chamber. Everything here was so neat, so purely clean, so scant and poverty-stricken, that I saw the sufferer with such a heartache as the poor feel for the poor. There was no clothing on the bed, which was only straw, but a snow-white spread and sheets. The weather was cold, and the sick lady had the dreadful chills that accompany the hectic fever of consumption. She lay on the straw bed, wrapped in her husband's great-coat, with a large cat in her bosom . . . The coat and the cat were the sufferer's only means of warmth, except as her husband held her hands and her mother her feet.

These circumstances being made known by the writer of the above, a paragraph appeared in the *New York Express*, to the effect that:

Edgar Poe and his wife are both dangerously ill with consumption, and that the hand of misfortune lies heavy upon their temporal affairs. We are sorry to mention the fact that they are so far reduced as to be barely able to obtain the necessaries of life. This is, indeed, a hard lot, and we hope that the friends and admirers of Mr Poe will come promptly to his assistance in his bitterest hour of need.

This appeal was followed by an article from Willis in the *Home Journal*, adverting to the dangerous illness of the poet and his wife, and their consequent sufferings for want of the commonest necessaries of life, and evidencing their case as a proof of a hospital being required for educated and refined objects of charity.

Here [he urges] is one of the finest scholars, one of the most original men of genius, and one of the most industrious of the literary men of our country, whose temporary suspension of labour, from bodily illness, drops him immediately to a level with the common objects of public charity.

The effect of this appeal was to bring instant aid to the poor suffering family; Poe's many friends reading it in a different spirit to that of his biographer who avers that the article by Willis was only 'an ingenious apology for Mr Poe's infirmities', and that the manly letter to its author from Poe, announcing his own gradual recovery from a long and dangerous illness, but his wife's hopeless condition, 'was written for effect. He had not been ill a great while,' continued his ruthless assailant, 'nor dangerously at all. There was no literary or personal abuse of him in the journals,' he adds, alluding to a paragraph in the poet's sad letter to Willis, to the effect that his wife's sufferings had been heightened by the receipt of an anonymous letter containing 'those published calumnies of Messrs ——, for which', says Poe, 'I yet hope to find redress in a court of justice.'

This letter, which, according to Griswold, 'was written for effect', is dated 30 December 1846, and was followed in a few weeks by his wife's death. Mrs Poe's last moments were soothed and her wants administered to, we believe, by the poet's good and noble friend, Mrs Lewis, in whose hospitable home, when the poet himself died, Mrs Clemm is said to have found a shelter. It is needless to follow the adventures of the poet through all the labyrinth of errors in which his biographer has enveloped them. On 9 February 1848 he delivered a lecture in New York on the Cosmogony of the Universe. This was the substance of his greatest work, and was subsequently published under the title of 'Eureka, a Prose Poem'. It has never been reprinted in England.

From this time to the day of his death Poe steadily worked with his pen and as a lecturer to obtain a livelihood. And he succeeded. But consumption had long been sapping his system, and enfeebled as it was by long suffering, constant and harassing literary labour, and, more than all, *want*, it was ready to succumb; and on the evening of Sunday, 7 October 1849, he died, if the correct date of his birth is given, in the thirty-eighth year of his age.

The present opportunity does not admit of a complete analysis of the 'Memoir' by Griswold – the memoir on which every English life of Edgar Poe has been founded; but it is believed that enough has been said to prove the biographer's animus. Mrs Whitman, in her clever little brochure of 'Poe and his Critics', states that 'some of the most injurious of these anecdotes' (i.e. in the 'Memoir') 'were disproved, during the life of Dr Griswold, in the New York *Tribune* and other leading journals, without eliciting from him any public statement or apology.' Quite recently we have had, through the columns of the *Home Journal*, the refutation of another calumnious story, which for ten years has been going the round of the English and American periodicals. 'Moreover,' adds Mrs Whitman, 'we have authority for stating that many of the disgraceful anecdotes, so industriously collected by Dr Griswold are *utterly fabulous*, while others are perversions of the truth, more injurious in their effects than unmitigated fiction.'

When Edgar Poe died a long account of his life and writings appeared in the New York *Tribune*, signed 'Ludwig'. Dr Rufus Griswold was subsequently obliged to acknowledge himself the author of it. It is the well-known paper beginning 'Edgar Allan Poe is dead. This announcement will startle many, but *few will be grieved by it . . . he had few or no friends*.' In November following the poet's death, a kindly notice of him and his writings was furnished to the *Southern Literary Messenger* by Mr John R. Thompson, his successor in the editorship of that magazine. It did not contain an unkind or disparaging word. A month or two later appeared a collection of Poe's works in two volumes, and it was most depreciatingly reviewed in the *Tribune* by a writer whose style is easily recognisable, and who signed himself 'R' (Rufus). In March 1840 appeared an extremely lengthy review of this same collection in the *Literary Messenger*; it is the so-called, by Griswold, 'Eulogium,' and beginning: 'These half-told tales and broken poems are the only records of a wild, hard life. . . . Among all his poems there are only two or three which are not execrably bad.' It then proceeds to vilify Willis and

Lowell for their tributes to the memory of Poe, the latter of the two, it avers, belonging to that 'minute species of literary insect which is plentifully produced by the soil and climate of Boston.' The writer then administers a gentle reprimand to Griswold, and forthwith proceeds to detail a life of Edgar Poe. Now comes the strange part of the story. Nearly the whole of this very lengthy life and critique was subsequently embodied in the 'Memoir' by Griswold as original matter, without any acknowledgement or inverted commas, save for the paragraph relating to the poet's quarrel with Mr Allan's second wife; we have, therefore, this conclusion before us: either Dr Griswold openly plagiarised wholesale from the recently published but anonymous article, or *he himself was the author of the paper in question.*

EDGAR ALLAN POE IN ENGLAND AND SCOTLAND

J. H. WHITTY

Poe's school at Stoke Newington, London

HAVING CONSIDERED some of the general elements of the Poe 'legend', we can now move on to deal with specific periods of his life beginning with his childhood years spent outside America in England and Scotland. This article, from the September 1916 issue of the British magazine, *The Bookman*, is by another leading expert on Poe, J. H. Whitty.

THERE REMAIN no incidents in the life of Edgar Allan Poe better known than the published episodes at Bransby's Manor House School, located in the London suburb, Stoke Newington, England. All biographers of Poe have drawn their conclusions of his early life abroad almost entirely from his tale of 'William Wilson', taking it for granted that Poe's descriptions of Schoolmaster Bransby and of the Manor House School were real, instead of fiction. The fact is, that this was the only thread the earlier Poe writer had in sight out of which to weave any story.

A disputed portrait of Poe's English schoolmaster, Doctor Bransby

Where Poe told so much, some suspicion might have been excited, for it was not his way to enter into minute particulars of his life. That later on he briefly wrote in a memorandum intended for 'Griswold's Poets', that his five years' stay about London was spent at the Bransby school, was more like Poe's methods. It was hardly to be expected, under the circumstances, however, that Poe would have mentioned a small London boarding school, or a stay for school in Scotland, when writing for public effect, and with limited space at his command.

In his tale of 'William Wilson', Poe styles the schoolmaster, 'Doctor' Bransby, but recent investigation fails to reveal such an academical degree for Bransby. The description of the Manor House School is also drawn along ideal lines in Poe's own imagination.

As Poe introduced Bransby, the schoolmaster, in his tale of 'William Wilson', likewise he has apparently taken his early London schoolmistress for a character in 'The Murders in the Rue Morgue', giving her real name of Pauline Dubourg. The records among the Ellis and Allan manuscripts, in the Library of Congress, now show that Poe's time spent at Bransby's school dates only from the latter years of his residence abroad, or from the autumn of 1817 until the summer of 1820, when he returned to America. Other records there also show that he attended a small London school kept by Miss Dubourg, located on the site of No 146 Sloane Street, adjoining which now stands the Holy Trinity Church. Poe was a pupil there from about April 1816 until probably early in December 1817. This leaves a hiatus in his school history of several months during the latter part of the year 1815 and a brief period early in the year 1816.

It must have been some time during one of these periods that Poe went for a short stay to the old grammar school at Irvine, Scotland, in which John Allan, his patron, had been a pupil, and where all his sons afterward attended school.

The story of Poe's Scotland visits has never been told until now. It has hitherto been a mooted question whether Poe ever crossed over into Scotland from England. But there can no longer remain any doubts upon that point. Poe went to Scotland, and was there a sufficient length of time for his visits to leave vivid marks of remembrance upon his memory of that classic region of which so many scenes and incidents are sketched with truth and beauty.

Who now knows but that the whisper of genius came into Poe's soul in the land of Burns? If not Scotland, it must have been England, for the leaven had already risen when he arrived home in America. It has been well said that 'true genius is a mind of large powers, accidentally determined to some particular direction.'

Among the English poets, Cowley, Milton, and Pope, might be said to 'lisp in numbers', and have shown such early proof, not only of powers of language, but of comprehension of other things, as to more tardy minds seem scarcely credible. Cowley had a volume of his poems printed in his fifteenth year, and Poe's first book of verse appeared when he was eighteen. There is sufficient evidence, however, to show that Poe while yet at school, seven years previous to the publication of his poems, was writing poetical compositions.

The confusion shown by biographers in the early events of Poe's life is now being gradually cleared away, and with newly discovered facts the future biographer of Poe may be able to point out with accuracy, like in Cowley's case, the circumstances that produced the particular designation of Poe's mind.

Sketch of the house in Stoke Newington where the Allan family stayed

The school playground

That Poe's mind was charmed and centred at an early age on some one of the earlier writers seems almost certain. Among the new discoveries is a letter written by John Allan, and dated 15 October 1815, in which he pictures Poe, then but six years of age, sitting before a snug fire in their London home, reading a story-book.

There are also recent new records showing Poe, while a mere stripling, and before his advent into the world of letters, with copies of Goldsmith, and Byron at his elbow trying to cheer his disconsolate spirits, which were much disheartened by enforced work in Ellis and Allan's establishment at Richmond, Virginia, as a salesman of 'calicoes and dimities'. It is now clear from Allan's letters that Poe arrived at Liverpool in the latter part of the year 1815, and with the Allan family proceeded at once to Scotland, to visit the Allan relatives. While the visit was partly one of pleasure, Allan was about to establish a London commission house, with tobacco as a main staple, and there were important connections to be made in Scotland.

The first journey was to Irvine, Ayrshire, the birthplace of John Allan, where Poe and the family stopped with a spinster sister of Allan's named Mary Allan. There were other near relatives of the Allans in Irvine named Galt. Among them was James Galt, then about fifteen years old, who came to America with the Allan family when they returned home. He settled in Virginia, and was afterward John Allan's executor and the progenitor of the well-known family of Goldsboroughs of Maryland. He lived to a ripe old age, and a son named after Allan, Major John Allan Galt, not so long deceased, has left interesting unpublished reminiscences of his father, which also throw new light upon Poe's early career.

Irvine is a seaport, twenty-three miles south-east of Glasgow, and has a present population of upward of five thousand. At the time of Poe's visit the town differed somewhat from the present day. An idea of Old Irvine, and how it looked at the period of Poe's visit, may be had from the accompanying illustration shown here. The house where John Allan was born in 1780 faced the High Street, the main thoroughfare of the town, and was also the Kirkgate, an old rambling street leading to the Parish church. This locality remains practically the same as in Allan's day. In one of the houses on the opposite side of the street to the Allan house was born Henry Eckford, who constructed the American Navy during the War of 1812. Not far distant was the Blue Bell tavern, and upon its steps stood the town crier twice a week who, after tapping his old-fashioned drum, read aloud the news-letter, just arrived with the coach, for the benefit of the motley crowd about him.

At the head of the old Kirkgate was the ancient grammar school, where Allan was educated with John Galt, the novelist, father of the Kailyard School, and Henry Eckford. The school was famous in its day and the masters had many pupil boarders from America. Within its confines Poe's stay must have been brief. The school was a continuation of the Pre-Reformation School in connection with the Church, with which it was no doubt coeval.

The Kirk was there in 1205, but for how long before is not known. James VI, of Scotland, by a deed of 8 June 1572, granted to the magistrates and community of Irvine certain revenues belonging to the Church for the support of a school to be called 'The King's Foundation of the School of Irvine'. This was continued until July 1816, when a new Academy was erected.

It was John Allan's early hopes to have Poe remain there while abroad for his education, but his wife demurred, and Poe was also opposed to being left so far away from the family. James Galt expected to go to London at a later date, so it was arranged that he was to bring back Poe to Irvine for school.

Nearly opposite to the Allan house stood the old Townhouse and Tollbooth, now removed. James Montgomery, the Christian poet, was a native of Irvine, but left for the Morvia school renowned in Yorkshire, shortly before Allan was born. Only a few doors from the Allan house was the printing office and bookshop of David Macmillan, the founder of the well-known publishing house of that name. He served his apprenticeship under the erratic publisher, Maxwell Dick. Judge Hughes, author of *Tom Brown's School Days*, in his life of David Macmillan refers to the town of Irvine.

Anonymous engraving of a scene from 'William Wilson' the story which Poe based on his London schooldays

In this same square was Templeton's bookshop, where Burns, the poet, delighted to browse among old sheets of song. It was in the year 1781 that Burns went to Irvine to learn flax dressing, and the old shop stands within a stone's throw of where Allan was born. It was two years later that the strange sect, The Buchanites, arose at Irvine. Elspeth Simpson Buchan believed that she was the woman of Revelation xii, in whom the light of God was restored to man. The sect was expelled a year later, and became extinct in 1848. John Galt, the novelist, whose writings, by the way, are becoming more in vogue, in his autobiography tells that he followed the erratic crowd, till his mother brought him back by the 'lug of the horn'. Galt's well-known book, *Annals of the Parish*, is taken from old Irvine, and the parish minister of Galt's day mentioned the town:

> as dry and well aired, with one broad street running through it from the south-east. On the south of the river, but connected with the town by a stone bridge, there was a row of houses on each side of the road, leading to the harbour. These were mostly of one storey with finished garrets and occupied by seafaring people. To the north-west of the town there was a commonty of three hundred acres of a sandy soil and partly covered with whin and broom.

The town of Irvine in the seventeenth and succeeding century was a port of some consequence, being at these periods the third port in Scotland and port for Glasgow, goods being transferred to and from Glasgow on pack horses. In the days of the so-called Tobacco Lords, it did a considerable trade to America, and it was the ambition of the town lads to fill a position in Virginia. With the rise of Greenock, and Port Glasgow the trade gradually left Irvine. In the earlier days Irvine was a veritable 'Sleepy Hollow' for smugglers, and filled with retired shipmasters.

Beside the river Irvine stands the parish church and alongside it the graveyard, in which all the Allan ancestors are buried. The Allan section adjoins that of 'Dainty Davie', the friend of Burns. The first graveyard Poe probably ever entered was the historic St John's at Richmond, Virginia, where Patrick Henry delivered his patriotic speech, and where Poe's mother is buried. The Irvine churchyard was the second, and the third, Shockoe Cemetery, at Richmond, Virginia, where pleasant legends relate he kept vigils during his youth with the spirit of his first Helen.

'Of all melancholy topics,' Poe once asked himself, 'what, according to the universal understanding of mankind, is the most melancholy?' 'Death,' was the obvious reply.

There was much about this old Scottish kirkyard to inspire Poe with awe, and with his love for the odd, the rhyming tombstones, and the 'dregy', or lengthy funeral services must have left lasting impressions on his mind. The epitaphs on the tombstones hereabouts are most original, and in the olden time the grammar school scholars are said to have been required to write them out for their examinations. Here is a sample, vouched for by Galt, which may have met with Poe's gaze:

> A lovely Christian, spouse, and friend,
> Pleasant in life and at her end –
> A pale consumption dealt the blow
> That laid her here with dust below.

In Irvine, near the printing office of Maxwell Dick, was a house where Dr Robertson, 'the poet preacher', lodged. Here one day the well-known writer, De Quincey, came from Glasgow to visit him, but unfortunately the genial doctor was out. The canny Scots landlady took De Quincey, with a suspicious looking volume he usually carried under his arm, for a tramp book-canvasser, and would not permit him to come in and await Robertson's return. De Quincey in high dudgeon returned to the station and took the first conveyance back to Glasgow. On the way to and from the station De Quincey had to pass the house where Poe stopped.

In this connection it might be recalled that Poe later on proved an admirer of De Quincey, whose declamatory interpolations may be detected in his writings, especially in the tale of 'William Wilson'.

While in Irvine, Poe lived in a Bridgegate house, shown in the illustration (p33). It was a two-storey tenement dwelling owned by the Allan family. It was taken down about thirty years ago to make room for a street improvement. At the time of Poe's visit it was occupied by Mary Allan, who afterward removed to the Seagate house, which had been previously tenanted by Dr John MacKenzie, the friend of Burns, and who is reputed to have been a connection of William MacKenzie, of Richmond, Virginia, into whose family Poe's sister Rosalie was adopted.

The next visit made by Poe in Scotland was to Kilmarnock, about seven miles distant from Irvine. He remained at that town about two weeks, and while there

THE EDGAR ALLAN POE SCRAPBOOK

Left: **Irvine Cross, circa 1900**
Above: **Irvine Cross today**
Below: **The High Street, Irvine, circa 1900**

stopped with another of Allan's sisters, named Agnes, but called Nancy, who married a nurseryman, named Allan Fowld. The site of the old nursery is now Fowld, Clark and Prince Streets. The house stood on Nelson Street, on the present site of the building occupied by the Kilmarnock *Standard*; and opposite was the Townsend house, occupied by a family named Gregory, who perfectly remembered the visit of John Allan and his family, and little Edgar Allan Poe. In the rear of the Nelson house ran the grounds of Kilmarnock, in the crook of which was the shop where executed for his share in the '45 Rebellion. There stands near by a large grove of trees, and a beautiful walkway, where the Lord's widow passed much of her time after his death. Here is also what was afterward called the Ghosts' Walk, and there it is said the Lord's widow might be seen after sundown in her pensive perambulations, alone, and again in company with her murdered husband. No doubt Poe heard of this incident, and perchance looked himself for what they called the 'Allagrugous bawsy-broon', or the ghastly, grim hobgoblin.

Nelson Street extended by a crooked lane to the cross of Kilmarnock, in the crook of which was the shop where Burns's first edition of his poems was issued, a copy of which now fetches about two thousand dollars. There are relics of Burns still exhibited by the town, which was once also noted for its manufacture of Kilmarnock cowls.

One end of Nelson Street led to the old Irvine road, and a number of visits to and from Irvine were made by Allan during his stay, on which occasions Poe invariably accompanied him. The old red riding carts, then abounding about Irvine and Kilmarnock, with their creaking wheels, are said to have had a special attraction for Poe. He was most happy in one of them, sitting beside the driver, usually attired in a coarse woollen cloth 'green duffle apron', and thick nap 'red Kilmarnock cap'.

Close to the Fowld house in Kilmarnock lived William Anderson, an intimate neighbour of the family. His son, James Anderson, died 26 December 1887 aged eighty-four years. In early life he was an accountant in the Union bank and for a long period auditor for the corporation of Kilmarnock, as well as chairman of the Bellford Trust. He had vivid recollections of Poe's visit to Kilmarnock and spoke with pride of having played in the streets of the town with Poe. He recalled Poe as 'much petted by the Allans, and a "curmudgeon", or forward, quick-witted boy, but self-willed'. A portrait of Anderson is preserved in the art gallery of the Dick Institute in Kilmarnock.

Poe went from Kilmarnock with the Allan family to Greenock, situated on the Clyde. There remains a letter of Allan's written from there 21 September 1815, in which he says: 'Edgar says, "Pa, say something for me; say I was not afraid across the sea".' The family with Poe went from Greenock to Glasgow, thence to Edinburgh, and also called at Newcastle and Sheffield, as mentioned in a letter of Allan's, dated Blake's Hotel, London, 10 October 1815, where he arrived on the 7th, and wrote also of the attractions of the Scotland trip as 'high in all parts'.

Among Poe's boyhood journeys no other scenes could have left deeper impressions on his young mind than what he saw and heard in Scotland. In a land so full of the olden time and among people so enthusiastically devoted to their 'ain mither-land' and full of reverence for 'days o' auld syne', it is but natural that lasting impressions would be left on his memory. He might well have said:

> Old tales I heard of woe or mirth,
> Of lovers' slights, of ladies' charms,
> Of witches' spells, of warriors' arms;
> Of patriots' battles, won of old,
> By Wallace wight and Bruce bold.

When Poe published his tale, the 'M Valdemar Case', a

THE EDGAR ALLAN POE Scrapbook

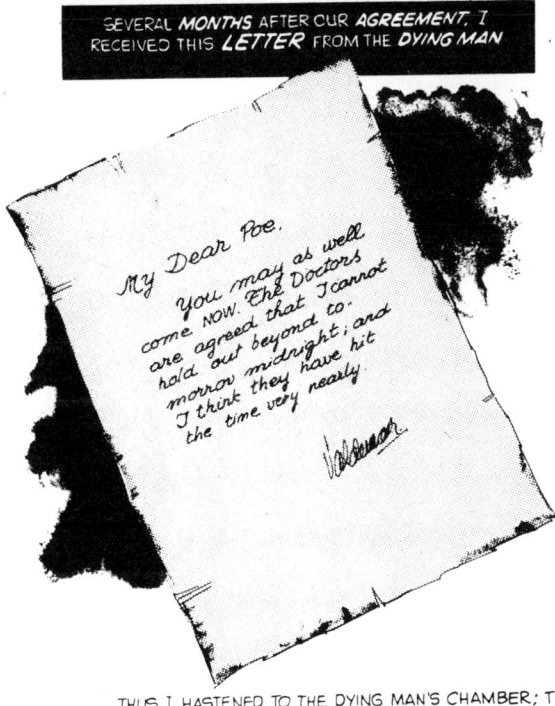

From *Psycho* magazine, October 1974

31

druggist at Stonehaven, Scotland, named Alexander Ramsay, to make sure the story was true, wrote a letter to Poe. This letter of Ramsay's to Poe has been published, but no reply of Poe's has ever appeared in print until now. The writer found a relative of Ramsay's still occupying the old Stonehaven warehouse. He had many of his relative's old letters, but none from Poe. The search, however, was continued and finally the reply from Poe was found with another relative in the same town. This letter is now first published, and is interesting in connection with this story of Poe's Scotland visits. It reads:

New York, 30 December '46

Dear Sir: Hoax *is* precisely the word suited to M Valdemar Case. The story appeared originally in the *American Review*, a monthly magazine published in this city. The London papers, commencing with the *Morning Post* and the *Popular Record of Science*, took up the theme. The article was generally copied in England and is now circulating in France. Some few persons believe it – but *I* don't – and don't you.

Very Resp'y, yr Ob St,
EDGAR A. POE

PS – I have some relatives, I think, in Stonehaven of the name of Allan, who again are connected with the Allans and Galts of Kilmarnock. My name is Edgar *Allan* Poe. Do you know any of them? If so, and it would not put you to too much trouble, I would like it as a favour if you could give me some account of the family.
To A. Ramsay, Esq

The postscript to this letter, written at so late a day in Poe's lifetime, in which he claims relationship with the Allans, reads a bit odd. It is said that Poe felt bitterly until the end that Allan should have brought him up, and educated him as an only child, until he had reached the advanced age of fifteen years, and then turn suddenly against him and make him feel a menial instead of a member of his family. This was the view Poe gave to 'Mary', his Baltimore sweetheart of the year 1832, who published her recollections in *Harper's Magazine*, many years after Poe's death. Her identity has recently been discovered by Professor Killis Campbell, as a Miss Deveraux, mentioned in the writer's latest, *Complete Poems of Poe*. [This article appears on page 94].

Above: **The Kirkgate, circa 1900**

Below: **Nelson Street, Kilmarnock, circa 1880**

She stated that Poe read her a letter from Allan, in which he threatened to disown him if he married her, which would indicate that Allan showed some disposition at that late date to lead Poe to be hopeful for some final recognition. John Allan told his sister, Mrs Fowld, of Kilmarnock, that he had willed his money to his sisters in Scotland, after providing for his wife during her lifetime and making adequate provisions for Edgar.

It is a curious fact that there are now families named Poe in and about Irvine, Scotland, who claim relationship with Poe, and stranger still that these families in turn, are also connected with the Allan family. The mother of John Spiers, who presented a statue of Burns to the town of Irvine, was named Poe.

Bridgegate, circa 1900

Bridgegate today

There is reason to believe that Poe must have met John Galt, the novelist, while visiting Scotland. Galt was a connection of John Allan's, and a school companion. There are many persons now in Irvine who have heard the statement handed down from their ancestors, that Edgar Allan Poe, the American poet, was a pupil in the old Irvine grammar school. This is confirmed by James Galt, although the stay of Poe must have been brief. James Galt lived in Irvine while Poe was on his first visit there. It had been the original intention of Allan to leave Poe at the school there for his education. To this Poe and Mrs Allan did not take kindly. As there was further holiday journeying it was decided to postpone school matters, and allow Poe to finish out the trip with the family, and return later to Irvine with Galt, who had planned to be in London later on.

The exact time of this second trip to Scotland was not mentioned, but there are several gaps in Poe's school record. It is presumed that the visit was toward the close of the year 1815.

There were pleadings from the women folks, as well as Poe, 'not to go', when the time for departure for Scotland arrived. It was the opinion, however, that Poe would be better satisfied after settling down, and out of sight of the home folks. The start on the part of Poe was unwilling and Galt said that he kept up 'an unceasing fuss all the way over'. His foster aunt Mary sent him to the school, but there he sulked, and no manner of coaxing or threats could induce him to enter into any studies. At Miss Allan's home he talked boldly about returning home to England alone, and fearing that he might carry out his threat young Galt, a typical tall Highlander, was required to remain there on guard. He slept in the same room with Poe in the Bridge-gate house; was impressed with Poe's old-fashioned talk for one so young, and believed that if he had not been restrained, that he would have attempted to make the trip to England alone.

LANDMARKS OF POE IN RICHMOND

CHARLES MARSHALL GRAVES

THIS FASCINATING article deals with Poe's early years in the town of Richmond and the influence some of its citizens were to have on his life. It appeared in the March 1904 issue of the popular American magazine, *The Century.*

EARLY IN the seventies a strange-looking woman, with a look of poverty and wretchedness in her shallow eyes, appeared upon the streets of Richmond, Virginia, trying to sell little photographs. They were likenesses of her brother, she said.

People stared at her and passed on. Once or twice an elderly man or woman stopped to speak to her, and she would almost cry with joy at sight of a familiar face. Before she let them go she spoke of her want and loneliness, and they readily bought the picture she offered. The brother was Edgar Allan Poe; the woman, Rosalie MacKenzie Poe, his only sister.

Poe loved Richmond as he loved no other place on earth. His happy childhood was spent there – the only period of his troubled life which was free from want. Here he found his foster-father, John Allan, who was proud of the orphan boy, and the only mother he ever knew, who was sweet and gentle with him to the end. Here were the friends and playmates of his boyhood, and here lived the gentle woman who was the 'Helen' of the most beautiful of his early poems. Here, after a first ceremony in Baltimore, he was married by a second to lovely and youthful Virginia Clemm, and here they spent the happiest year of their married life. Here, as editor of the *Southern Literary Messenger*, he did much of his best work.

At one time Richmond was full of houses and localities closely associated with the poet. It is a wonder and a pity, it would seem, that his biographers have not pointed these out. The theatre in which Poe's mother played stood on the north side of Broad street, between Twelfth and College streets. It was burned on the night of 26 December 1811. It was the benefit performance of Mr Placide, one of the most popular actors of Green's company, of which Mrs

33

The Allans' house in Richmond, Virginia

Poe had been a member, and as it was in the Christmas holidays the theatre was crowded. That night seventy-two perished in the flames. Scarcely a family of prominence in the city but lost a member or a close connection. Three years after the burning of the playhouse, the Monumental Church was erected on the site. The ashes of those who perished in the theatre are preserved in a marble urn in the vestibule of the church, and their names are inscribed upon it.

Mrs Poe appeared for the last time on her benefit night early in the October preceding the fire. Rosalie Poe was only a few months old, having been born in the summer of the same year; Edgar was nearly two, and William Henry four. Mrs Susan Archer Tally Weiss, who knew Poe intimately during his last visit to Richmond, in 1849, and to whom, says Professor Woodberry, in his excellent life of Poe, 'is due the most lifelike and detailed portrait of him that exists', has given me a connected and unquestionably correct account of the last days of Poe's father and mother.

David Poe, his father, died of consumption late in the spring of 1811, while the family was living in Norfolk. Mrs Weiss says that her mother's sister, Mrs Butt, and the Poes occupied a double tenement-house on Bermuda street, Norfolk, and that David Poe was buried in one of the cemeteries of Norfolk. Rosalie Poe was born about this time, whether before or after the death of her father, Mrs Weiss does not remember. In the summer of that year Mrs Poe came to Richmond that she might take her place in Green's company, which opened its engagement at the Richmond Theatre in September. Mrs Weiss says that the widowed actress, broken in health and utterly ruined in fortune, engaged a cellar for herself and her children under the store of a milliner named Phillips. She does not remember this man's Christian name, and there are no directories of Richmond as far back as that. His place was on the south side of Main street, in the Bird in Hand district, consequently near where Shockoe Creek now flows, going under the street, but then through it. In her damp cellar the delicate actress contracted pneumonia, and on Sunday, 8 December 1811, died. She was probably buried at the expense of the city. Her grave, says Mrs Weiss, is in the burying-ground of old St John's Church, by the eastern wall, but one looks for it in vain. This church is known to all the world for the immortal words spoken there by Patrick Henry: 'Give me liberty, or give me death.'

The good people of Richmond had been considerably wrought up by the appeal made through the Richmond *Enquirer* of 29 November. Mrs Poe was desperately ill and in great want, the paper said. The little paragraph, which is addressed to 'The Human Heart', concludes by saying that this would probably be her last plea for assistance. It was.

The children were not long homeless. William was sent to his grandfather in Baltimore. Mrs Jane MacKenzie took Rosalie. Mr and Mrs John Allan took Edgar. Dr John F. Carter, who obtained his information from his mother and other elderly ladies who were intimate with the Allan family, says that Mr and Mrs Allan had then no idea of adopting the boy, but were to take care of him until his mother's relatives in Baltimore could be reached.

The biographers are mistaken when they say that Mr Allan was then a wealthy man. He and Charles Ellis were doing a general merchandise business at the corner of Fourteenth street and Tobacco Alley, on a site opposite that of the Exchange Hotel, on Fourteenth street, where,

St John's Church, Richmond

many years after, Poe made his two appearances before Richmond audiences. Mr and Mrs Allan lived over the store. This was the modest temporary home which they gave the boy.

Dr Carter says that for weeks correspondence was conducted by Mr Allan with the Baltimore connections of the orphan. Their responses were not at all satisfactory, and in the meantime Edgar, no longer a baby skeleton, had grown to be such an attractive child that Mrs Allan begged her husband to keep him. They had no children though they had been married several years, and Mr Allan consented. But Dr Carter insists that Mr Allan never adopted the orphan in a legal way.

Mrs MacKenzie was at the time conducting a school for girls in a frame house at the north-west corner of Fifth and Main streets, just opposite the house which Mr Allan bought in the summer of 1825, and which was Poe's home for some months before he went to the University of Virginia. She had a number of children of her own, and her motherly heart could not turn the baby Rosalie into the street. So Poe and his sister were destined to grow up very near each other, and to see each other daily, as the families were intimate.

Mr William Galt, Mr Allan's uncle, had a store on Franklin street, between Fourteenth and Fifteenth, and did an immense tobacco business. His success probably turned the thoughts of Ellis & Allan toward an exclusive trade in tobacco, and with a view to opening a market for the famed Virginia leaf, Mr Allan went to England in 1814, taking with him Mrs Allan, her sister Miss Valentine, and Edgar. As every one knows, the boy was put at school in Stoke Newington. While Mr Allan was away, the Four-teenth-street store was given up. The first directory of Richmond ever published – that of John Maddox, 1819 – places the store of Ellis & Allan on the east side of Fifteenth street, south of Main, second door from the corner. It is interesting to note that while the first building is now long in the dust, it stood just across the alley from where now rises the big printing-house of Mr John W. Fergusson, who was a 'devil' in the office of the *Southern Literary Messenger* when Poe was its editor: and the second stands today adjoining the *Messenger* building, where Poe wrote his spiciest criticisms and the early instalments of 'Arthur Gordon Pym'.

The biographers carelessly say that, when Mr Allan came back, his house was leased and he went to Mr Ellis's residence. The fact is that Mr Allan had no residence upon his return in the summer of 1820. Mr Ellis had a comfortable home on Franklin street, between First and Second. The residence was on the south side of Franklin, while opposite he had a fine vineyard. Mr and Mrs Allan and Edgar remained with the Ellises nearly a year, when Mr Allan rented a small frame dwelling on North Fifth street, near the corner of Clay. This cottage – for it was scarcely more – was standing within the last ten years, and was torn down to make room for a more pretentious brick residence. A livery-stable stands on a part of the yard in which Poe played.

It was while in this house that the poet attended the classical school of Joseph H. Clarke. Clarke, a fiery Irishman from Trinity College, Dublin, gave up teaching in the fall of 1823. Poe was selected by the boys to deliver the farewell ode, and did so with grace and with satisfaction to all. Master William Burke succeeded Master Clarke. Dr Creed

Thomas, who was Poe's desk-mate at Burke's, and who lived until 23 February 1899, said in an interview a short time before his death that the school was at the south-east corner of Broad and Eleventh streets, where the Powhatan Hotel now stands.

It was while under these masters that Poe accomplished the swim from Richmond to Warwick Park, six miles down the James. This famous swim was made later by Mr Charles M. Wallace, the Richmond antiquarian. One of Poe's playmates told this gentleman that he started the swim with Poe, but the imperious youth was so furious that another should attempt to rival him that he yielded to Poe and got into the boat accompanying them.

Rare tintype of Poe's sister, Rosalie (POE FOUNDATION INC)

Portrait of Sarah Elmira Royster Shelton (POE FOUNDATION INC)

Poe, Dr Creed Thomas, Beverly Anderson, and William P. Ritchie, all destined to be men of note, were at that time members of the Thespian Society, and gave their amateur theatrical performances in the old wooden house which stood at the north-east corner of Marshall and Sixth streets, where the Second Police Station now is. It was from Burke's school that one afternoon Poe went home with Monroe Stanard, one of his few intimate friends, to meet that lad's mother, the gentle Jane Stith Craig Stanard, whom the boy loved at first sight, and who became the 'Helen' of one of the most exquisite poems ever written. He thought the name of Jane ugly, and addressed his lines 'To Helen' instead. When Mrs Stanard died, his young heart was almost broken, and night after night he would go to her grave and weep upon it. Mrs Stanard was the wife of the Hon Robert Stanard, a lawyer of great ability and for a number of years United States attorney for the district of Virginia.

Dr Carter tells me the story of 'Don Pompioso', one of the early poems, now lost. A young man had hurt Poe's feelings. He held himself too high to associate with the son of an actress and a pauper, and let the high-strung boy understand it. Soon a poem appeared on the street ridiculing this young man unmercifully. The girls at Mrs MacKenzie's school, then at No 506 East Franklin street, got hold of the poem and were laughing over it and wondering who its author was. That evening about dusk Poe dropped in at the school, where his sister lived and where he came and went at pleasure, a privilege denied to other young men of the city. A number of young people were in the parlour, and one of the girls asked him to read the poem aloud. This he did by the fading light, reading with a readiness that one could not possibly have shown without really repeating it from memory. 'You wrote it!' they all cried, and he did not deny it. When the young man who had drawn such fire appeared on the street, he was peppered with allusions from the poem, with jests and gibes, and at length he was driven from the city. The MacKenzie school is standing yet, and is in good condition, considering its age. Dr Carter identifies it positively, as he knew the MacKenzies intimately.

In March 1825, Poe left Burke's school and began his preparation for the University of Virginia. It was about this time that he met Miss Sarah Elmira Royster, his first sweetheart, afterward Mrs Shelton.

This year was also eventful to Mr Allan. His uncle, Mr Galt, died in March, and Mr Allan came in for one third of his estate, valued at approximately one million dollars. Mr Robert Lee Traylor of Richmond has a certified copy of Mr Galt's will. It shows that Mr Allan received more than three hundred thousand dollars in money and property, a great fortune in that day. This was really the first time in his life that Mr Allan had more than a comfortable living. Less than two months after Mr Galt's death Mr Allan bought the house at the south-east corner of Fifth and Main streets, long known locally as the 'Allan house'. He did not give up the cottage home, however, for two or three months.

Poe lived in the new home from late in the summer of 1825 until the middle of February 1826, when he entered the University of Virginia.

He came back to the Allans in December of the same year, but, not liking the counting-room work which Mr Allan set him doing, after a few days' trial he ran away. He returned when Mrs Allan died, 28 February 1829. Mr Woodberry says it was not until some days after her death. He was seeking appointment to the West Point Academy, and had been advised to get Mr Allan's influence. Mr Allan gave it in a letter in which he took pains to disown him.

Mrs Weiss and Dr Carter assert with equal positiveness that Edgar Poe left the Allans on account of unpleasant words with the second Mrs Allan. Mrs Weiss says that this lady took Poe's room from him and gave him one in the back of the house, not nearly so attractive. This made him furious, as it is easy to imagine, and a wordy war followed. This was the reason, say she and Dr Carter, that Mr Allan sent Poe away. But it is apparently impossible, with the admitted dates before one, to reconcile the inconsistencies. If these two reputable persons are right, there are yet some missing links in the poet's biography; for the second Mrs Allan is said to have stated that, in all, she saw the poet but twice.

The Allan house was torn down fifteen years ago. For a long time the lot remained vacant. Until a year ago the Young Men's Christian Association had an athletic field on it, but now it has been built up with residences fronting on Fifth street and with stores fronting on Main.

On St Valentine's day of 1826, Poe entered the University of Virginia. His happy days in the Allan household were gone. He came back to Richmond under a cloud, but soon ran away, breaking for ever the tie which bound him to his benefactor.

Tradition says that Mrs Allan made an appeal to Mr Allan on her death-bed to do all he could for Edgar, and this was the reason Mr Allan consented to use his influence to get the appointment to West Point. The story of his life there and his movements for five years afterward belongs to his biographers. He came to Richmond only once in this period. That was just before the death of Mr Allan. The story is that he rushed to Mr Allan's room and found him sitting in a chair. Upon seeing the wayward young man, Mr Allan, it is said, seized his walking-stick, and waving it menacingly, bade him leave the house forever.

Mr Allan died in the latter part of March 1834. In the summer of the next year Poe came to Richmond to help Mr Thomas W. White edit the *Southern Literary Messenger*. The old *Messenger* building is not only standing yet, but is in excellent condition. The *Messenger* was printed on the first floor, while Mr White and the poet had their offices on the second floor, overlooking the street.

Below: **Copper plate engraving of 'The Burning of the Theater in Richmond' December 1811** (POE FOUNDATION INC)
Below right: **Offices of the** *Southern Literary Messenger* **where Poe worked**

In the spring of 1836 Mrs Clemm and Virginia came to Richmond and obtained board with Mrs James Yarrington, whose house was at the corner of Twelfth and Bank streets. The flames of 1865 swept it away. It is virtually certain that here Edgar and Virginia were married. The date, 16 May 1836, is well known. The Rev Amasa Converse, editor of the *Southern Religious Telegraph*, a Presbyterian weekly, performed the ceremony. Thomas W. Cleland went on the marriage bond, swearing that Virginia was twenty-one when she was but fourteen.

'There never was a more perfect gentleman than Mr Poe when he was sober,' says Mr Fergusson, 'but he was a very devil when drunk. He would just as soon lie down in the gutter as anywhere else.'

It was on account of 'lying down in the gutter' too often that Mr White announced in the first number of the

Title page of first issue of the *Southern Literary Messenger,* **August 1834** (POE FOUNDATION INC)

Important page from the *Southern Literary Messenger,* **December 1835 announcing Poe's arrival on the staff** (POE FOUNDATION INC)

Messenger of 1837 that 'Mr Poe's attention has been called in another direction.'

Early in August 1849, Poe was again in Richmond.

One of his new friends was John R. Thompson, the poet, who two years before had purchased the *Messenger*. Another new friend was little Miss Susan Archer Talley, who, though but seventeen years old, had written some admirable poems. She had heard much of the distinguished poet from her mother, the MacKenzies, and Rosalie, and had read almost everything he had written. Miss Talley is now the Mrs Weiss who has already been mentioned in this article. She is still living and is a beautiful old lady.

Poe took lodgings at Swan Tavern, on the north side of Broad, between Eighth and Ninth streets. This famous old building was erected about 1795 and was the leading tavern in Richmond for a quarter of a century. But when Poe came there in 1849 the prestige of the place was gone. It was hardly more than a cheap boarding-house. The poet did not go there first, but to the United States Hotel, at the south-west corner of Nineteenth and Main streets, in the Bird in Hand neighbourhood, where his mother had died. The building is standing, and is now used as a Methodist mission house.

Poe changed to the Swan, to be nearer his friends the MacKenzies, who were living at Duncan Lodge, a mile out on the Broad-street road. The Swan building is in bad condition and is soon to be torn down. In exterior appearance it has changed but little since Poe's eyes saw it – just a little older and a little more battered.

Naturally, Poe went at once to see the MacKenzies, for they had ever been faithful to him, and his sister was there. Here he met many of his old friends and was introduced to others who knew him by reputation and soon became warmly attached to him. One of the latter was Dr John F. Carter. Dr Carter is still living in Richmond. He says that one night, when no one was there but the family and two or three intimate friends, the poet recited 'The Raven'. He did it so admirably that he was persuaded to give a public reading at the Exchange Hotel. Dr Carter and ten other persons attended, and this was Poe's first audience in his old home. There is no accounting for the small attendance. Poe certainly did not understand it. Dr Carter says he never saw any one more cast down. He went through the reading in a mechanical way, and at once went out.

Poe was asked some time later to deliver his lecture on 'The Poetic Principle'. He was assured of a good attendance, and the lecture was announced. Financially it was a tremendous success. Three hundred tickets were sold at five dollars each. The proprietor tendered the parlours of the Exchange free of charge, and so the poet's pocket was replenished, and he was as deeply gratified now as he was downcast before.

One of the eleven persons who attended the reading of 'The Raven' was Mrs Elmira Shelton, already referred to as Poe's first sweetheart, Sarah Elmira Royster. When he came to Richmond in 1849 he sought her out, then a widow with youthful comeliness retained and an abundance of this world's goods. She was living on Grace street between Twenty-fourth and Twenty-fifth streets, directly behind St John's Church.

The place where Poe felt most at home was Duncan Lodge, the home of the MacKenzies. The old place looks today very much as it did during that summer and autumn fifty-four years ago. The only alteration to the house since Poe knew it is the addition of a storey. It is now used as an industrial home for men.

On the south side of Broad street the girlhood home of Mrs Weiss yet stands. The poet was a frequent visitor there. The house is unchanged in appearance, though Mrs Weiss tells me that the surroundings are greatly altered. All the beautiful trees are gone. It was at this house that Poe spent the evening of his last night but one in Richmond. Sitting with the Talley family until bedtime, he came down Broad street to Duncan Lodge and spent the night. The poet met some gay friends in Sadler's Old Market Hotel the next night, and they talked, laughed, and drank together until early morning, when the boat left for Baltimore. It carried Poe away from Richmond for ever.

The American artist, Frederick Simpson Coburn's illustration for 'The Oval Portrait', 1902

RISE INFERNAL SPIRITS!

A POEM BY EDGAR A. POE

THIS POEM was written by Poe when he was thirteen years old and is probably the earliest completed example of his youthful work. It was written in 1822 and discovered among the files of Ellis & Allan, the firm run by Poe's stepfather, John Allan. Although it was unsigned, experts are convinced it was the work of young Edgar because it is characteristic in both style and penmanship.

> Flow softly – gently – vital stream;
> Ye crimson life drops, stay;
> Indulge me with this pleasing dream
> Thro' an internal day.
>
> See – see – my soul, her agony!
> See how her eyeballs glare!
> Those shrieks delightful harmony,
> Proclaim her deep despair.
>
> Rise – rise – infernal spirits, rise,
> Swift dart across her brain
> Thou Horror with blood chilling cries
> Lead on thy hideous train.
>
> O, feast my soul revenge is sweet
> Louisa, take my scorn –
> Curs'd was the hour that saw us meet
> The hour when we were born.

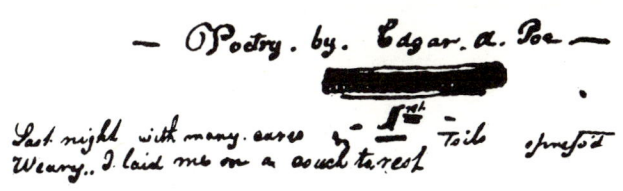

The earliest known lines of poetry and signature of Poe written when he was still a boy in November 1824 and found among papers in his foster-father's shop

THE UNIVERSITY STORY-TELLER

T. G. TUCKER

THIS IS one of the few reports by a contemporary of Poe at the University of Virginia and it is interesting in that it shows young Edgar to be already a lover of the weird and the macabre. Tucker also recalled that his friend liked drinking – though his capacity was limited – and although he gambled, rarely won. The extract is taken from the *University of Virginia Magazine*, 1880.

Poe's room at the University of Virginia

WHATEVER POE may have been in after years, he was at the University as true and perfect a friend as the waywardness of his nature would allow. There was never then the least trace of insincerity, and never the least indication of that fickleness of disposition with which he was afterwards so often – although in the main, we think, unjustly – accused.

Poe showed his warm appreciation and high respect for his friend Tucker by reading to him the early productions of his youth – productions that his critical hand afterwards destroyed, thinking them unfit for publication. Sometimes, when he had written an article that Tucker would especially praise, he would call in a few of his friends and read it to them. Those men who were fortunate enough to hear these impromptu readings never forgot them, and those of the number who were still living in 1880 declared that there was no impression on their minds more strikingly vivid. They were mostly stories characterised by that same weirdness of style, graphically picturing horrible scenes and incidents, that so strongly marked all of his published writings. His little room on West Range was often filled with a small, select audience of his most particular friends who, spell-bound, scarcely breathed while they eagerly listened to some story – strange and wild, like all the rest – that he had just written and that he read with his whole soul thrown into every action and intonation of his voice – now loud and rapid, like the mad rush of many waters, and now sinking into a scarcely audible whisper, of some terrible sentence of incantation or curse sending a shiver over all that heard.

On one occasion Poe read a story of great length to some of his friends who, in a spirit of jest, spoke lightly of its merits, and jokingly told him that his hero's name, 'Gaffy', occurred too often. His proud spirit would not stand such open rebuke; so in a fit of anger, before his friends could prevent him, he had flung every sheet into a blazing fire, and thus was lost a story of more than ordinary parts which, unlike most of his stories, was intensely amusing, entirely free from his usual sombre colouring and sad conclusions merged in a mist of impenetrable gloom. He was for a long time afterwards called by those in his particular circle 'Gaffy' Poe, a name that he never altogether relished.

Unusual portrait of Poe when he was a young man and published in *Graham's Magazine*, **February 1845**

POE'S LEGENDARY YEARS

GEORGE WOODBERRY

THE GROWTH of the Poe legend has been helped not only by his bizarre lifestyle, but the puzzling six-year period from Christmas 1826 (when he was seventeen) to 1833, when his whereabouts and occupation are in the main shrouded in mystery. These years have come in for much study and discussion, and perhaps one of the most interesting early articles to consider all the scraps of legend, rumour and half-truth was this essay by the noted Poe scholar and biographer, Professor George Woodberry. It appeared in *Atlantic Monthly* of December 1884.

THE LEGEND of Edgar Allan Poe would not be an inappropriate title for his biography. The most striking of the few things that the narratives of Poe's life have in common is a mythological strain, as if some subtle influence were at work in the minds of men to transform his career into a story stranger than truth, and to make his memory a mere tradition. It appears in that first newspaper article which Griswold wrote before the earth had chilled the body of the dead poet:

He walked the streets, in madness or melancholy, with lips moving in indistinct curses, or with eyes upturned in passionate prayer for their happiness who at the moment were objects of his idolatry; or with his glances introverted to a heart gnawed with anguish and with a face shrouded in gloom, he would brave the wildest storms, and all night, with drenched garments and arms beating the winds and rains, would speak as if to spirits that at such times only could be evoked by him from the Aidenn.

It is as plain to be seen in Baudelaire's declamatory eulogy over him as the martyr of a raw democracy. In Gilfillan he is the archangel ruined; in Ingram he is the ruined archangel rehabilitated; in all the biographies there is a demoniac element, as if Poe, who nevertheless was a man and an American, were a creature of his own fancy. This change which is worked upon Poe's human nature by the lurid reflection of his imagination is almost justifiable, since the true impression of him must be not only of a man who ate, slept, and put on his clothes, but of a genius as well, whose significant life was thought. In the legend of him, however, there is also a romantic element, not springing from any idiosyncrasy of his own character, but purely literary, historic; belonging to the time when our fathers wore Byron collars and were on fire for adventure in the corsair line, and all for dying in the sere and yellow leaf of their thirty-sixth year. Thus, in what would sentimentally be called his *Wanderjahre*, Poe is represented as a young Giaour in Greece, or as a Don Juan in some French provincial town; but always as a scapegrace of the transcendent order, impetuous, chivalric, unfortunate – in a word, Byronic.

The young stowaway is found. A moment from 'Arthur Gordon Pym', illustrated by A. D. McCormick from an edition of the novel published in 1898

It is an amiable human weakness to believe those we love better than they are; and he, even the humblest of us, who has not profited by such fond idolatry must be a very pitiable creature. The idealisation of the illustrious dead is wrought similarly, though rather by the imagination than the heart; and this refining and exalting power is a great privilege of our nature, for it strengthens and supports our faith in perfection, and brings a light of promise on our own lives. Of old, Hercules and Perseus, Roland and St Francis, were golden names on the lips of youth, and the modern age has not been a mean heir of history. There is a light around Shelley's head that any saint, the noblest and purest in the calendar, might righteously envy. No man would deny to Poe the honour or affection won by his manhood or his genius, if, in however less a degree, his purpose was of the same high kind. Nay, if the memory that gathers about his name were merely picturesque, were that of a boy-Byron, who rode on until he drank waters of Marah quite different from those mock ones for which the noble lord found hock and soda a sufficient remedy, we would welcome the romance and regret the sorrow of it, and never disturb the tradition of a fine folly. Let the myth increase and flourish if the root be sound and the flower sweet, and let a leaf from it decorate our sober annals; but if the bloom be *fleurs du mal*, and the root a falsehood, let us keep our literary history plain and unadorned, raw democracy though we be. In the worship of genius, we know, as in that of the gods, there springs up now and then a degraded cult.

'In a biography,' wrote Poe, 'the truth is everything' but he was thinking of other people's biographies. The speediest discovery that a student of his life makes is that Poe was his own myth-maker. He had a habit of secrecy, and on occasion he could render silence more sure by a misleading word. Thus it happens that in the various versions of his story the incidents seem to share in the legendary character of the hero. The record belongs, one would say, to that early period of literature when our ancestors first termed biographies *Veracious Hystories*. The three white stones of life, even – birth, marriage, and death – are, in Poe's case, graven with different dates; the first bearing four from his own hand, to which Mr R. H. Stoddard has thoughtfully contributed a fifth. The most obscure period, however, extends from the Christmas holidays of 1826, when he was just under eighteen years old, to the fall of 1833, when Kennedy found him starving in Baltimore. During this time, from 1 July 1830 to 7 March 1831, he was in the light of day at West Point. To the remainder of the period on each side of his cadet life the romantic element in his myth belongs, and to it this paper will be devoted in order to elucidate somewhat more in detail than was possible in a limited volume the facts of his career.

Poe left his home at Mr Allan's in the beginning of 1827, and he entered West Point in July, 1830. The story which was accredited throughout his lifetime as a true account of his doings during the intervening years first appeared in print in the sketch of him included in Griswold's *Poets and Poetry of America*, published in 1842, the materials for which, Griswold said, were furnished by Poe himself. It was as follows:

Mr Allan refused to pay some of his [Poe's] debts of *honour*. He hastily quitted the country on a Quixotic expedition to join the Greeks, then struggling for liberty. He did not reach his original destination, however, but made his way to St Petersburg, in Russia, where he became involved in difficulties, from which he was extricated by the late Mr Henry Middleton, the American minister at that capital. He returned home in 1829, and immediately afterward entered the military academy at West Point.

The next year, H. B. Hirst, a young Philadelphia poet, repeated this statement in a more extended sketch of Poe:

With a young friend, Ebenezer Burling, he endeavoured to make his way, with scarcely a dollar in his pocket, to Greece, with the wild design of aiding in the revolution then taking place. Burling soon repented his folly, and gave up the design when he had scarcely entered on the expedition. Mr Poe persevered, but did not succeed in reaching the scene of action; he proceeded, however, to St Petersburg, where through deficiency of passport, he became involved in serious difficulties, from which he was finally extricated by the American consul. He returned to America, only in time to learn the severe illness of Mrs Allan, who, in character, was the reverse of her husband, and whom he sincerely loved. He reached Richmond on the night after her burial.

The huge, shrouded figure which confronts Arthur Gordon Pym in the icy wastes at the conclusion of the novel – another picture by A. D. McCormick

This was published in the *Philadelphia Saturday Museum*, with which Poe then had close connections, and the article was written for the express purpose of advancing a scheme which he had in hand, in partnership with the owner of this newspaper, to establish a new periodical. Poe sent the sketch to Lowell a year later as authority for a new life which the latter was to prepare for *Graham's Magazine*, and wrote that Hirst had obtained his information from Mr T. W. White, owner of the *Southern Literary Messenger*, and Mr F. W. Thomas, a littérateur, both intimates of Poe; and he added that he believed it was 'correct in the main'. Lowell therefore introduced the story as here told into his own article, and sent it to Poe, who revised it with his own hand and forwarded it to *Graham's*, where it appeared in February 1845. Griswold naturally embodied the reiterated and uncontradicted account in his 'Memoir' after Poe's death.

This, however, was the established version long before 1842. A gentleman who saw Poe last at some time earlier than 1831, at Baltimore, writes to me, 'I remember he told me he had left Richmond in a coal vessel, and made his way to Europe, to Russia.' Allan B. Magruder, Esq, who was with him at West Point, also writes:

I am unable to remember whether I derived the information I gave you in a former letter, as to Poe's rambles in the East and his whaling voyage before the mast, from Poe himself while a classmate at West Point, or from some mutual friend who received the account from him. I certainly learned it while he was at the military academy.

Mr Magruder goes on to give the story then current as follows:

> He made a voyage to sea on some merchant vessel, before the mast. Finding himself in the Mediterranean, he debarked at some Eastern port, and penetrated into Egypt and Arabia. Returning to the United States, he enlisted as a private in the United States Army at Fortress Monroe. After some months' service his whereabouts and position became known to Mr Allan, who, through the mediation of General Scott, obtained his release from the army, and sent him a cadet's warrant to West Point.

These letters fix the date of the alleged adventures before July, 1830. The voyage to Greece and the journey to St Petersburg, however, are stated by Mr Didier, in his biography, to belong to the life of Poe's elder brother, William, and have consequently been discredited by later writers.

A second story is at hand, and for it we are indebted to Mr Ingram, the English biographer. After mentioning that Poe's first book was printed at Boston, in 1827, on which account he supposes that the young man visited that city in the spring, he continues his narrative as follows:

> Toward the end of June 1827, Edgar Poe would appear to have left the United States for Europe. It is very problematical whether he ever reached his presumed destination, the scene of the Greco-Turkish warfare... Edgar Poe was absent from America on his Hellenic journey about eighteen months. The real adventures of his expedition have never, it is believed, been published. That he reached England is probable, although in the account of his travels, derived from his own dictation, that country was not alluded to any more than was the story of his having reached St Petersburg, and there having been involved in difficulties that necessitated ministerial aid to extricate him. The latter incident is now stated to have occurred to his brother, William Henry Leonard, whilst Edgar himself, it has been suggested by a writer claiming personal knowledge of him, resided for some time in London, formed the acquaintance of Leigh Hunt and Theodore Hook, and, like them, lived by literary labour.

According to Poe's own story, which apparently accounts only for a portion of his time, he arrived, eventually, at a certain seaport in France. Here he was drawn into a quarrel about a lady, and in a fight which ensued was wounded by his antagonist, a much more skilful swordsman than he was. Taken to his lodgings, and possibly ill tended, he fell into a fever. A poor woman, who attended to his needs and pitied him, made his case known to a Scotch lady of position, who was visiting the town in the hope of persuading a prodigal brother to relinquish his evil ways and return home with her. This lady came to see the wounded stranger, and for thirteen weeks had him cared for; providing for all his wants, including the attendance of a skilled nurse, whose place, indeed, she often took herself. Whilst Poe was in a precarious condition she visited him daily, and even persuaded her brother to come and see the young Englishman, as his language led them to believe he was. When the patient became convalescent he was naturally intensely grateful to his generous benefactor. As the only means he possessed at that time of showing his gratitude, he wrote a poem to her, which he entitled 'Holy Eyes', with reference to the trust, sympathy, and faith which he deemed her blue eyes typical of. Indeed, according to Poe's description, the lady's eyes were her chief personal attraction, she being otherwise plain, large-featured, and old-maidish. Owing to the peculiarity of her position in this foreign seaport, she did not wish her name made public, and impressed this upon the youthful poet. She made him promise to return to America – and perhaps supplied the means for him to do so – and adopt a profession, in which she expressed a hope of some day hearing that he had become famous.

During his stay in France – so runs Poe's narration – he wrote a novel, in which his own adventures were described under the garb of fiction. The manuscript of this story he carried back with him to America, and retained it in his possession until at least some few years before his death. When asked why he had not published it, he replied that a French version of it had been published, and had been accredited to Eugène Sue, but that he would not sanction its publication in English because it was too sensational; that it was not to his taste; that it had too much of 'the yellow-cover-novel style' for him to be proud of it; and, moreover, that it contained 'scenes and pictures so personal that it would have made him many enemies among his kindred, who hated him for his vanity and pride already and in some respects very justly – the faults of his early education.' The truth in his story, he asserted, was yet more terrible than the fiction. *The Life of an Artist at Home and Abroad* was the title by which Poe at one time designated this youthful novel: it was written entirely in the third person, and was pronounced by its author to be 'commonplace'.

This circumstantial narrative was dictated by Poe to Mrs Maria L. Shew, of New York 'from what', says Mr Ingram, 'it was deemed at the time might be his death-bed'. That biograher finds it hard to decide whether the story 'was fact, or fact and fiction deliriously interwoven, or mere fiction, invented in such a spirit of mischief as, like Byron, he frequently indulged in at the expense of his too inquisitive questioners.' A death-bed is not the place where one expects to find a spirit of mischief, and there is more truth, though not perhaps in the sense meant, in what Mr Ingram elsewhere remarks of this same matter: 'There does not appear to be any reason for doubting the accuracy of this any more than of any other of the poet's statements.

A third story develops the tradition referred to by Mr Magruder, that Poe was in the army; but instead of placing this in the period before he went to West Point, his biographers assign it to the time after he was dismissed from the academy. The first mention of it in print occurs in Griswold's 'Memoir' as follows:

> His contributions to the journals attracted little attention, and, his hopes of gaining a living in this way being disappointed, he enlisted in the army as a private soldier. How long he remained in the service I have not been able to ascertain. He was recognised by officers who had known him at West Point, and efforts were made privately, but with prospects of success, to obtain for him a commission, when it was discovered by his friends that he had deserted.

An illustration by W. Heath Robinson in 1900 for a poem which typified Poe's life, 'Alone'

THE EDGAR ALLAN POE SCRAPBOOK

Mr Gill supports this version, on the authority of Mrs Clemm, Poe's mother-in-law:

In a fit of desperation, the poet on leaving Mr Allan's house [in 1831] enlisted in the army. He soon became seriously ill from the exposure incident to the unwonted hardship of barrack-life, and, being recognised by friends while at the hospital, his discharge was promptly secured. Griswold's statement that he deserted is, like others made by him, a malicious invention. The facts are, on the written testimony of Mrs Clemm, that at this time his friends were seeking for him a commission.

Mr Ingram remarks on this period:

All attempts hitherto made to explain what Poe did and whither he wandered during the next two years [1831-1833] succeeding his expulsion from his godfather's home have signally failed. The assertion that he was residing at Baltimore with his aunt, Mrs Clemm, is not in accordance with fact, her correspondence proving *that she never did know* where her nephew was during this interregnum in his history . . . Another biographer, of proven unreliability [Griswold], suggests that Poe enlisted in the army, but after a short service deserted.

Of other writers who have dealt with the problem, Powell states that Poe went to help the Poles against Russia (but this is evidently a misquotation from Hirst); Mr Didier places him at Richmond in the first period, and at Baltimore in the second; and Mr Stoddard, while discrediting the early rupture with Mr Allan on the ground that the latter probably paid for the Boston edition of the poems, discreetly disclaims any faculty for writing imaginary biographies.

In all that has been laid before the reader in opening the state of the question there is but one sure fact. A book, *Tamerlane and Other Poems*, by 'A Bostonian', was published in Boston by Calvin F. S. Thomas in 1827. A copy is in the British Museum, and its contents consist of the first drafts of poems since known as Poe's. On the threshold of investigation, however, I was met by the opinion that the author was John Howard Payne; but this suggestion was altogether too startling, it disclosed too dismal a view of my hero, to be entertained. The volume had contemporary mention in *The United States Review and Literary Gazette*, August 1827; *The North American Review*, October 1827; and Kettell's *Specimens of American Poetry*, 1829. In all these it was only named, but that is enough to show that it was issued before August and had some circulation. The name of Calvin F. S. Thomas is in the *Boston Directory*, 1827, where he is described as a printer at 70 Washington Street; but he was not a member of the Franklin Typographical Union, nor does any Boston printer of that time remember him except one now in Wisconsin, who merely thinks that he recalls him. His name is found also, crossed off, in a trial tax-list of 1827, in which he is assessed only for a poll-tax. These are meagre facts, nor is much added to them by the statements of his daughter, who, I learned through some obliging strangers, is living in Missouri. She writes that her father resided in Boston with his widowed mother and a sister in 1827, and, being then nineteen years old, had a printer's shop there; he left the city in 1828, and afterwards lived in New York, Buffalo, and Springfield, Mo, and died in 1876. 'None of us', she says (his wife and sister being still alive), 'can remember ever having heard him speak of himself as the publisher of Poe's early poems;

no copy of the book is in the possession of any member of the family – neither account-books nor letters of that period.' In view of the almost universal publication of reminiscences by those who knew Poe, and of the extraordinary interest of this portion of his life, it may fairly be inferred that Thomas never identified the author of the first book he printed with Poe, or, in other words, that the latter dealt with him under an assumed name.

One other source of information, besides this volume, would naturally occur to the mind, but it is so obvious that resort to it would seem superfluous. If Poe was in the army, the records of the War Department would show the facts. Secretary Lincoln had a search made for the name of Poe, or any name with his initials whose bearer's career in the army corresponded in time and character with that ascribed to him. Adjutant-General Drum took up the subject with great kindness, and it is to his personal efforts, Secretary Lincoln informs me, that the recovery of Poe's army record is due. The examination of documents both at Washington and elsewhere has been exhaustive.

From these papers it appears that on 26 May 1827 Poe enlisted at Boston in the Army of the United States as a private soldier, under the name of Edgar A. Perry. He

Aubrey Beardsley produced this restrained but striking illustration for *The Fall of the House of Usher*, **1894**

stated that he was born at Boston, and was by occupation a clerk; and although minors were then accepted into the service he gave his age as twenty-two years. He had, says the record, gray eyes, brown hair, and a fair complexion; was five feet eight inches in height. He was at once assigned to Battery H of the First Artillery, then serving in the harbour at Fort Independence; on 31 October the battery was ordered to Fort Moultrie, Charleston, SC, and exactly one year later to Fortress Monroe, Va. The officers under whom he served are dead, but it appears that he discharged his duties as company clerk and assistant in the commissariat department so as to win the goodwill of his superiors. On 1 January 1829, he was appointed Sergeant-Major, a promotion which, by the invariable custom of the army, was given only for merit. He now made his circumstances known to Mr Allan, and shortly after Mrs Allan's death, 28 February 1829, he returned to Richmond on leave of absence. Of this furlough there is no record, but on 28 February he is reported on the rolls as present for duty.

The result of his visit is told in the following letter, which is, however, extraordinarily inaccurate in its details:

Fortress Monroe, 30 March '29

General: I request your permission to discharge from the service Edgar A. Perry, at present the Sergeant-Major of the 1st Reg't of Artillery, on his procuring a substitute.

The said Perry, is one of a family of orphans whose unfortunate parents were the victims of the conflagration of the Richmond theatre, in 1809. The subject of this letter, was taken under the protection of a Mr Allan, a gentleman of wealth and respectability, of that city, who, as I understand, adopted his protégé as his son and heir; with the intention of giving him a liberal education, he had placed him at the University of Virginia from which, after considerable progress in his studies, in a moment of youthful indiscretion he absconded, and was not heard from by his Patron for several years; in the meantime, he became reduced to the necessity of enlisting into the service and accordingly entered as a soldier in my Regiment, at Fort Independence, in 1827. Since the arrival of his company at this place, he has made his situation known to his Patron at whose request, the young man has been permitted to visit him; the result is, an entire reconciliation on the part of Mr Allan, who reinstates him into his family and favour, and who in a letter I have received from him requests that his son may be discharged on procuring a substitute. An experienced soldier and approved sergeant is ready to take the place of Perry so soon as his discharge can be obtained. The good of the service, therefore cannot be materially injured by the discharge.

I have the honour to be, with great respect,
Your obedient servant,
JAS HOUSE, Col 1st Art'y.
To the General Commanding the E. Dept. USA, New York.

The reply to this was a special order:

Office Head Quarters Eastern Dept
New York, 4 April 1829

Special Order No 28.
Sergt Major Edgar A. Perry of the 1st Reg't of Arty ... will be discharged the service of the United States, on their furnishing, each, an acceptable substitute without expense to the Government.

By order of Major General Gaines.
(Sd) R. LOWNDES,
A A Adjt Gen'l.

In accordance with this Poe was discharged, by substitute, April 15. Before leaving his post he obtained the following letters from his officers, which show conclusively that he had already formed the plan of entering West Point, and indicate that this entered into the understanding on which Mr Allan took him into favour:

Fortress Monroe, 20 Ap 1829

Edgar Poe, late Serg't-Major in the 1st Art'y, served under my command in H company 1st Regt of Artillery from June 1827 to January 1829, during which time his conduct was unexceptionable. He at once performed the duties of company clerk and assistant in the Subsistent Department, both of which duties were promptly and faithfully done. His habits are good, and entirely free from drinking.

J. HOWARD.
Lieut 1st Artillery.

In addition to the above, I have to say that Edgar Poe [originally written *Perry*, but changed to read *Poe*] was appointed Sergeant-Major of the 1st Arty, on the 1st of Jan'y, 1829, and up to this date, has been exemplary in his deportment, prompt and faithful in the discharge of his duties – and is highly worthy of confidence.

H. W. GRISWOLD.
Bt Capt and Adjt 1st Art'y.

I have known and had an opportunity of observing the conduct of the above mentioned Sergt-Major Poe some three months during which his deportment has been highly praiseworthy and deserving of confidence. His education is of a very high order and he appears to be free from bad habits, in fact the testimony of Lt Howard and Adjt Griswold is full to that point. Understanding he is, thro' his friends, an applicant for cadet's warrant, I unhesitatingly recommend him as promising to acquit himself of the obligations of that station studiously and faithfully.

W. J. WORTH.
Lt Col Comd'g, Fortress Monroe.

With these credentials in his pocket the discharged Sergeant-Major, aged twenty, went to Richmond, where no time was lost in attempting to place him at West Point.
The following letters were obtained for him:

Richmond, 6 May 1829

Dr Sir: I beg leave to introduce to you Mr Edgar Poe, who wishes to be admitted into the military academy and to stand the examination in June. He has been two years in the service of the U States, and carries with him the strongest testimonials from the highest authority. He will be an acquisition to the service and I most earnestly recommend him to your especial notice and approbation.

Very respy yr obt serv't.
A. STEVENSON.
To Honble. J. H. Eaton,
Secy of War.

Richmond, 6 May 1829

D Sir: The history of the youth Edgar Allan Poe is a very interesting one as detailed to me by gentlemen in whose veracity I have entire confidence, and I unite with great pleasure with Mr Stevenson and Col Worth in recommending him for a place in the Military Academy at West Point. My friend Mr Allan of this city by whom this orphan and friendless youth was raised and educated is a gentleman in whose word you may place every confidence and can state to you more in detail the character of the youth and the circumstances which claim for him the patronage of the Government.

With great respect, your obdt sevt.
JOHN CAMPBELL.
The Honbl John H. Eaton,
Sec of War, Washington City.

Richmond, 13 May 1829

Sir: Some of the friends of young Mr Edgar Poe have solicited me to address a letter to you in his favour believing that it may be useful to him in his application to the Government for military service. I know Mr Poe and am acquainted with the fact of his having been born under circumstances of great adversity. I also know from his own productions and other undoubted proofs that he is a young gentleman of genius and talents. I believe he is destined to be distinguished, since he has already gained reputation for talents and attainments at the University of Virginia. I think him possessed of feeling and character peculiarly intitling him to public patronage. I am entirely satisfied that the salutary system of military discipline will soon develop his honourable feelings, and elevated spirit, and prove him worthy of confidence. I would not unite in his recommendation if I did not believe that he would remunerate the government at some future day, by his services and talents, for whatever may be done for him.
I have the honour to be

Very respectfully your obt serv't,
JAMES P. PRESTON.
Major John Eaton,
Sec'y of War, Washington.

Of more interest than all these, however, is Mr Allan's own communication:

Richmond, 6 May 1829

Dr Sir: The youth who presents this, is the same alluded to by Lt Howard, Capt Griswold, Col Worth, our representative and the speaker the Hon'ble Andrew Stevenson, and my friend Major John Campbell.

He left me in consequence of some gambling at the University at Charlottesville, because (I presume) I refused to sanction a rule that the shopkeepers and others had adopted there, making Debts of Honour, of all indiscretions. I have much pleasure in asserting that he stood his examinations at the close of the year with great credit to himself. His history is short. He is the grandson of Quartermaster-General Poe, of Maryland, whose widow as I understand still receives a pension for the services or disabilities of her husband. Frankly Sir, do I declare that he is no relation to me whatever: that I have many [in] whom I have taken an active interest to promote theirs; with no other feeling than that, every man is my care, if he be in distress. For myself I ask nothing, but I do request your kindness to aid this youth in the promotion of his future prospects. And it will afford me great pleasure to reciprocate any kindness you can show him. Pardon my frankness: but I address a soldier.

Your obdt servt,
JOHN ALLAN.
The Hon'ble John H. Eaton,
Secy of War, Washington City.

From the tenor of these letters it would seem that Poe delivered them in person. On his return from this journey to Washington he made the closer acquaintance of his blood relations at Baltimore, where he remained, engaged in

Superb painting by Edmund Dulac for Poe's evocative piece, 'Eldorado'

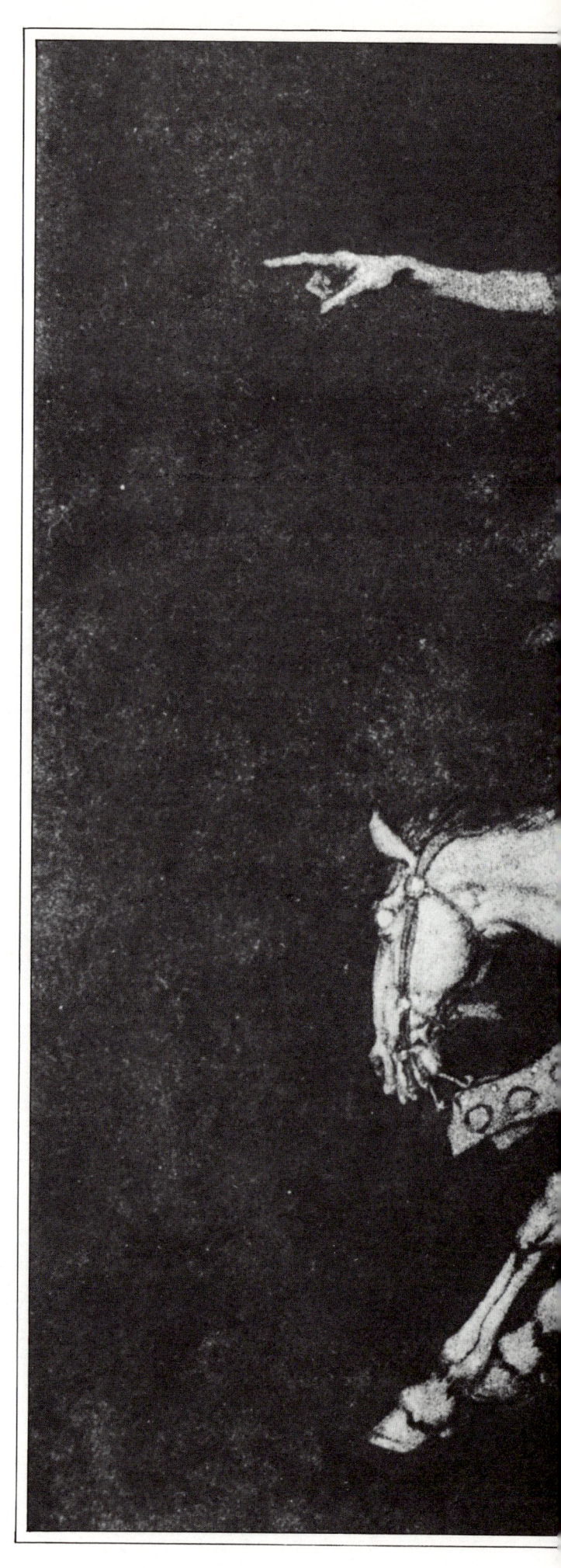

THE EDGAR ALLAN POE SCRAPBOOK

publishing a new edition of his poems and corresponding with John Neal, the editor of *The Yankee*, until the end of the year. It must have been at this time that he received help from my unnamed correspondent, and said he had been in Russia, and that he entered into some obscure relations with William Gwynn, the editor of the *Baltimore American*, and showed him the manuscript of 'Al Aaraaf'. On the issue of his volumes, in which it was stated that the Boston edition had been suppressed through circumstances of a private nature, he went back to Richmond, about Christmas time, and waited for his cadet warrant. His birthday came and went; he was twenty-one, and hence past the legal limit within which he could receive an appointment. This circumstance did not disturb him: he had grown four years older in 1827; he now grew two years younger in 1829, and relying on the fiction he solicited the favour of Powhatan Ellis, a younger brother of Mr Allan's partner, and then Senator from Mississippi, who wrote to the Secretary of War on his behalf:

Washington, 13 March 1830

Hon John H. Eaton.

Dear Sir: I have received a letter from a young gentleman in Richmond by the name of Edgar A. Poe stating, that he was an applicant for a situation in the Military Academy at West Point. He requested me to ask you, if there was any probability of his receiving a warrant to enter that institution. I am not personally acquainted with Mr Poe, but from information I would say his capacity and learning eminently qualify him to make in a few years a distinguished officer.

I am sir, with great respect,
Your obdt servant,
POWHATAN ELLIS.
Hon Mr Eaton,
Secretary of War.

This letter received immediate attention. The appointment was made, and Mr Allan, as Poe's guardian, gave his formal consent to his ward's enlistment.

Richmond, 31 March 1830

Sir: As the guardian of Edgar Allan Poe I hereby signify my assent to his signing articles by which he shall bind himself to serve the United States for Five years, unless sooner discharged, as stipulated in your official letter appointing him a cadet. Respectfully

Your obt servant,
JOHN ALLAN.
The Hon: Sec'y of War,
Washington.

There is no evidence that General Scott, Judge Marshall, or John Randolph had any hand in securing the appointment, as has been asserted since Hirst wrote his early sketch of Poe. Scott's wife was a cousin of the young lady whom Mr Allan was now preparing to marry, but his interest in Poe belongs to a later time. Powhatan Ellis's letter was plainly the determining influence. The young cadet was furnished by Mr Allan with whatever was necessary, and started north. He stopped at Baltimore, where he called upon Dr N. C. Brooks, as that gentleman told me, and read, and engaged to send to him, a poem for a forthcoming annual, and at length entered West Point 1 July 1830 – his age being recorded as at the time of entrance nineteen years and five months – and there he figured among his classmates as an adventurous boy who had run away from home and sown his wild oats in the East.

In further elucidation of Poe's life at this period an extract should be added which has only lately been brought within my reach, by the courtesy of Colonel Thomas H. Ellis, the son of Mr Allan's partner. It is from an open letter 22 April 1880, from himself to the *Richmond Standard*, and contains in my judgement the only account of the relations between Poe and Mr Allan that can pretend to any authority whatever. In this Colonel Ellis quotes from a letter of the second Mrs Allan to himself (and this is the only published utterance of the Allan family upon the subject) as follows:

Mr Poe had not lived under Mr Allan's roof for two years before my marriage, and no one knew his whereabouts; his letters, which were very scarce, were dated from St Petersburg, Russia, although he had enlisted in the army at Boston. After he became tired of army life, he wrote to his benefactor, expressing a desire to have a substitute if the money could be sent to him. Mr Allan sent it, Poe spent it; and after the substitute was tired out, waiting and getting letters and excuses, he (the substitute) enclosed one of Poe's letters to Mr Allan, which was too black to be credited if it had not contained the author's signature. Mr Allan sent the money to the man, and banished Poe from his affections; and he never lived here again.

Mrs Allan was an interested witness, and her prejudices were strongly excited against Poe. If her story be true in its essential part, it explains where Poe might have obtained the money to pay for his second volume of poems – a bill which Mr Allan was not likely to meet voluntarily; and since it indicates that his purse was not liberally supplied, it also explains how it happened that during his long stay in Baltimore he was now and then out of funds. This incident, however, may be left to one side; nor would it have been revived here had it not seemed necessary to include in this article everything which has been alleged regarding Poe during this period.

The natural construction to be placed on the foregoing story would seem to be this: that Poe's officers, becoming interested in him, advised him to go to West Point, the only way in which he could rise in the service; and that in compliance with the dying request of Mrs Allan, with whom Poe kept up some correspondence, Mr Allan recalled him, provided a substitute, and agreed to befriend him further, on the distinct understanding that he should go to West Point, but with no intention of ever making him his heir; and, finally, that during the fifteen months intervening between his discharge at Fortress Monroe and his entrance at West Point Poe lived mainly apart from Mr Allan, and gave no reason for the latter to trust him more than in years past. It would also appear that Poe invented the account of his travels in the East or in Russia at once, possibly appropriating something from the adventures of his brother, who died in Baltimore, in July 1831, and that he used this tale in later years to conceal his enlistment. If he ever went on a voyage before the mast, as is not altogether unlikely, it must have been on his way from Richmond to Boston, when he first left Mr Allan's counting-room, in 1827. He would then have as the basis of the nautical knowledge he displays in his works his early ocean voyages in boyhood, this hypothetical one, and those with his regiment in its changes from post to post, besides the in-

Judge Neilson Poe, the writer's cousin, who helped him during his last years

formation he would naturally acquire during a two years' residence by the sea; nor is it to be forgotten that his later journeys between the North and South were largely by water. His seamanship thus seems to be amply accounted for without assuming that he derived it from any long practical service in the merchant marine. As to Mr Ingram's legend of the duel in France, the Scotch lady, and the novel ascribed to Eugène Sue, it requires no discussion.

In the seventh month of his cadet life Poe was courtmartialled for neglect of duty, and dismissed the service. The sentence went into effect 6 March 1831. The version of this affair that was circulated by Poe has been universally adopted. This was that the birth of an heir to Mr Allan by his second wife having destroyed Poe's expectations of inheriting his patron's estate, and Mr Allan having refused to allow him to resign his place, he intentionally so acted as to be dismissed, in order to be free to follow some other profession better suited to a poor man than was that of arms. This may be substantially true. Nevertheless, as Mr Allan was not married until 5 October 1830, there was no heir born in January, when Poe's offences against discipline were committed: the marriage alone, therefore, determined him to take so extreme measures, and as it was a near event when he entered West Point he was probably apprised of it from the first. From the tone of Mr Allan's letter to the Secretary of War it would seem that he had most likely made it clear to Poe that he did not look upon him as his heir, and meant merely to start him in a military career. Poe left West Point, one can be quite sure, not because he had lost the hope of a large fortune, but because he was restless, wilful, and discontented. There is, however, nothing improbable in the statement that his dismissal was sought by him as his only way of exit from army life.

On the morning of 7 March 1831 he was thus a free man. He had, left over from his pay, twelve cents to begin that career which was better fitted for a poor man than the military profession. Possibly additional funds were provided from the subscription of the cadets, at seventy-five cents each, to the new edition of his poems; this money was allowed to be deducted from their pay, but a part only was advanced. Poe went to New York, and may have stayed in the city awhile attending to his forthcoming volume, which was not delivered to the cadets until some time after he had departed. It is commonly said that he now went to Richmond to Mr Allan's, where he was coldly received, and after a short time banished from the house. One hesitates to reject entirely so generally received a tradition, though it has no evidence in its support. It is unlikely that Poe who had now made Mr Allan's renewed efforts in his behalf wholly futile by violent and disgraceful methods, should present himself as if he expected to remain an inmate of the home where he had not lived for five years past, and to which in the meantime a young wife of thirty had come; nor would Mr Allan's letters to him have invited such a course. At all events, the only fact in the matter is that two months after leaving West Point he was in Baltimore, and perhaps that was as far south as he got upon this present journey. On 6 May 1831, he addressed his old acquaintance, William Gwynn, the editor, as follows:

6 May 1831

Mr W. Gwinn.

Dear Sir: I am almost ashamed to ask any favour at your hands after my foolish conduct upon a former occasion – but I trust to your good nature.

I am very anxious to remain and settle myself in Baltimore as Mr Allan has married again and I no longer look upon Richmond as my place of residence.

This wish of mine has also met with his approbation. I write to request your influence in obtaining some situation or employment in this city. Salary would be a minor consideration, but I do not wish to be idle.

Perhaps (since I understand Neilson has left you) you might be so kind as to employ me in your office in some capacity.

If so I will use every exertion to deserve your confidence.

Very respectfully yr ob st,
EDGAR A. POE.

I would have waited upon you personally, but am confined to my room with a severe sprain in my knee.

Poe's application to Mr Gwynn was apparently fruitless, and shortly afterwards he wrote to another acquaintance, Dr Brooks – to whose Annual, it will be remembered, he had promised a contribution – and asked for a position as teacher in that gentleman's school at Reisterstown, but there was no vacancy. Dr Brooks, who told me the incident, recalls perfectly well the time of its occurrence. This is, however, the last definitely dated event in Poe's life until 12 October 1833, when his name was printed as the winner of a prize for the best story contributed to the *Saturday Visiter*, a Baltimore literary weekly. During this period, the tradition of the Poe family and the sketches of his life published before he died place him at Baltimore, and there is not in any quarter the slightest bit of evidence on which to base a doubt of the truth of this belief. The fact that Judge Neilson Poe was then living in another town, and that Mrs

Clemm, Poe's future mother-in-law, had apparently also moved away, may explain why our knowledge of his whereabouts is not more exact, and how he came to fall into such circumstances of poverty as he did. A cousin, however, then Miss Herring, whose reminiscences of Poe have been carefully obtained for me by a member of the Poe family, says that Poe called on her at this time, in the morning or afternoon, when he could see her alone, and used to entertain her by reading, or by writing verses in her album; but her father discouraged these attentions because of the relationship and of Poe's habits of drinking. These calls were made at frequent intervals, on flying visits from Philadelphia and other places, and this lady is positive that they extended from 1830 to 1834, when she was herself married. She never heard of his leaving this country during these years. A date that depends only on the memory of a long-past event is always open to question. In this case it was in 1830 that Poe called on his relatives as he passed through Baltimore to West Point; in 1834 he visited Richmond, and possibly Philadelphia, where he was endeavouring to get a book published: and such absences, though few, may have left the impression that he was given to travelling. However this may have been, such are the statements of the only person who claims any personal knowledge of Poe between the summers of 1831 and 1833.

Some inferences may be drawn from the condition in which Poe was found by Kennedy, who befriended him on his reappearance as a prize story-teller. Griswold may have exaggerated the meanness of Poe's poverty, but notwithstanding the strenuous denials of Mr Ingram and others, who seem to think Poe degraded by misfortune, there is not the least doubt that he was in extreme distress, as is conclusively shown by this extract from Kennedy's diary:

> It is many years ago, I think, perhaps as early as 1833 or '34, that I found him in Baltimore, in a state of starvation. I gave him clothing, free access to my table, and the use of a horse for exercise whenever he chose; in fact, brought him up from the very verge of despair. (Tuckerman's *Life of Kennedy*)

It is further illustrated by the following self-explanatory note from Poe to that kind-hearted gentleman, who throughout life was seeking out and advancing merit:

> Your invitation to dinner has wounded me to the quick. I cannot come for reasons of the most humiliating nature – my personal appearance. You may imagine my mortification in making this disclosure to you, but it is necessary. (Tuckerman's *Life of Kennedy*)

And if further proof be needed it is furnished by a letter of Poe's, written years afterwards to Thomas Stoddard, in which he says, 'Mr Kennedy has been at all times a true friend to me – he was the first true friend I ever had – I am indebted to him for *life itself*.'

If this extreme destitution of Poe be considered in connection with the fact that he had sent in to the competition for prizes six tales, so well finished that the committee advised him to publish all of them, it may fairly be thought that he had been devoting himself to literature for some time previous, and that his garret was in Baltimore. Nevertheless, if any one chooses to suppose that Poe was starving elsewhere, there can be no check to the vagaries of his fancy; for if the unappreciated genius who had now found out what a poor man's career was like was not at

Another of W. Heath Robinson's outstanding designs. This is for 'Lenore'

Baltimore, there is as much reason to imagine him in Hong Kong as in any other place.

One other source of information must be glanced at, since it has been relied on to clothe Poe with more respectability when he was in his worst disgrace with fortune and men's eyes. Mr Lambert A. Wilmer, whose books, at least, do not entitle him to much regard, since they are scurrilous and filthy, was one of the projectors of the *Saturday Visiter*. He published reminiscences of Poe several times, but the only article which need be referred to here is one, 'Recollections of Edgar A. Poe', contributed to the *Baltimore Daily Commercial*, 23 May 1866. He writes:

> My acquaintance with Poe commenced in Baltimore, soon after his return from St Petersburg, 'covered with debt and infamy, and confirmed in habits of dissipation,' as one of his biographers represents. I can most conscientiously declare, however, that at the time referred to, and a long time afterwards, I heard nothing of his debts and infamy, and saw nothing of his dissipated habits. His time appeared to be constantly occupied by his literary labours; he had already published a volume of poems, and written several of those minor romances which afterwards appeared in the collection called *Tales of the Grotesque and Arabesque*. He lived in a very retired way with his aunt, Mrs Clemm, and his moral deportment, as far as my observation extended, was altogether correct. 'Intemperance', says the biographer quoted above, 'was his master-passion.' How then did it happen that during an intimate acquaintance with him, which continued for more than twelve years, I never saw him intoxicated in a single instance?
>
> His personal appearance and equipments at the time I speak of have been thus described: 'He was thin and pale even to ghastliness; his whole appearance indicated sickness and the utmost destitution. A well-worn frock-coat concealed the absence of a shirt, and imperfect boots

discovered the want of hose.' This description is wholly incorrect. In his youthful days, Poe's personal appearance was delicate and effeminate, but never sickly or ghastly, and I never saw him in any dress which was not fashionably neat, with some approximation to elegance. Indeed, I often wondered how he could contrive to equip himself so handsomely, considering that his pecuniary resources were generally scanty and precarious enough.

My intercourse with Poe was almost continuous for weeks together. Almost every day we took long walks in the rural districts near Baltimore, and had long conversations on a great variety of subjects; and however dry might be the subject of our discourse, and however dusty the road we travelled, we never stopped at any hotel for liquid refreshment, and I never observed any disposition on the part of my companion to avail himself of the liberal supplies of alcoholic beverage which were always to be had in the vicinity of Baltimore. In short, his general habits at that time were strictly temperate, and but for one or two incidents I might have supposed him to be a member of the cold-water army. On one occasion when I visited him at his lodgings he produced a decanter of Jamaica spirits, in conformity with a practice which was very common in those days, especially in the Southern and Middle States, where one gentleman would scarcely visit another without being invited to drink. On the occasion just referred to, Poe made a moderate use of the liquor; and this is the only time that ever I saw him drink ardent spirits. On another occasion I was present, when his aunt, Mrs Clemm, scolded him with some severity for coming home intoxicated on the preceding evening. He excused himself by saying that he had met with some friends, who had persuaded him to take dinner with them at a tavern, where the whole party had become inebriated – a circumstance for which many a poetical gentleman's experience might furnish a parallel. I judged from the conversation between Mrs Clemm and Poe that the fault for which she reproved him was of rare occurrence, and I never afterwards heard him charged with a repetition of the offence.

This is all that Wilmer has to say with regard to this particular time. The twelve years' intimate acquaintance with Poe which he asserts is an absurd claim. He knew Poe well only for a very few months at this time; during six of the twelve years he did not see Poe at all, and for the last five of them he met him only incidentally in Philadelphia. Other statements in this article – for example, the circumstantial account of Poe's attempt to learn lithographing in Philadelphia about 1841 – are entirely fictitious. Wilmer, therefore, is not a scrupulous and careful witness, and his word would not for a moment stand against Kennedy's as recorded in his diary. From Wilmer's book, *Our Press Gang*, in which he gives an account of his life, but without dates, it appears that he went from Washington to Baltimore to start the *Visiter*, and was its editor not much longer than six months; he lost his place, and was soon forced to go away from Baltimore in search of a living elsewhere, and did not return until after Poe had left the city. It is possible, of course, that Poe offered his services to the new weekly at once, and that an acquaintance sprang up between the editor and contributor, but this supposition cannot be verified, as no file of the paper is known to exist. It is quite as likely, and the hypothesis reconciles all the facts, that Wilmer's intimacy with Poe grew out of the latter's winning the prize, and his reminiscences therefore cover the months just subsequent to Kennedy's charity, when, after Mrs Clemm again settled in Baltimore, he went to reside with her. Poe was then, under the stimulation of Kennedy's friendship and active interest, trying to retrieve his reputation and break off his bad habits.

Whether during these hard years Poe made any application for assistance to Mr Allan has never been publicly known. The account which Colonel Ellis (whose article, as has been said, is the only one of the slightest authority) has given of the final scene between Poe and his old patron, though it took place six months after Poe's literary adoption by Kennedy, seems to belong here:

A short time previous to Mr Allan's death, on 27 March 1834, he was greatly distressed by dropsy, was unable to lie down, and sat in an armchair night and day; several times a day, by the advice of his physician, he walked across the room for exercise, leaning on his cane, and assisted by his wife and a man servant. During this illness of her husband, Mrs Allan was on an occasion passing through the hall of this house, when, hearing the front door bell ring, she opened the door herself. A man of remarkable appearance stood there, and without giving his name asked if he could see Mr Allan. She replied that Mr Allan's condition was such that his physicians had prohibited any person from seeing him except his nurses. The man was Edgar A. Poe, who was, of course, perfectly familiar with the house. Thrusting her aside, and without noticing her reply, he passed rapidly upstairs to Mr Allan's chamber, followed by Mrs Allan. As soon as he entered the chamber Mr Allan raised his cane, and, threatening to strike him if he came within his reach, ordered him out, upon which Poe withdrew; and that was the last time they ever met.

In this article all that has ever been alleged or is now known in regard to Poe's life, from his desertion of Mr Allan's home in 1827 to his expulsion from it under the circumstances just related, has, I believe, been included. His story, stripped of its fabulous incidents, has turned out to be the commonplace one of a runaway boy, who persistently rejected and at last forfeited the honest kindness of his friends. There is nowhere in it a generous, noble, or picturesque incident. If one desires to build up a transforming legend and to perpetuate the romance of a bygone literary fashion, he can do so only by suppressing the facts and elaborating the myth in the direction of a tawdry and foolish sentimentality. Whether or not, as Poe said, the truth is everything in a biography, justice has a supreme right there as elsewhere: I do not mean the justice that is expressed in verdicts, but that ideal justice, which, however obscured, or lost, or overborne, it may be, by the intrusion of extraneous influences, is nevertheless discernible in human affairs, and brings about a certain consistency in life and character. Shelley's youth was full of error, and at his death his name was held in dishonour; but, the nobility of his nature always remaining undefiled, ruin could not touch him nor shame live beside his grave. If Poe, on the other hand, was the victim, he was also the servant, as he was the poet, of the evil gods; and the same consistency, the same ideal justice, working itself out to a different end, is to be seen in his life as in Shelley's. It is not the career of a youth between the ages of eighteen and twenty-five that has been so minutely examined in this paper; it is rather the sowing-time of a man of genius, whose harvest proved so black a growth that it is deemed hardly natural. But so far from learning to credit any part of the legend that strives to turn Poe into the object of an exceptional fatality, one rises from the exhaustive study of his days from birth to death, with only the more profound conviction that nothing but a man's own acts can plunge him into the worst of life.

CADET POE OF WEST POINT

THOMAS GIBSON

THIS IS another intimate portrait of the young Edgar Allan Poe by a room-mate at the West Point Military Academy. Poe attended the Academy for two years until he deliberately had himself courtmartialled and expelled in 1831. Gibson's account was published in the distinguished American monthly, *Harper's Magazine*, of November 1867.

Edgar A. Poe was one of the occupants of the room. 'Old P——' and the writer of this sketch completed the household. The first conversation I had with Poe after we became installed as room-mates was characteristic of the man. A volume of Campbell's *Poems* was lying upon our table, and he tossed it contemptuously aside, with the curt remark: 'Campbell is a plagiarist'; then without waiting for a reply he picked up the book, and turned the leaves over rapidly until he found the passage he was looking for.

'There', said he, 'is a line more often quoted than any other passage of his: "Like angel visits few and far between", and he stole it bodily from Blair's "Grave". Not satisfied with the theft, he has spoiled it in the effort to disguise it. Blair wrote: "Like angel visits *short* and far between". Campbell's "Few and far between" is mere tautology.'

Poe at that time, though only about twenty years of age, had the appearance of being much older. He had a worn, weary, discontented look, not easily forgotten by those who were intimate with him. Poe was easily fretted by any jest

NUMBER 28 South Barracks, in the last months of the year of our Lord 1830, was pretty generally regarded as a hard room. Cadets who aspired to high standing on the Merit Roll were not much given to visiting it, at least in daytime. To compensate in some measure for this neglect, however, the inspecting officer was uncommonly punctual in his visits, and rarely failed to find some object for his daily report of demerit. The old barracks have passed away, and are now only a dream of stone and mortar; but the records of the sins of omission and commission of Number 28 and its occupants remain, and are filed carefully away among the dusty archives of the Academy.

West Point Military Academy at the time Poe attended there

at his expense, and was not a little annoyed by a story that some of the class got up, to the effect that he had procured a cadet's appointment for his son, and the boy having died, the father had substituted himself in his place. Another report current in the corps was that he was a grandson of Benedict Arnold. Some good-natured friend told him of it, and Poe did not contradict it, but seemed rather pleased than otherwise at the mistake.

Very early in his brief career at the Point he established a high reputation for genius, and poems and squibs of local interest were daily issued from Number 28 and went the round of the classes. One of the first things of the kind that he perpetrated was a diatribe in which all of the officers of the Academy, from Colonel Thayer down, were duly if not favourably noticed. I can recall but one stanza. It ran thus:

> John Locke was a very great name;
> Joe Locke was a greater in short;
> The former was well known to Fame,
> The latter well known to Report.

Joe Locke, it may be remarked by way of explanation, was one of the instructors of tactics, and *ex officio* Inspector of Barracks, and supervisor of the morals and deportment of cadets generally. In this capacity it was his duty to report to headquarters every violation of the regulations falling under his observation; a duty in which he was in nowise remiss, as the occupants of Number 28 could severally testify.

The studies of the Academy Poe utterly ignored. I doubt if he ever studied a page of Lacroix, unless it was to glance hastily over it in the lecture-room, while others of his section were reciting. It was evident from the first that he had no intention of going through with the course, and both the professors and cadets of the older classes had set him down for a 'January colt' before the corps had been in barracks a week.

Poe disappointed them, however, for he did not remain until the January examination, that *pons asinorum* of *plebe* life at West Point. He resigned, I think, early in December, having been a member of the corps a little over five months.

Some month or two after he had left, it was announced that a volume of his poems would be published by subscription, at the price of two dollars and fifty cents per copy. Permission was granted by Colonel Thayer to the corps to subscribe for the book, and as no cadet was ever known to neglect any opportunity of spending his pay, the subscription was pretty nearly universal. The book was received with a general expression of disgust. It was a puny volume, of about fifty pages, bound in boards and badly printed on coarse paper and, worse than all, it contained not one of the squibs and satires upon which his reputation at the Academy had been built up. Few of the poems contained in that collection now appear in any of the editions of his works, and such as have been preserved have been very much altered for the better.

For months afterward quotations from Poe formed the standing material for jests in the corps, and his reputation for genius went down at once to zero. I doubt if even 'The Raven' of his after years ever entirely effaced from the minds of his class the impression received from that volume.

The unfortunate habit that proved the bane of his after-life had even at that time taken strong hold upon him, and Number 28 was seldom without a bottle of Benny Haven's best brandy. I don't think he was ever intoxicated while at the Academy, but he had already acquired the more dangerous habit of constant drinking.

Keeping up the communications with our base of supplies at Old Benny's was one of the problems that occupied a good deal more of our thoughts than any of the propositions in Legendre; but, upon the whole, this branch of the commissary department of Number 28 was a success; and many a thirsty soul, with not enough of pluck to run the blockade himself, would steal into our room between tattoo and taps to try the merits of the last importation.

The result of one of these foraging parties after supplies created for a time no little excitement in the South Barracks. People had been burned and hung in effigy, from time immemorial, but it was reserved for Number 28 to witness the eating of a Professor in effigy.

It was a dark, cold, drizzling night, in the last days of November, when this event came off. The brandy bottle had been empty for two days, and just at dusk Poe proposed that we should draw straws – the one who drew the shortest to go down to Old Benny's and replenish our stock. The straws were drawn, and the lot fell on me.

Provided with four pounds of candles and Poe's last blanket for traffic (silver and gold we had not, but such as we had we gave unto Benny), I started just as the bugle sounded to quarters. It was a rough road to travel, but I knew every foot of it by night or day, and reached my place of destination in safety, but drenched to the skin. Old Benny was not in the best of humours that evening. Candles and blankets and regulation shoes, and similar articles of traffic, had accumulated largely on his hands, and the market for them was dull in that neighbourhood. His chicken

'The Young Poe at Fort Monroe' – a drawing by Shirley S. Hogge
(FORT MONROE CASEMATE MUSEUM)

suppers and bottles of brandy had disappeared very rapidly of late, and he had received little or no money in return.

At last, however, I succeeded in exchanging the candles and blanket for a bottle of brandy and the hardest-featured, loudest-voiced old gander that it has ever been my lot to encounter. To chop the bird's head off before venturing into barracks with him was a matter of pure necessity; and thus, in fact, Old Benny rendered him before delivery. I reached the suburbs of the barracks about nine o'clock. The bottle had not as much brandy in it as when I left Old Benny's; but I was very confident I had not spilled any. I had carried the gander first over one shoulder and then over the other, and the consequence was that not only my shirt front, but my face and hands were as bloody as the entire contents of the old gander's veins and arteries could well make them.

Poe was on the look-out, and met me some distance from the barracks, and my appearance at once inspired him with the idea of a grand hoax. Our plans were perfected in an instant. The gander was tied, neck and feet and wings together, and the bloody feathers bristling in every direction gave it a nondescript appearance that would have defied recognition as a gander by the most astute naturalist on the Continent. Poe took charge of the bottle, and preceded me to the room. 'Old P——' was puzzling his brains over the binomial theorem, and a visitor from the North Barracks was in the room awaiting the result of my expedition.

Poe had taken his seat, and pretended to be absorbed in the mysteries of *Leçons Françaises*. Laying the gander down at the outside of the door, I walked or rather staggered into the room, pretending to be very drunk, and exhibiting in clothes and face a spectacle not often seen off the stage. 'My God! What has happened?' exclaimed Poe, with well-acted horror.

'Old K——, old K——!' I repeated several times, and with gestures intended to be particularly savage.

'Well, what of him?' asked Poe.

'He won't stop me on the road any more!' and I produced a large knife that we had stained with the few drops of blood that remained in the old gander. 'I have killed him!'

'Nonsense!' said Poe. 'You are only trying one of your tricks on us.'

'I didn't suppose you would believe me,' I replied; 'so I cut off his head and brought it into barracks. Here it is!' and reaching out of the door I caught the gander by the legs, and giving it one fearful swing around my head dashed it at the only candle in the room, and left them all in darkness with what two of them believed to be the head of one of the Professors. The visitor leaped through the window and alighted in the slop-tub, and made fast time for his own room in the North Barracks – spreading, as he went, the report that I had killed old K——, and that his head was then in Number 28. The story gained ready credence, and for a time the excitement in barracks ran high. When we lit the candle again, 'Old P——' was sitting in one corner, a blank picture of horror, and it was some time before we could restore him to reason.

The gander was skinned – picking the feathers off was out of the question – and after taps we cut him up in small pieces, and cooked him in a tin wash-basin, over an anthracite fire, without seasoning of any kind. It was perhaps the hardest supper on record, but we went through with it without flinching. We had set out to eat old K—— in effigy, and we did it; whether he ever learned of the honours we paid him that night I never learned.

Upon the whole the impression left by Poe in his short career at West Point was highly favourable to him. If he made no fast friends, he left no enemies behind him. But up to that time he had given no indications of the genius which has since secured for him a world-wide fame. His acquaintance with English literature was extensive and accurate, and his verbal memory wonderful. He would repeat both prose and poetry by the hour, and seldom or never repeated the same passage twice to the same audience.

The whole bent of his mind at that time seemed to be toward criticism – or, more properly speaking, cavilling. Whether it were Shakespeare or Byron, Addison or Johnson – the acknowledged classic or the latest poetaster – all came in alike for his critical censure. He seemed to take especial delight in cavilling at passages that had received the most unequivocal stamp of general approval. I never heard him speak in terms of praise of any English writer, living or dead. I never met him after he left the Academy in December 1830; and hence my recollections and impressions of him are wholly uninfluenced by his after-life.

Alexandre Dumas

DID EDGAR ALLAN POE VISIT PARIS?

A Dumas Manuscript

THE APPEARANCE in a Paris autograph dealer's catalogue of a manuscript by Alexandre Dumas père, with a definite claim that he was on intimate terms with Edgar Allan Poe, has opened a problem which is not likely to be readily solved. The manuscript itself is of an article which Dumas seems to have written for an Italian paper; but it does not bear any traces of printers' or sub-editors' marks, and so may never have been printed. It, and many others in Dumas's autography, remained in Italy until recently, when they were taken to Paris and sold there. The manuscript with the Poe reference was purchased from the French dealer on the eve of the publication of the catalogue and resold to Mr Gabriel Wells. Mr Wells has kindly placed it in my hands.

It is hardly necessary to say that anything bearing on the career of Edgar Allan Poe is of the highest interest – English and American. A large number of books have been written about him; but in spite of the most exhaustive researches into archives, printed and otherwise, in the United States, there are yet many blanks in the story of his life, often of a year or two. He was born in Boston in 1809, and was at school in England 1815-20, when he was taken back to the United States. Hitherto there has been no indisputable evidence that he ever revisited Europe. There is a story or legend that after his disgrace at the University of Virginia he went to Europe with the intention of going to Greece to assist in the overthrow of the tyranny of the Turks, but that he never got to his destination; he is further said to have wandered about the Continent until he was seized by the police at St Petersburg for having engaged in a drunken riot, but was rescued and sent home by the American Minister in Russia. There does not seem to be a grain of reliable evidence in support of this story, and it may be only one of the many legends which have grown up around his erratic career.

He was certainly at home in 1827 when he published *Tamerlane*, his first work. He was at West Point Military Academy from July 1830 to March 1831, when he was dismissed; and he is supposed to have been in Baltimore for the following two years or so; but hardly anything definite is known of his life there. It is at about this period that Alexandre Dumas comes into the story with the manuscript referred to. This manuscript, on fourteen quarto slips of light-blue paper (two are missing, but these do not affect the main points), is headed 'Préface dédiée Comme le Reste de la Publication a MMrs les Préfets de Police de Naples'. He starts with declaring that not only are theft and murder common in Naples, but that both go unpunished. The then *Préfet* of Naples apparently was a M Spaventa, 'which is a capital name for a Chief of Police' (*spavento* = terror), 'but a name is not enough to scare away robbers'. Dumas then goes on at considerable length to deal with *Préfets* of Police, mostly in France, mentioning, among others, Vidocq, with much concerning the duties of, and qualities necessary in, a *Préfet*. All this leads up to a narrative concerning a murder case which 'presented a widely different problem from the case of Piero Falcone or of Largo San Pasquale'.

Before coming to the narrative Dumas breaks off into 'a few words of explanation' which 'I owe my readers', and these 'few words' entirely relate to Poe. They are here translated and set out in Dumas's staccato paragraphs:

It was about the year 1832.

One day a young American presented himself at my house with an Introduction from his fellow-countryman, the famous novelist, Fenimore Cooper.

Needless to say, I welcomed him with open arms.

His name was Edgar Allan Poe.

From the outset I realised that I had to deal with a remarkable man: two or three remarks which he made on my furniture, the things I had about me, the way my articles of everyday use were strewn about the room, and on my moral and intellectual characteristics, impressed me with their accuracy and truth. On the very first day of our acquaintance I freely proferred him my friendship and asked for his. He must certainly have entertained for me a sympathy similar to that I felt for him, for he held out his hand to me and the understanding between us was instantaneous and complete.

At this time my mother's ill-health [she died 1 August 1838] required that she should enjoy a purer air than that afforded by the more central parts of Paris; she was living in the Luxembourg district, while I had a little house all to myself in the Rue de l'Ouest.

I offered to let Edgar Poe have two rooms in this house for the duration of his stay in Paris.

Edgar Poe accepted my offer, confessing that his financial resources amounted to no more than three hundred francs a month, accruing to him from a credit on M Lafitte, and that in consequence I was, without being aware of it, doing him a greater service than I suspected.

Only, he made his acceptance conditional upon one essential stipulation, which was that in his mode of life under my roof, he should be free to do entirely as he wished, and to comport himself as if the house were his and not mine.

I was too much afraid of losing his agreeable companionship to hesitate about complying with everything he desired. From the very first day of our association, I realised why he had laid down the conditions to which I have referred.

Poe had one curious idiosyncrasy: he liked the night better than the day. Indeed, his love of the darkness amounted to his passion. But the Goddess of Night could not always afford him her shade and remain with him continually, so he contrived a substitute. As soon as the day began to break, he hermetically sealed up the windows of his room and lit a couple of candles. In the midst of this pale illumination he worked, or read, or suffered his thoughts to wander in the insubstantial regions of reverie, or else he fell asleep, not being always able to indulge in waking dreams. But as soon as the clock told him that the real darkness had come, he would come in for me, take me out with him if I was there, or go forth alone if I was not.

As a general rule, I must confess I was ready waiting for him, for these nocturnal expeditions in his company were a source of veritable pleasure. In these rambles, I could not help remarking with wonder and admiration (though his rich endowment of ideas should have prepared me for it) the extraordinary faculty of analysis exhibited by my friend. He seemed to delight in giving it play, and neglected no opportunity of indulging himself in that pleasure. He made no secret of the enjoyment he derived from it, and would remark with a smile of proud

Aubrey Beardsley sketch for 'The Murders in the Rue Morgue'

satisfaction, that for him every man had an open window where his heart was. And as a rule, he accompanied that assertion with an immediate demonstration, which, having me for its object, could leave no doubt in my mind concerning Edgar's power of divination.

This, but for a few lines of no particular importance, concludes Dumas's reflections on Poe, whilst the two missing pages clearly dealt with the crime which, according to the next page or two of the manuscript, was that which furnished Poe with the material for his story of 'The Murders in the Rue Morgue' which first appeared in *Graham's Magazine* (Philadelphia) in 1841.

Was the expansive author of *The Three Musketeers* romancing in this apparently very circumstantial account of his association with Edgar Allan Poe? Anyone familiar with his career knows that his 'facts' have often to be taken with large grains of salt. Poe's grim story above named might have been written by one who had never been in Paris, but it is difficult to read 'The Mystery of Marie Roget' (the story of a New York murder converted by Poe into a Parisian one) without feeling convinced that the author was intimately associated with the topography and physiognomy of Paris.

Dumas wrote these real or imaginary recollections of Poe some years later than the year 1832. The paper is flimsy and has no watermark, but it dates from the late forties or early fifties. Poe died in 1849, and even then – assuming that the recollections are purely fictions – Dumas could have known little or nothing of Poe's life and habits. It was not until 1859 that Baudelaire published his translation of the *Nouvelles Histoires Extraordinaires*, whilst his *Notes Nouvelles sur Edgar Poe* are critical rather than biographical. Except to his intimates and associates, Poe was merely a poet and writer of stories, and it was only in after years that the, often sordid, details of his tragic life came into prominent notice.

The accuracy or otherwise of the Dumas story concerning Poe's stay with him in Paris need not be discussed here. It can only be given 'without prejudice' as Alexandre himself had related it.

W. ROBERTS
The Times Literary Supplement, 21 November 1929

DUMAS AND POE

IF POE really visited France and stayed with Dumas, he or his work may have suggested the use of detective business in detail founded on small hints. D'Artagnan, in *Le Vicomte de Bragelonne* Vol 4, Chapter 23, provides an early and little known example of this now popular method. He deduces the course of the duel between de Guiche and de Wardes and the tactics of the two by examining the ground and the dead horse left there. The long course of the *Bragelonne* series appeared between 1848 and 1850, and this would be after Poe's visit and the publication of his famous detective stories. So it is possible that Dumas, being interested in Poe, had knowledge of them. Again, it is possible that both Poe and Dumas took a hint from Voltaire's *Zadig*, the first known source, I believe, of such methods in fiction. It has been suggested that Poe found his inspiration in the French-Canadian trackers; but this visit to France, if substantiated, may point to *Zadig*. His detective is a Frenchman.

V. RENDALL
The Times Literary Supplement, 28 November 1929

Jules Verne, a Poe admirer and 'collaborator'

THE LEADER OF THE CULT OF THE UNUSUAL

JULES VERNE

THE FRENCH were among the first to recognise the genius of Poe and the great Charles Baudelaire not only translated his *Tales of Mystery and Imagination* but prefaced it with an Introduction which is still regarded today as one of the finest essays on the American and his work. Another leading French writer who was much influenced by Poe was Jules Verne, who was to develop several of the themes Poe had begun. In 1864, Verne expressed his admiration for Poe in an essay published in the *Musée des Familles* which, until now, has never been translated into English. It is appropriate that Verne, of all Frenchmen, should discuss Poe's stories, both because of the common interest he had with Poe in the unusual, and the fact that Verne actually completed one of Poe's stories, 'The Narrative of Arthur Gordon Pym'.

The translation of this essay has been made by I. O. Evans, one of the leading experts on Verne and the man who has already put many of his novels and short stories into English. It should perhaps be pointed out that Verne's facts about Poe (whom he refers to as Edgard Poe) are not always correct – indeed they reflect the beliefs of the time about him – and that in the translating of Poe into French (Verne uses

Baudelaire's translation) and then back into English again, some distortions of the original have occurred, but it was felt best that these should be retained. This apart, I. O. Evans has splendidly captured Verne's idiosyncratic and urgent style of writing and shown him to be a fervent and appreciative admirer of the much maligned American.

HERE, MY dear readers, is an American novelist with a great reputation; many of you, no doubt, will be familiar with his name, but few will know his work. Permit me, then, to tell you something about the man and his work; both occupy a high position in the history of the imagination, for Poe has created a distinct species of this, originating with himself, and of which he seems to have borne away the secret. You might call him 'The Leader of the Cult of the Unusual'; he has thrust back the bounds of what is impossible. He will certainly have imitators: those who seek to go beyond him, to exaggerate his style; but plenty of those who fancy that they have surpassed him, and will not even have equalled him.

Vivid moment from 'Arthur Gordon Pym' by an unknown turn-of-the-century artist

First I want to tell you what a French critic, M Charles Baudelaire, has written at the start of his translation of Edgard Poe's works, a preface which is not less unusual then the works themselves. This preface may, of course, exaggerate in its turn some of his explanatory comments. However that may be, this has been well spoken of in the world of letters; it has been noticed, and with good reason: M Charles Baudelaire is well worthy to explain this American author in his own way, and I should never hope for this French author any other comment than his being the present and future works of a new Edgard Poe. In fact, the two are made to understand one another. Certainly, M Baudelaire's translation is excellent and I'm going to borrow from him the passages quoted in the present article.

I shall not try to explain the inexplicable for you – the elusive, the impossible, product of an imagination which Poe sometimes carried even to the edge of delirium; yet we shall follow this step by step; I shall describe the most extraordinary events with illustrative quotations; I shall show you how it develops, and to which of the human emotions it appeals in producing its strange effects.

Edgard Poe was born in Baltimore, USA, in the midst of the most matter-of-fact country in the world. His family, who for some time had filled a high position, had strangely degenerated by the time it reached him; his grandfather had distinguished himself in the War of Independence as a quartermaster-general under Lafayette; his father died, a mere actor, in utter destitution.

A certain Allan, a merchant of Baltimore, adopted the young Edgard and sent him to travel in England and Ireland and Scotland; the youth does not seem to have visited Paris, some of whose streets he describes rather inaccurately in one of his stories.

Returning to Richmond in 1822, he resumed his education, showing a remarkable aptitude for physics and mathematics. His dissipated behaviour led to his being expelled from Charlottesville University – and, what is more, from the family which had adopted him; he next set out for Greece during that war which seems only to have been waged for the greater glory of Lord Byron. It may be noticed, by the way, that Poe showed remarkable skill in swimming, like the English poet, but failed to make anything out of this.

Poe went on from Greece to Russia and reached St Petersburg; he was much embarrassed because of certain matters of which we do not know the secret; then he returned to America, where he entered the Military Academy. But his temperamental aversion to discipline soon led to his being expelled; it was then that he tasted poverty – and poverty in America is the most frightful of all. Next we see him escaping from this by consecrating himself to literary activities; he was fortunate enough to gain two prizes from a competition for the best story and the best poem, and then was appointed to run the *Southern Literary Messenger*. Under his control it prospered; he gained a sort of factitious ease, and he married his cousin Virginia Clemm.

It was only two years later that he quarrelled with the owner of his journal; it must be confessed that the unfortunate Poe often gave way to intoxication, and it was brandy which gave him the most extravagant of his inspirations. His health gradually gave way; let us skip these moments of poverty, these struggles, of success giving way to despair, of a novelist supported by his wretched wife and especially by his mother-in-law, who loved him as though he were a son on the edge of the tomb. Let us simply say that, after a long stay in a Baltimore inn, on 6 October 1849 a body was found on the street, that of Edgard Poe; the unhappy wretch was still breathing; he was rushed into hospital, where delirium tremens set in and he died next day at the early age of thirty-six.

Such was the life of this man; let us now examine his works. I will leave on one side the Journalist, the Philosopher, the Critic, so as to stick to the Novelist; for it is the novel, indeed the story, that displays the strange genius of Edgard Poe.

People have sometimes compared him with two other authors; one is English, Anne Radcliff, the other German, Hoffman; but Miss Radcliff has exploited the *terrible type*, which explains everything by natural causes; Hoffman has indulged in fantasy, for which no natural cause can be adduced. This is not the style of Poe; his characters seem really to exist; they are pre-eminently human, though sometimes they show that they were endowed with an over-excitable sensibility – super-nervous, exceptionally individualistic, one might say galvanised, as people are who have breathed air too rich in oxygen, and whose life seems always to be actually on fire. If they are not insane, the characters of Poe seem likely to become insane through having abused their brain just as others have abused alcoholic liquors; they push to the limit the urge to ponder and deduce; they are the most formidable analysts that I know of, and when seized by a brilliant idea they reach an irrefutable truth.

I will seek to define them, to depict them, to delineate them, for they elude the forceps of definition; it will be better, my dear readers, to show them using their ability, which seems almost to be superhuman. That is what I will seek to do.

The works of Edgard Poe have come to us in his *Tales of Mystery and Imagination*, which M Charles Baudelaire has translated; *The Unpublished Stories*, translated by

Charles Baudelaire, who did much to promote Poe's work in Europe

William Hughes; and a story entitled 'The Narrative of Arthur Gordon Pym'. I intend to select from these collections those which are most likely to interest you, and I shall not find it hard to succeed for I shall leave Poe to speak for himself for most of the time. So please be good enough to hear me with confidence.

First I am going to offer you three stories in which his skill in analysing and deducing reached the utmost bounds of intelligence. These are 'The Murders in the Rue Morgue', 'The Purloined Letter', and 'The Gold Bug'.

Here is the first of these stories, and this is how Edgard Poe prepares the reader for this strange romance.

After making acute observations, by which he will show that 'the *truly* imaginative man is never otherwise than the analytic', he brings upon the stage a friend of his, Auguste Dupin, with whom he stayed in Paris in an obscure and forsaken part of the Faubourg Saint Germain:

It was a freak of fancy in my friend to love the night; the night was his passion; and into this bizarrerie, as into all his others, I quietly fell; giving myself up to his wild whims with a perfect *abandon*. The sable divinity would not herself dwell with us always; but we could always counterfeit her presence. At the first dawn of the morning we closed all the massy shutters of our old building; lighted a couple of tapers which, strongly perfumed, threw out only the ghastliest and feeblest of rays. By the aid of these we then busied our souls in dreams – reading, writing, conversing, until warned by the clock of the advent of the true Darkness. Then we sallied forth into the streets, arm in arm, continuing the topics of the day, or roaming far and wide until a late hour, seeking amid the wild lights and shadows of the populous city, that infinity of mental excitement which quiet observation can afford.

At such times I could not help remarking and admiring (although from his rich ideality I had been prepared to expect it) a peculiar analytic ability in Dupin . . . His manner at these moments was frigid and abstract; his eyes were vacant in expression; while his voice, usually a rich tenor, rose into a treble . . .

And now, before reaching the subject of his story, Poe describes the way in which Dupin embarked upon his strange feats of analysis:

We were strolling one night down a long dirty street, in the vicinity of the Palais Royal. Being both, apparently, occupied with thought, neither of us had spoken a syllable for fifteen minutes at least. All at once Dupin broke forth with these words:

'He is a very little fellow, that's true, and would do better for the Théâtre des Variétés.'

'There can be no doubt of that,' I replied unwittingly, and not at first observing (so much had I been absorbed in reflection) the extraordinary manner in which the speaker had chimed in with my meditations. In an instant afterwards I recollected myself, and my astonishment was profound.

'Dupin,' said I, gravely, 'this is beyond my comprehension, I do not hesitate to say that I am amazed, and can scarcely credit my senses. How was it possible you should know I was thinking of . . . ?' Here I paused, to ascertain beyond a doubt whether he really knew of whom I had thought.

'. . . of Chantilly,' said he, 'why do you pause? You

Charles Raymond Macauley illustration for 'The Murders in the Rue Morgue' showing the detective Auguste Dupin (right) and a companion who looks just like Poe!

were remarking to yourself that his diminutive figure unfitted him for tragedy.'

This was precisely what had formed the subject of my reflections. Chantilly was a quondam cobbler of the Rue St Denis, who, becoming stage-mad, had attempted the role of Xerxes, in Crébillon's tragedy.

'Tell me, for Heaven's sake,' I exclaimed, 'the method – if method there is – by which you have been enabled to fathom my soul in this manner.'

It is obvious that this remark was indeed strange; here begins a discussion between Poe and Dupin, and the latter, disclosing his friend's train of thoughts, showed him that they had followed in this order: *Chantilly, the cobbler, Orion, Dr Nichols, Epicurus, stereotomy, the paving stones, the fruiterer*.

Here are the ideas which have no relation between themselves, and yet Dupin went on to show quite easily how they were connected, beginning with the last-named.

Indeed, as they walked down the street, a *fruiterer* had jostled Poe brusquely; the latter, startled by the impact, had stepped upon a loose stone and slightly strained his ankle while cursing that defective stone. When he reached the part where they had tried to make a wooden pavement the word *stereotomy* had come into his mind, and this word had led him inevitably to think of the theories of *Epicurus*. Now he had recently had a discussion with Dupin about these, in which it transpired that he had heard of the recent cosmographic discoveries of *Dr Nichols* which confirmed the theories of the Greek philosopher. In thinking about this, Poe would have been bound to raise his eyes to see the constellation *Orion*, which was shining then in all its brilliance. Then the Latin line: *Perdidit antiquum literis prima sonum* had discussed *Orion*, which was originally *Urion*, and this verse a critic had said in his latest article was quite applicable to the cobbler *Chantilly*.

'This association of ideas', Dupin explained, 'I could see from the *style* of the smile which passed over your lips. You thought of the poor cobbler's immolation. Up to this you had walked bent almost double, but now you regained your full height. I was quite sure that you were thinking of the poor little figure of Chantilly. It was at this moment that I interrupted your reflections to remark what a poor little mite this Chantilly was, and that he would do better at the Théâtre des Variétés.'

What could be more ingenious and novel, I ask you; to what could a zeal for observation lead a man with a gift like Dupin's? That's what we're going to see.

A frightful murder had been committed in the rue Morgue; an old lady, L'Espanaye and her daughter, living on the fourth storey, had been assassinated at about three in the morning. Several witnesses, including an Italian, an Englishman, a Spaniard, and a Dutchman, attracted by these terrible cries, forced their way into the room. There, in the midst of a wild disorder, they had found the two victims, one strangled, the other attacked with a razor which was still dripping with blood. The doors and windows which had been firmly closed, did not disclose the means of entry used by the murderer. The most careful investigations the police had made were quite fruitless, and nothing had turned up to reveal the circumstances of the crime.

This terrible affair, completely wrapped in the deepest mystery, excited Dupin's profound interest; he decided that to investigate this, it would not be enough to use his ordinary methods; he knew the Prefect of Police, who authorised him to visit the scene of the crime in order to examine it carefully.

Poe was allowed to go with him as Dupin, followed by a gendarme, examined the street, the rear of the building and its façade with minute care. Next he went into the room where the two bodies lay. His investigation took him until evening; then, without saying a word, he stopped for a moment or two in the office of a daily paper.

He remained silent all night, and not till noon on the following day, did he ask his companion if he had noticed anything *special* at the scene of the crime.

This was how Dupin started his analysis:

'Well,' he said, 'I'm waiting for someone who, even if he were not the person who committed the crime, might find himself implicated to a certain extent in it; it is quite likely that he was innocent of this atrocious crime ... I'm waiting for someone here, in this room, from minute to minute. If he does come, then we shall have to detain him. Here are some pistols, and we shall know how to use them if we have to.'

I leave you to think how amazed Poe was at these words. Dupin then told him that if the police, after taking up the floor, pulling down the ceiling, testing the solidity of the walls, could not explain how the murderer had entered, he himself, who had proceeded in quite a different manner, knew what to think about it. Indeed, while ferreting about in every corner, and especially near the rear window which *must* have allowed the assassin to enter, he had found a spring; this spring, badly fastened by a rusty nail, could have closed itself and secured the window after this had been pushed shut from outside by the foot of the fugitive. Near this window was a lightning-conductor, and Dupin never doubted that this could have provided the murderer with an aerial pathway.

Yet this was a trifle; from the path followed by the assassin, whether before or after the crime, nobody could succeed in knowing who the criminal was. So Dupin, who was certain as to this, embarked upon a strange method of deduction, and began in quite another method, not asking how such things had happened, but what had been remarkable about it in everything that had occurred so far. The money left untouched in the room showed that robbery had not been the motive of the crime.

It was at this point that Dupin called Poe's attention to something which had not been reported in the evidence and which was enough to show the ingenuity of the American novelist.

The witnesses, who had run up when the crime took place, had noticed that there had been two distinct voices; they had all recognised one as speaking French – but as for the other, a very sharp voice, there had been complete difference among these witnesses, all of whom were of different nationality.

'This', Dupin explained, 'formed the distinctive nature of the evidence. Each of the witnesses had said that this voice had not been that of one of their own compatriots; they had compared it not to the voice of anyone whose tongue he could recognise, but just the reverse. The Frenchman guessed that it was that of a Spaniard, and said *he could have distinguished a few words if he had known Spanish.* The Englishman thought that it was the voice of a German, and *he didn't understand German.* The Dutchman declared that it was the voice of a Frenchman; but it had been established that this witness, who couldn't speak French, had been examined through an interpreter. The Spaniard was *positively sure* that it was the voice of an Englishman, but he had judged only by the intonation, for *he was totally ignorant of English.* The Italian thought that it was the voice of a Russian, but he had *never spoken* to anyone who came from Russia. Another Frenchman, *however,* judged differently from the first, and he was certain that it was the voice of an Italian; but never having had any knowledge of that language, he had, like the Spaniard, *been certain of the intonation.* So the voice was then so impossible to identify and so strange, what could be deduced from witnesses such as these? A voice in whose accent these natives of five great regions of Europe had not distinguished anything familiar! You will say that it might have been the voice of a native of Asia or Africa. Africans and Asiatics are not very plentiful in Paris, but without denying the possibility of this, I would simply call your attention to three points. One witness had described the voice thus: *harsh rather than sharp,* two others had spoken of a voice as *abrupt and broken.* These witnesses had not been able to distinguish any words – *nothing resembling speech.*'

Dupin continued: he reminded Poe about the details of the crime, the immense power it had shown, for whole strands of grey hair had been torn from the old lady's head, and you know what strength it would have taken to tear from the head twenty or thirty hairs at once; he pointed out the agility shown by the climb up the lightning conductor, the bestial ferocity displayed during the murder, that '*grotesquerie* in horror, absolutely alien from humanity,' and throughout that voice in tones foreign to the ears of humanity, that voice which was devoid of any clear and intelligible syllabification! 'So what does this seem to you?' Dupin then asked his friend. 'What impression has it made on your imagination?'

I declare that at this stage of the story, like Dupin's friend, I felt my flesh creep! You can see how this amazing story-teller has gripped you! Has he mastered your imagination? Do you feel the excitement of his story? Do you now realise *what* had committed this amazing crime?

For my own part, I had guessed everything: but I shall end briefly by quoting the few lines which Dupin had inserted on the previous evening in the journal *Le Monde*, a paper devoted to maritime interests, and very popular among the sailors:

NOTICE. On such and such a morning (the morning of the murder) soon after dawn, an immense tawny orang-outang, apparently from Borneo, was found in the Bois de Boulogne. The owner (who is ascertained to be a sailor, belonging to a Maltese vessel) may regain the animal, after identifying it satisfactorily, and repaying a few charges to the person who captured and is looking after it. Enquire at rue—no—Faubourg St-Germain – *au troisième.*

Dupin had inferred that the man was a Maltese from a small piece of ribbon found at the foot of the lightning-conductor, tied with a knot peculiar to the sailors of Malta; as for the wearer, his voice and words had been that of a Frenchman; this was what all the witnesses had said. As for the notice, this had not mentioned any connection between the escape of the orang-outang and the crime – that would be seen when he appeared.

And he did appear: he was a sailor, a tall, stout and muscular-looking person, looking as fierce as any devil, and after a short conversation he revealed all. The ape had escaped from his room, taking his razor, for he had been shaving. The sailor, somewhat frightened, had followed the animal; this had taken a fantastic route and reached the rue Morgue; finding the lightning-conductor, it scrambled up it quickly. Its master hurried after it; the ape, seeing the open window, went through it and fell into the room of those wretched women. You know what followed. That sailor had to watch a tragedy without being able to do anything to stop it, an accessory before the fact, calling and shouting; then, losing his head, he made off, followed by the beast, which, shutting the window with its foot, slid down into the street; then it too made off.

There is that strange story and its true explanation. It is

Illustration by F. Darley from *The Dollar Newspaper* **for Poe's prize story 'The Gold Bug' (1843)**

Front page of *The Dollar Newspaper* **containing Poe's $100 prize story, 'The Gold Bug'**

easy to see what wonderful gifts it has shown its author to possess. It has so convincing an air of truthfulness that it seems to be an accusation taken in its entirety from the *Gazette des Tribunaux*.

Edgard Poe did not forsake that very strange fellow Auguste Dupin, the man who could make such wonderful inferences; we find him again in 'The Purloined Letter'. This story is quite simple: a compromising letter had been abstracted by a minister from a personage noted in political life. This minister D—— would be able to make an evil use of this document, and it must be recovered at any price. The Prefect of Police had been entrusted with this delicate mission. It was certain that the letter always stayed in the personal possession of D——. While he had been away from home the police had ransacked his home several times, inspected it room by room, examined all the furniture, opened every drawer, found all the so-called *secret* drawers, sounded the cushions with long needles, taken the tops off the tables, pulled the beds to pieces, looked into the smallest cracks, searched through the curtains, the carpets, the flooring, the picture-frames. Finally the entire surface of the house was divided into compartments, which they numbered; every square inch was scrutinised with the microscope and the fiftieth part of a pin would never have escaped such an examination. In case D—— had been carrying that compromising letter, he had been stopped and searched twice by the so-called thieves. But nothing had been discovered.

The Prefect, completely discouraged, came to find Dupin; he explained the business to him. Dupin promised to continue the hunt. A while later, the Prefect again visited Dupin; he had not been any more fortunate.

THE
CONCHOLOGIST'S FIRST BOOK:
OR,
A SYSTEM
OF
TESTACEOUS MALACOLOGY,
Arranged expressly for the use of Schools,
IN WHICH
THE ANIMALS, ACCORDING TO CUVIER, ARE GIVEN
WITH THE SHELLS,
A GREAT NUMBER OF NEW SPECIES ADDED,
AND THE WHOLE BROUGHT UP, AS ACCURATELY AS POSSIBLE, TO
THE PRESENT CONDITION OF THE SCIENCE.

BY EDGAR A. POE.

WITH ILLUSTRATIONS OF TWO HUNDRED AND FIFTEEN SHELLS,
PRESENTING A CORRECT TYPE OF EACH GENUS.
PHILADELPHIA:
PUBLISHED FOR THE AUTHOR, BY
HASWELL, BARRINGTON, AND HASWELL,
AND FOR SALE BY THE PRINCIPAL BOOKSELLERS IN THE
UNITED STATES.
1839.

Title page of an unknown book on shells which Poe was commissioned to write in 1839 – a surprising subject for him!

'I would really give fifty thousand francs', he said, 'to anyone who could get me out of this business.'

'In that event,' replied Dupin, opening a drawer and producing a cheque-book, 'you may as well fill up a cheque for the amount mentioned. When you have signed it, I'll give you the letter.'

And he handed the precious document to the Prefect of Police – to his complete surprise. When he had gone, Dupin explained to Poe how he had come into the possession of the letter; and to show him that the means to use could vary according to the person with whom he had to deal, he had related what follows:

'I once knew a child of eight whose success at palying heads or tails delighted everyone. He had a method of guessing which consisted in simply observing and understanding the way his opponents acted. Supposing that the fellow was a complete simpleton and when he showed him his closed fist, asking "Heads or tails?" our scholar replied "Tails" and lost. Then in the second game he won, because he thought "The ninny had gone heads the first time, and on the second all he could think of was to go tails, so I'll say 'tails'"; – he said "tails" and won.

'Now with an opponent who was a little less naïve, he would have thought: "This lad saw that I said 'tails'" and for the second game he would have adopted a slight variation from that of the first ninny; but his next thought was that this would be too obvious, and he would end by deciding to go heads as he had done the first time. "So I'll go heads"; – he said "heads" and won.'

Working on this principle, Dupin had begun by finding out something about the minister D——, and had learned that he was both poet and mathematician.

'As poet and mathematician', he reflected, 'he is bound to reason correctly; had he been merely a mathematician he would not have reasoned at all, and so he would have been at the mercy of the Prefect.'

This is very sound thinking, my dear readers; the mathematician had been astute enough to make a hiding-place, but the poet was bound to proceed on different lines and his method was completely simple. It is a fact that there are some objects which elude the eyes through the simple fact that they are so clearly present. So upon geographical maps the names in large letters, stretching from end to end of the map, are much less obvious than names in tiny, almost imperceptible letters. D—— had accordingly tried to throw the police agents off the scent by the sheer simplicity of his concealment.

Dupin quite realised this; he had a facsimile of the letter in question; he went to the minister's home, and the very first thing he saw on the desk was this elusive letter clearly in evidence. The poet had realised that the best way of eluding the search was not to hide it at all. D—— had done this easily, and by substituting the facsimile the game was over. There, where the sleuth-hounds had failed, a mere theorist had succeeded, and that quite easily.

This story is charming and packed with interest and M Victorien Sardue has made an excellent play from it, *Les Pattes de Mouche*, of which you must have heard and which had a great success at the Gymnase.

I now come to 'The Gold Bug' and in this Edgard Poe's hero gives proof of a very rare sagacity; I shall be forced to quote at length from the story, but I fancy that you won't complain of this.

Poe had shown himself as intimately associated with a Mr William Legrand, who, ruined by a series of misfortunes, had left New Orleans and had just settled down near Charlestown, in South Carolina, on Sullivan's Island, formed of nothing but sea-sand, about a quarter of a mile long. Legrand was a misanthropic character, subject to alternations of enthusiasm and melancholy; one would have thought him a little deranged, and his parents had seen that he was accompanied by an old negro answering to the name of Jupiter.

You can see them already – this Legrand, Poe's friend, who once more was an unusual character, with a temperament readily over-excitable and subject to crises.

Poe had gone to visit him one day and found him in an indescribable contentment. Legrand, who was making a collection of shells and entomological specimens, had just found a beetle of a strange species. But he had not got the insect just then; he had lent it to one of his friends, Lieutenant G——, staying at Fort Moultrie.

Jupiter swore that he had never seen such a beetle; it was a brilliant gold colour and was enormously heavy. The negro never doubted that it was made of solid gold throughout. Legrand wanted to give his friend a drawing of the insect; he looked for a scrap of paper, and, not finding any, he pulled out of his pocket a piece of very dirty parchment, on which he began to draw the animal. But – and this was queer – when he had finished and passed the parchment to Poe, the latter saw, not a beetle but a death's head very

A rather 'unlifelike' but extremely rare French etching of Poe produced towards the end of the nineteenth century

THE EDGAR ALLAN POE SCRAPBOOK

A beautifully detailed illustration by Harry Clarke for Poe's essay 'Lionising', published in a collection of his works in 1919

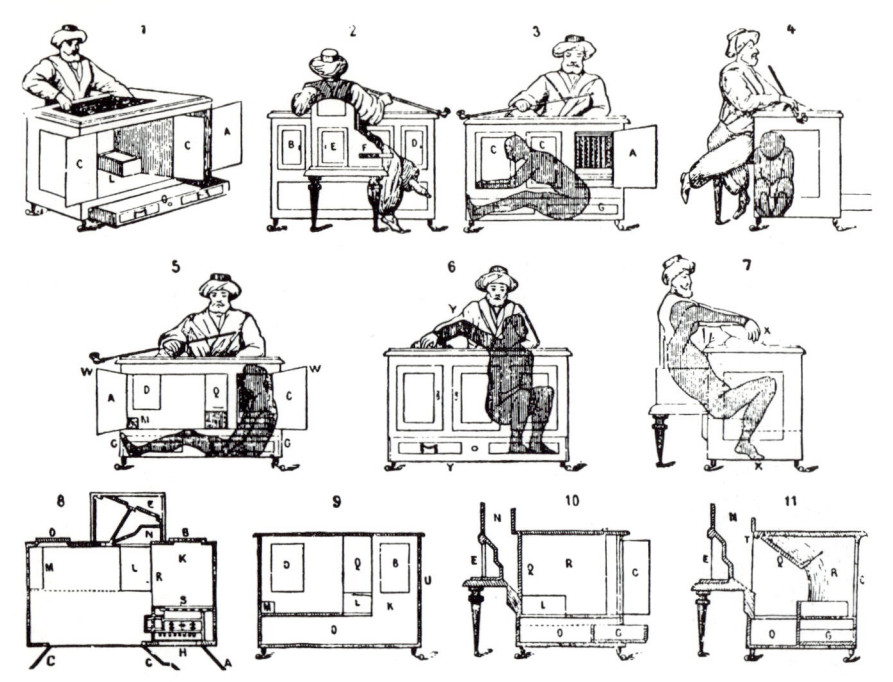

Left *and* right:
Poe was also a brilliant exposure journalist. He explained how the 'Automaton Chess Player', which astounded audiences on both sides of the Atlantic, was actually worked by a concealed man – as this sequence of pictures shows

clearly sketched. He commented on this, but William would not agree; but after a brief discussion, he had to admit that his pen had drawn a skull, perfectly recognisable. He took the drawing very peevishly; then he picked it up again, examined it thoughtfully, and shut it up in his desk. They talked about other things, and Poe went away, without Legrand making the slightest effort to keep him.

A month later, Poe received a visit from the negro; the latter, very uneasy, spoke about the sickly state of his master, who had become weak, pale, and taciturn; he thought this was due to his having been bitten by the beetle. All this time, every night, he had dreamed about gold. Jupiter had been given a letter in which William begged Poe to visit him.

'*Come ! Come !*' he said. 'I want to see you about something very important. I assure you that it is of *the highest* importance.'

You can see how the action is developing, and of what *singular* interest this story must be. A monomaniac who *dreams of gold* after being bitten by a beetle!

Poe accompanied the negro to his boat, where he found a scythe and three spades bought by William's orders. This purchase astonished him. The two men reached the island about three in the afternoon. Legrand was waiting for him impatiently, and he shook his hand with a nervous *empressement*. 'His face was ghastly pale, and his eyes, naturally deeply set, glared with unnatural lustre.'

Poe asked him for news about his beetle. William replied that this beetle was destined to make his fortune, and that by using it properly he would find the gold *of which it was the index*.

He then showed him a remarkable insect unknown at that time to naturalists; it bore, at one end of its back, two black round spots, and at the other a longer stain. Its wing-covers were exceedingly hard and glossy, and really looked like burnished gold.

'I sent for you', William told Poe, 'to ask for your advice and help in furthering the views of Fate and the beetle . . .'

Poe interrupted William and felt his pulse; he could not find the slightest symptom of fever; all the same he wanted to divert the flow of his ideas; but William announced his firm intention to make, that very night, an expedition into the hills, an expedition in which that beetle would play an important part; all Poe would have to do was to follow with Jupiter.

The three set off; they crossed the creek which separated the island from solid land, and then the little expedition, crossing the high ground on the bank, proceeded across some horribly wild and desolate country. At sunset they came to a sinister-looking region, trenched with deep ravines. On a narrow natural platform there grew a wild tulip tree in the midst of a dozen or so oaks. William ordered Jupiter to climb this tree, carrying the beetle on a long cord. In spite of his repugnance, and in the face of William's threats, Jupiter obeyed, and he reached a large branch of the tree, about seventy feet above ground.

Then William told him to climb out on the largest branch on that side; soon Jupiter had vanished into the foliage. When he had passed seven branches, his master told him go climb out on the seventh as far as he could, and to say if he found something unusual there. After some hesitation, for the wood seemed rotten, but encouraged by the promise of a silver dollar, he went out to the end of the branch.

'Oh! Oh! Oh!' he exclaimed. 'Lord God! Have mercy! What is this here upon the tree ?'

'Well,' exclaimed Legrand in a transport of delight, 'what is it ?'

Jupiter had found himself in the presence of a skull, fastened by a large nail and stripped of flesh by the beaks of the crows. William told him to lower through the left eye of the skull the cord attached to the beetle, and to lower it to the ground.

Jupiter obeyed, and the insect was soon swinging a few inches above the ground. William cleared the ground, let the beetle drop on to it, and drove a wooden peg in the precise spot where it dropped. Then, taking a tape-measure from his pocket, and fastening it to the part of the tree nearest to the peg, he unrolled it for fifty feet, following the direction indicated by the tree and the peg. Next he fixed a second peg at the end of the tape, drew a circle four feet in diameter, and helped by Poe and Jupiter, he quickly dug

MAELZEL'S EXHIBITION,
No. 29, St. James's Street.

The Automaton Chess Player

Being returned from *Edinburgh* and *Liverpool*, where (giving the Pawn and Move) it baffled all Competition, in upwards of 200 Games, although opposed by ALL THE BEST PLAYERS.

Has opened its Second Campaign,
WITH THE ADDITION OF THE
AUTOMATON TRUMPETER,
AND THE
Conflagration of Moscow,

In which Mr. M. has endeavoured to combine the ARTS of DESIGN, MECHANISM, and MUSIC, so as produce, by a novel Imitation of Nature, a perfect Fac Simile of the real Scene. The View is from an elevated Station on the Fortress of the *Kremlin*, at the Moment when the Inhabitants are evacuating the Capital of the Czars, and the Head of the French Columns commences it Entry. The gradual Progress of the Fire, the hurrying Bustle of the Fugitives, the Eagerness of the Invaders, and the Din of warlike Sounds, will tend to impress the Spectator with a true Idea of a Scene which baffles all Powers of Description.

The MORNING EXHIBITIONS begin at 1 and 3 o'Clock, and the EVENING EXHIBITION at 8 precisely, when GAMES will be played AGAINST ANY OPPONENT, to whom the double Advantage of A PAWN AND THE MOVE WILL BE GIVEN.

Admission 2s.6d.   Children 1s.6d. each.

☞ Each Exhibition lasts One Hour. Should a Game not be finished in that Time, the Party will be at Liberty to take it down with a View to its being resumed at another Opportunity.

Mr. M. begs leave to announce that the ORCHESTRION, the AUTOMATON TRUMPETER, the CONFLAGRATION OF MOSCOW, and the Patent for the METRONOMES, are to be disposed of.

away the soil; the work continued for two hours. But no signs of the treasure appeared and William was discouraged. Without saying a word, Jupiter picked up his tools, and they began to return westwards.

They had hardly gone a dozen steps when Legrand hurled himself on Jupiter.

'You scoundrel!' he said, hissing out the syllables between his teeth. 'Which is your left eye?'

The unfortunate negro pointed to his right eye.

'I was sure of it!' shouted Legrand. 'Come on! Come on! We've got to start again!'

The negro had indeed been mistaken, and he had lowered the cord attached to the beetle through the right eye instead of the left. So the work started again; the first peg was moved several inches more to the west, and the tape was unrolled to mark a new point several yards from the site which had already been dug into.

Then once more they began to dig. Soon they had brought to light fragments of a skeleton, metal buttons, a few gold or silver coins, and at last an oblong wooden chest secured by bands of wrought iron; the lid was fastened by two bolts which William, panting with anxiety, soon drew back.

The chest was filled with incalculable treasures: 60,000 dollars in French, Spanish, German and English money; 110 diamonds, 18 rubies, 310 emeralds, 21 sapphires, and one opal, an immense fortune of ornaments in massive gold, rings, ear-rings, chains, 85 golden crucifixes, 5 censors, 197 superb watches, in all a value of one and a half million dollars.

All this wealth was taken little by little to Legrand's cabin. Poe was dying with impatience to learn how his friend had come to know about this treasure, and the latter hastened to explain.

This version gives the reader only a very imperfect idea of the genius of the author; I cannot describe the sickly over-excitement of William throughout that night. The discovery of the treasure is more or less similar to the discoveries of the kind which you have read about; the part which the accessories had played, the beetle and the skull, could not be more ordinary. But we shall now reach the picturesque and strange part of the story, the series of deductions which had led William to the discovery of the treasure.

He began by reminding his friend of that crude sketch of the beetle that he had made on his first visit, and which he had found represented a death's head. The drawing had been traced on a fragment of very thin parchment.

Now these are the circumstances in which William had picked up that parchment; it was on a corner of the island near the remains of a shipwreck, and found on the very day when he had seen the beetle, which he had wrapped up in a piece of rag.

The stranded fragments aroused his attention and he had remembered that the skull or death's head was an emblem well known among the pirates. There were also two rings off a long chain.

Yet this skull had not appeared on the parchment when William had drawn the beetle, so how had it been seen there when it was handed over to Poe? It was because just at the moment when the latter had been going to examine it, William's dog had leaped on Poe to play. He, in pushing

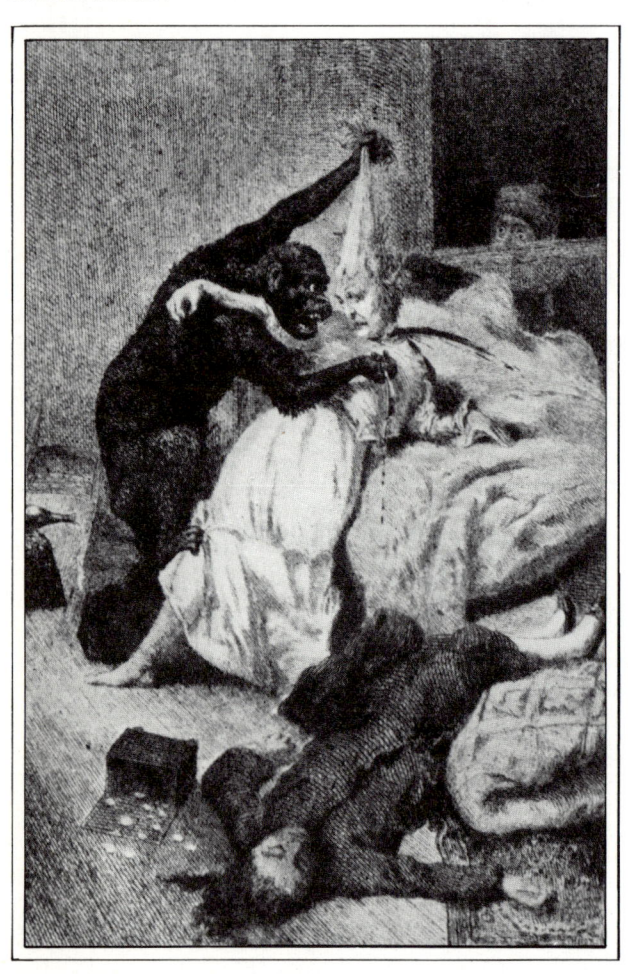

Two illustrations by an unknown French artist for Baudelaire's translation of Poe's Works. The amusing 'The Devil in the Belfry' (right) **and the gruesome 'Murders in the Rue Morgue'** (left)

him off with his hand, had put the parchment rather close to the fire, and the heat of the flame, as the result of some chemical preparation, had brought to light that drawing hitherto invisible.

After his friend had left, William again picked up the parchment, exposed it to the action of heat, and then saw appearing in a corner of the strip – a corner diagonally opposite to the one on which the death's head was drawn – a figure representing a goat.

But what had pirates to do with a goat? This. There used to be a certain Captain Kidd, (*kid*, the English for 'goat') who had given rise to many stories. Why should this figure not have been his logographic signature, while the death's head filled the use of a seal or trademark? William was thus brought naturally to look for a letter between the stamp and the signature. But the text seemed to be totally missing.

But the stories about Kidd kept returning to his head; he recalled that the captain and his cronies had vanished with enormous sums gained by their piracy on some point on this side of the Atlantic. The treasure must exist somewhere in its cache – because, but for this, the present rumours would never have sprung up. So William had gained the conviction that this scrap of parchment contained an indication of the place of the cache.

He cleaned it, carefully uncreased it, and set a saucepan on the glowing coals. After a few minutes he saw that the strip of vellum was speckled in several places with signs which resembled a line of figures. After heating it again, William saw the appearance of characters crudely traced in red.

Poe, on seeing this series of figures, of signs, of full stops and commas, of brackets, declared that this did not take him further. You would have said the same, dear readers; well, the novelist unravels this chaos with admirable logic if you follow him . . .

It is needless for us to follow the solution in all its detail here. It only remains for me to give you the translation of the document and I invite my readers to study the calculations – they will admit that these are exact.

The enigma thus solved, William returned to the tree, identified *the seventh branch, east side*, and realised that *a bullet* had to be dropped *through the left eye* of the skull, and *that a bee-line*, or rather a straight line, taken from the trunk *of the tree through the bullet*, to a distance of *fifty feet beyond*, would show him the exact spot where the treasure had been buried. Conforming to his fantastic nature, and wishing to mystify his friend a little, he had replaced the bullet by the beetle, and he had become rich by over a million dollars.

Such is this strange and astounding story, arousing interest by methods hitherto unknown and by strictly logical deductions, and which, in itself, is enough to illustrate the American novelist.

To my mind it is the most remarkable of all his strange stories; for in this is revealed the supreme degree of that kind of literature which has became *the Poe type*.

I now come to 'The Balloon Hoax' which I will tell you in a few lines is about a flight across the Atlantic. The report of this voyage appeared in the *New York Sun*. Many people believed in it who certainly hadn't read it, for the method Poe described, the Archimedean screw, which acted as a propeller, and the rudder, would have been absolutely insufficient to steer a balloon. The aeronauts, who had set out from England for Paris, were swept into America as far as Sullivan's Island and during their voyage they attained

An illustration for 'The Gold Bug' from Baudelaire's translation of Poe

a height of 25,000 feet. The story was short, and the incidents of the voyage were reproduced in an account more strange than it is true.

I prefer 'The Unparalleled Adventures of One Hans Pfaall', which I shall discuss with you rather more fully. The only thing is that I must hasten to tell you that, here again, the most elementary laws of physics and mechanics are boldly transgressed; this has always seemed astonishing to me as coming from Poe, who, by a few inventions, could have made his story more plausible; after all, as it deals with a voyage to the moon, the mode of transport need not have been too difficult.

This certain Hans Pfaall was a reckless criminal, a sort of dreaming assassin, who, as he couldn't pay his debts made up his mind to escape to the moon. He set out one fine morning from Rotterdam, after having taken the precaution of blowing up his creditors by means of a mine set for that purpose.

I must tell you now how Pfaall accomplished that impossible flight. To meet his needs, he had filled his balloon with a gas invented by himself, produced by the combination *of a certain metallic substance,* or *demi-metal,* and of a very common acid. This gas was one of the constituents of azote, hitherto considered irreducible, and its density was thirty-seven times that of hydrogen. Here we are, then, speaking physically, in the realm of phantasy; but that's not everything.

As you know, it is the pressure of the air which lifts the aerostat. Reaching the upper limits of the atmosphere, six thousand fathoms or thereabouts, a balloon, if it could reach it, would stop short, and no human force could make it go higher; it was there that Pfaall, or rather Poe himself, enters into long arguments to show that outside the layers of air there extends another medium, the ether. These discussions are made with a remarkable assurance, and the arguments are based on what are almost fallacies with the most illogical force. Briefly, he arrives at the conclusion that there is a strong probability that at no period of its flight would the various weights of that immense balloon and its accessories, of the inconceivably rare gas that it contains, its car and its contents, be exactly equal to the surrounding atmosphere which it displaces.

Here is the basic assumption; but that is not sufficient. Indeed to rise, always to rise, that is all very well; but it is also necessary to breathe; so Pfaall takes along a certain contrivance made to condense the atmosphere, however rare it may be, sufficiently for the needs of respiration.

Very well, here is an air which it is necessary to condense to supply the lungs, and which, however, will be dense enough in its natural state to raise the balloon. You will understand how these facts contradict one another.

Nevertheless, once the basic assumptions are admitted, the journey of Pfaall is wonderfully described, packed with unexpected comments and strange observations. The aeronaut takes his reader with him into the highest regions of the air; at a height of nine and a half miles he speeds through a stormy cloud; it seems that his eyes, no longer held by the atmospheric pressure, are thrust outside their orbits, and that the objects in the car appeared in a monstrous and misleading aspect; he kept getting excited; a spasm gripped him; he had to bleed himself with his penknife, and this relieved him at once.

So here, then, is an air which he had to condense for the supply of his lungs, which, nevertheless, will be dense enough to support the balloon in its natural state. You will realise the contradiction in these facts, and I need say no more.

'At a height of seventeen miles', says Pfaall, 'the appearance of the Earth was really magnificent. To the west, to the north or south, my eyes could see so far as to include an endless layer of sea, to all appearances still – which, from second to second, assumed a deeper blue colour. Far away, towards the east, the British Isles could be indistinctly seen stretched out, and the western shores of Spain and France, as well as a small portion of the north of the African Continent. It was impossible to recognise any buildings, and the proudest cities of mankind had completely vanished from the face of the earth.'

Soon Pfaall reached a height of twenty-five miles; he set up his condensing apparatus; he enclosed himself and his whole car in a veritable rubber bag. Here he condensed the air and invented an ingenious apparatus which, by means of drops of water falling on his face, aroused him every hour to replenish the air vitiated in that narrow space.

Day by day he kept the log of his voyage. He had set off on April the first; on the sixth he found himself above the pole where he watched the immense ice-banks and saw the horizon gradually getting larger. On the seventh he estimated his height at 7,254 miles; it exposed to his gaze all of the Earth's broad diameter with its horizon on the equator.

Then our planet began to get smaller every day; but he couldn't see the Moon, which was almost at its zenith and hidden by his balloon. On the fifteenth a terrible noise stunned him; he supposed that he had crossed the path of an immense meteor. On the seventeenth when glancing downwards he was much terrified; the Earth's diameter had suddenly become immensely greater. Could his balloon have burst? Was he falling with the most impetuous, the most incomparable, speed? His knees trembled, his teeth chattered, his hair stood up on his head . . . But second thoughts reassured him, and you can imagine his delight when he realised that this globe spread beneath his feet, and towards which he was rapidly descending, was the Moon in all her glory!

While he was asleep the balloon had turned completely upside-down and it was then descending towards the brilliant satellite, whose mountains projected all around him in volcanic masses.

On the nineteenth of April, in contradiction to modern discoveries, which have demonstrated the complete absence of air on the moon, Pfaall noticed that the surrounding air gradually became more and more dense; the work of his condenser had diminished noticeably; he could even remove his rubber prison. Soon he realised that he was falling with horrible speed; he quickly threw overboard his ballast and the other objects which garnished his car, 'and at last he dropped like a cannon-ball into the very heart of a city of fantastic aspect, and right in the midst of a multitude of little ugly people, not an individual of which spoke a word nor did anything to help him.'

The journey had lasted nineteen days, and Pfaall had crossed a distance of about 231,920 miles. Looking up at the Earth, he saw it:

in the shape of a vast dark copper shield about two degrees in diameter, fixed and motionless in the heavens, and garnished along one of its edges with sparkling golden crescent. It was impossible to see any trace of sea or land, and it was all fly-specked with variable stains and traversed like belts by the tropical and equatorial zones.

Here finishes the amazing adventure of Hans Pfaall. How did this story appear to the bourgeois of Rotterdam, Mynheer Superbus von Underduck? For an inhabitant of the Moon, no more and no less, asked to return to the Earth; this privilege granted, he undertook to communicate his curious observations on the new planet:

on the astonishing alternations of cold and heat; – on this solar brilliance which lasts for a fortnight scorching and merciless, and on that glacial temperature, greater than that of the poles, which fills the other fortnight; – on a continual movement of dampness which is produced by distillation, as though in empty space, from a point situated above the sun to that which is most distant from it; – even on the race of the inhabitants, on their customs, their dress, their political institutions; on their organism in particular, their ugliness, *their lack of ears, appendages which would be superfluous in an atmosphere so strangely modified*; in consequence their ignorance of the use and properties of speech; *on the strange method of communication which replaces speech*; *on the incomprehensible* rapport *which unites every citizen of the moon to a citizen of the terrestrial globe*; – rapport analogous to, and controlled by, that which no less rules the movements of planet and satellite, and as a result of which *the existences and destinies of the one are intertwined with the existences and destinies of the other*; – and, above all, on the dark and

Opening page of Le Sphinx des Glaces **in which Jules Verne continued Poe's story of 'Arthur Gordon Pym', dedicated to the American (1895)**

LE SPHINX DES GLACES

PREMIÈRE PARTIE

A la mémoire d'Edgar Poe.
A mes amis d'Amérique.

I

LES ILES KERGUELEN

Personne n'ajoutera foi, sans doute, à ce récit intitulé le *Sphinx des Glaces*. N'im-

The Edgar Allan Poe Scrapbook

terrible mysteries banished to the other lunar hemisphere, regions which, thanks to an almost miraculous correspondence of our satellite's rotation with its revolution round the Earth, are never turned towards us, and, by the mercy of God, are never exposed to the curiosity of the human telescope.

Ponder well over this, dear readers, and realise what magnificent pages Edgard Poe has written about these strange facts! He preferred to stop here; he even ended his novel in proving that it could be nothing but a *hoax*. He regretted, and we shall all regret, the ethnographic, physical and moral story of the Moon which still remains to be made. Until someone with more inspiration, or perhaps more cheek, undertakes this, we must give up hoping to understand the special organisation of the inhabitants of the Moon, the method by which they communicate between themselves in the absence of speech, and above all the correlation which exists between ourselves and these co-beings on our satellite. I love to think that, considering the inferior position of their planet, they will at most be good enough to become our servants.

As I said, Edgard Poe has drawn varied effects with his bizarre imagination and I'm going to sketch the main ones quickly, by quoting a few more of his stories such as 'Ms Found in a Bottle', the fantastic description of a shipwreck in which every wreck is collected by an impossible vessel manned by shades; 'A Descent into the Maelström', a dizzy exploit attempted by the Lofoden fishermen; 'The Facts in the Case of M Valdemar', the story of the death of a man deferred by a magnetic sleep; 'The Black Cat', the tale of an assassin whose crime is revealed by that animal, clumsily buried with the victim; 'The Man of the Crowd', an exceptional person who lives only in crowds, and whom Poe, attracted in spite of himself, follows in London from the morning onwards, through the rain and the fog, through crowded streets, in noisy bazaars, in groups of rioters, in secluded places where the drunkards collect, everywhere where there is a crowd, his natural element; finally 'The Fall of the House of Usher', a terrifying experience of a young girl who is believed to be dead, who is buried, and then recovers.

I shall end this list by citing the story entitled 'Three Sundays in a Week'. It is of a type not so sad but bizarre. How can there be a week with three Sundays? Easily for three individuals, and Poe demonstrates this. Briefly, the Earth is twenty-five thousand miles in circumference, and it turns on its axis from east to west in twenty-four hours; this is a speed of about a thousand miles an hour. Let us assume that the first person sets out from London, and goes a thousand miles towards the west; he sees the sun an hour before the person who stays where he is. At the end of a thousand more miles, he sees it two hours earlier; at the end of his tour around the world, returned to his point of departure, he will be just a whole day in advance of the second person. And if the third person carries out the same voyage in the same conditions, but in the opposite direction, by going towards the east, after his tour around the world he will be a day later. So what happens if the three of them meet on Sunday at their starting-point? For the first, *yesterday* was Sunday, for the second, *today*, and for the third it is *tomorrow*. As you see, this is a cosmographic joke explained in remarkable words.

Illustration by the renowned French artist, G. Rioux, for Verne's *Le Sphinx des Glaces* **(1895)**

Finally I reach the story with which I shall end this study of Poe's works. It is longer than the other stories and bears this title, 'Adventures of Arthur Gordon Pym'. Perhaps more *human* than the Strange Stories, it is no less unusual for all that. It shows situations which are not to be encountered anywhere, and its character is essentially dramatic. You can decide about this.

Poe begins by quoting a letter said to be from Gordon Pym, tending to show that his adventures are not in the least imaginary, as someone had tried to make them by signing them with the name of M Poe; he lays claim to their genuine nature; without probing so far, we are going to see if they are even probable, not to say possible.

Gordon Pym relates them himself and begins by describing his childhood and his desire to go to sea. He defies the wishes of his parents and aided by a friend embarks as a stowaway on a whaling ship. After a number of hair-raising exploits while he lies hidden and nearly goes mad from hunger and fear, the ship becomes the scene of a mutiny in which terrible butchery occurs. Almost immediately a tempest arises and Gordon and his friend find themselves masters of the ship.

However, as days pass the provisions run out and the survivors become desperate for food. They are all on the verge of starvation when they luckily run into a British schooner, the *Jane Guy*, on a sealing and trading voyage to the south. The captain, a gentleman named Captain Guy, takes Gordon and his friends on board and gives them places in his crew.

The *Jane Guy* then sails uneventfully on to the south until on 26 December they cross the 63rd parallel and find themselves in the midst of ice-flows. Now begins the really extraordinary events of Edgard Poe's narrative, for on 18 January, the crew fish up the body of a remarkable animal, evidently terrestrial:

It was three feet long by six inches high; but, with four very short legs, the feet armed with long claws of a brilliant scarlet and much resembling coral. The body was clothed with a smooth silky fur, completely white. The tail tapered like the tail of a rat, and was about a foot and a half long. The head resembled that of a cat, except for the ears, flattened and hanging down like a dog's. The teeth were the same brilliant red as the claws.

On the 19th of January, they discovered a land at 83° of latitude; some savages, a new type of men, jet black, came in front of the schooner, which they evidently took for a living creature. Captain Guy, encouraged by the good mood of these natives, decided to visit the interior of the country; so, followed by a dozen well-armed sailors, he reached the village of Klock-Klock after three hours walking. Gordon was with the expedition:

At each step which we took into the country we were forcibly struck by the conviction that we were on a land which differed essentially from all those visited up to then by civilised men.

Indeed, the trees did not resemble any of the products of the torrid Zones, the rocks were new both by their composition and their stratification; the water certainly offered the strangest phenomena!

Although it was as limpid as any water in existence, it lacked *the usual clear appearance* and showed all the possible varieties of purple, like the chatoyancy in the reflections of shot silk.

The animals of this land differed essentially from known animals, at least by their appearance.

The crew of the ship and the natives lived together thereafter on good terms. Later, they decided upon a second journey into the interior; six men stayed on board the schooner, and the others proceeded. The group, accompanied by some savages, worked their way into winding narrow valleys. The rocky walls reached very high, and were broken by certain fissures which attracted Gordon's attention.

As he was examining one of these with two men named Peters and Wilson,

I felt suddenly Gordon says: a shock which resembled nothing I was so far familiar with, and which gave me a vague idea that the foundations of our massive globe had suddenly split open, and that we were on the verge of universal destruction.

They were in fact buried alive. After they had recovered, Peters and Gordon realised that Wilson had been crushed; the two wretches found that they were inside a hill formed of a sort of soapstone, swallowed up by a cataclysm – but an artificial cataclysm. The savages had overthrown the whole mountain on the crew, and all had perished except Peters and Gordon.

By digging away into the soft rock, they arrived at an opening through which they could see that the country was swarming with the natives; these were attacking the schooner, which was defending itself with the cannon. But at last she was captured and set on fire, and soon she blew up with a terrible explosion which cost the lives of thousands of natives.

For long days Gordon and Peters lived in the labyrinth, feeding on nuts. After superhuman efforts, they finally succeeded in getting back on the plain; pursued by a horde of savages, they were lucky enough to find a canoe, in which a frightened native had taken refuge, so they were able to put out to sea.

They then found themselves upon the Antarctic Ocean 'immense and desolate, at a latitude of more than 84 degrees, in a frail canoe, without any other food than three turtles.' They made a sort of sail out of their shirts; the sight of the cloth affected their prisoner very strangely; he could never bring himself to touch it and seemed to have *a dread of white*; but they still sailed on and they were drawn into a strange and astonishing region:

A tall barrier of a grey light vapour appeared constantly at the horizon and was sometimes festooned with long, luminous rays, running mostly from east to west and then uniting again to make a crest of a single line . . .

A phenomenon more strange still – the temperature of the sea seemed to increase and was soon excessive; its milky appearance became more evident than before. Soon the sea was violently agitated. This was accompanied by a strange flaming of the vapour at its crest.

A very fine white dust, resembling ashes – though it was certainly not ashes – fell around the canoe, while the luminous trembling of the vapour disappeared and the commotion of the water died away.

Thus it continued for several days; forgetfulness and sleepiness suddenly gripped the three wretches; their hands could no longer bear the heat of the water.

I now quote the whole fragment which ends this astonishing narrative:

9 March. The cinder-like substance still rains incessantly round us in enormous quantity. The barrier of vapour to the south has risen to a prodigious height above the horizon, and its shape begins to get clearer. I can only compare it to an endless cataract, falling silently into the sea from the height of some immense rampart lost in the sky. The gigantic curtain occupied the whole expanse of the southern horizon. It did not emit any sound.

21 March. Gloomy shadows sweep around us – but the milky depths of the Ocean throw up a luminous brilliance which sweeps over the sides of the canoe. We are almost worn out by a white cindery shower which is piling upon us and upon the boat, but which melts upon falling into the sea. The top of the cataract is completely lost in the gloom and in space. Yet it is clear that we are approaching it with a horrible speed. At intervals we can see gaping rifts in that curtain, but this is only for moments, and through these rifts, behind which move a chaos of images, floating and indistinct, sweep currents of air, powerful but silent, which whip into foam the flaming Ocean in their flight.

22 March. The shadows had visibly thickened, and were no longer lessened by the clearness of the water, reflecting the white curtain before us. A host of gigantic birds, livid white in colour, flew endlessly behind that strange veil . . . And then we were hurled into the grip of the cataract, in which a gulf opened as though to receive us. But behold in front of our course a veiled human figure which towered up, much more gigantic than any inhabitant of the Earth. And the hue of the skin of the man was the perfect whiteness of the snow . . .

And the narrative closes in this way. Who will ever complete it? Someone bolder than myself, and more rash to advance into the domain of impossibilities. Yet we must believe that Gordon Pym managed to get away because he himself wrote this strange publication; but he died before having completed his work. Poe appears to regret this very sorely and declines the task of filling up the gap.*

Here then is a summary of the chief works of the American novelist; have I gone too far in calling them strange and supernatural? Has he not created a new form of literature, a form which demonstrates the delicacy of his *excessive* mind, to use one of his own words?

Leaving the incomprehensibilities on one side, that which we have to admire in the works of Poe are the originality of his situations, his discussion of little-known facts, his observation of the morbid faculties of man, his choice of subjects, the ever strange personalities of his heroes, their nervous temperament, their way of expressing themselves by bizarre interjections. And yet in the midst of these impossibilities, there can still sometimes exist a verisimilitude which grips the reader's credulity.

May I now be allowed to call attention to the materialistic

---

* Despite Verne's statement that it would take 'someone bolder than myself' to complete Poe's story, he was obviously unable to get it out of his mind, and in 1895 he did write a conclusion which he entitled, 'Le Sphinx des Glaces'. This work remained virtually unknown to readers outside France – its one appearance in English being as a serial in the juvenile publication, *Boys Own Annual*, before the turn of the century – until 1960 when two British Verne enthusiasts, Basil Ashmore and I. O. Evans, the translator of this article, brought the Poe original and the Verne conclusion together in one remarkable volume.

aspect of his stories; they never suggest providential intervention. Poe never seems to admit of this; he claims to explain everything by physical laws, which he will even invent if he has to; we never feel in him that faith which could have been given him by ceaseless contemplation of the supernatural. He creates his fantasies *coldly*, if I may express myself in this way, and the poor wretch is always an apostle of materialism; but I imagine that this is less the fault of his temperament than the influence of the exclusively practical and industrial society of the United States; he wrote, thought and dreamed as an American, this positivist of a man; this tendency being admitted, let us admire his work.

By his extraordinary stories, we can judge of the state of over-excitement in which Edgard Poe lived; unfortunately his nature was not adequate for this, and his excesses led him into *the terrible illness of alcoholism* which he had so well described and of which he died.

Unusual daguerreotype of Poe, probably taken in Baltimore in the early 1840s

POE'S ESSAY ON THE BEETROOT!

APART FROM writing for the publications on which he was employed, Poe, usually in desperate need of money, contributed work to other journals. Sometimes he was successful but more often not, and even when he did get into print, he was usually not even credited. Professor Thomas O. Mabbott, one of the leading Poe scholars of this century, has devoted much time and effort to investigating and authenticating 'lost' journalistic items by Poe, including the unfinished short story 'The Lighthouse' mentioned by Robert Bloch in his Foreword. He has written of his researches in both books and magazines, and here are two typical reports on 'finds' from the important publication *Notes and Queries*.

SEVERAL YEARS ago Professor Manly of the University of Chicago located a file of the rare Philadelphia newspaper, *Alexander's Weekly Messenger* for 1839 and in the issue of 18 December found the first of the essays on cryptography by Poe, which were known, from other publications of the poet, to have appeared in the paper. I later examined the file of the paper, and in the same issue found one other brief essay, unsigned, but demonstrably Poe's. No file for 1840 is yet known to me, nor did I recognise anything else in 1839 as from Poe's pen. Since my projected edition of Poe's Works is still far in the future I think it perhaps worth while to make accessible the following untitled paragraphs. The general tone of the essay and Poe's known friendship for the Pedder named attracted my attention to the article, but I only ventured to ascribe it to him definitely upon finding a close analogue – really a kind of repetition of the sixth sentence of the first paragraph – in Poe's 'Marginalia' (Harrison, ed xvi, 60), for such repetitions are the surest criterion of Poe's authorship of unsigned articles in magazines and papers of which he was an editor – or, as in the case of *Alexander's*, sub-editor. The paragraphs I copy from the second page of the paper named.

A controversy has been going on of late in the columns of the *Ledger*, on the subject of the beetroot. The opponents are a Mr T. M. (which letters may possibly stand for Tugmutton, or Trismegistus) and Mr James Pedder, a gentleman of sound sense and much practical knowledge, who is well acquainted with the subject which he discusses, having paid attention personally for many years to the whole system of beet-raising and beet-sugar making in France, and being at the same time an experienced sugar-refiner. As might be expected Mr P. has the battle all to himself, and makes sad exposure of his antagonist's ignorance. For our own parts we wonder at the good humour with which he has listened and replied to the rigmarole of Mr T. M. We allude to the platitudes of this latter person now merely as an instance of the *kind* of opposition which all new suggestions or discoveries, however reasonable, or valuable, have to contend with from that vulgar dunder-headed conceit which adheres, through thick and thin, to 'the good old way' and which so often calls itself by the name of 'common sense' that it sometimes passes for such among people who should know better. Time was, when credulity, and a blind adoption of raw schemes, were the distinguished [*sic*] traits of the rabble; but the rapid march of invention has altered all this, and *in*credulity and a dogged refusal to see or understand, are now more properly the popular features. The simple truths which science unfolds, day after day, are in fact, far stranger, apparently, than the wildest dreams in which imagination used to indulge of old.

When we spoke of new propositions and discoveries, we did not mean to insinuate that the cultivation of the beetroot was any thing very new, or even the manufacture of sugar therefrom. It is now an old story – at least it is old to everybody but Mr T. M. To this gentleman it appears very novel and chimerical only because he views it through the darkened glasses of his gross ignorance, or rather because he looks at it with the eyes of an owl. France derives a very considerable revenue from an impolitic impost on the manufacture; and nearly all the sugar consumed in the country, is sugar of the beetroot. Her climate is not better adapted to the culture than our own; and our manufacture[r]s are not less skilful than hers. What she has done, we can do – and, what is more we surely will do it, in spite of the whole race of the Tugmuttons.

Poe's interest in scientific discovery showed itself in many comments in the papers to which he contributed. The incredibility of the 'simple truths' gave rise to 'The Thousand-and-Second Tale of Scheherazade'.

15 December 1934

POE ON INTEMPERANCE

IN 1931, Miss Annie Edward Barcus announced the discovery in *Sterling's Southern Fifth Reader*, 1866, at pp 254f of an article of four paragraphs, entitled 'Intemperance' and ascribed to Poe. This she quoted only in part. Subsequent 'bibliographies' of Poe have noticed the item, and Dr Robertson gave a facsimile of the full text, but almost all students of Poe have practically forborne to discuss the authenticity of the item. In the circumstances of a posthumous ascription, such as this, where the ascriber failed to give any reason for the attribution, this is not surprising. The chances of a hoax were obviously great, but it is known that almost at the end of his life, Poe had joined the Washingtonians, and it seemed possible that he had made a speech on that occasion, of which a copy had in some way come to the hands of the editor of the schoolbook, perhaps in MS. I know this view was held by my friend, Mr David K. Jackson, of Duke University, and that I inclined to share it. The other possibilities were, of course, that the compiler had selected the lines from some review he thought to be Poe's, or had found it in print in some earlier and unknown place.

Recently Mr E. J. Wessen, in the Bookseller's Catalogue, Midland Notes, No 17, 1941, pointed out that the article had appeared, ascribed to Poe, far earlier than had been supposed. It occurs at pp 300-301 of *The Southern First Class Book; or exercises in reading and declamation*. Selected principally from American Authors. By M. M. Mason, AB, Principal of the Vineville Academy. Macon: [Georgia] 1839. Of the first edition there is a copy in the Library of Congress; of a second, dated 1840, the New York Historical Society has a copy, apparently from the same plates as the first. I here reprint the full text of the earliest version copied from a photostat. I believe there are probably other copies and later issues in existence. The Mason text shows slight verbal differences from the Sterling text; the latter probably was revised by the later editor.

LESSON CLXXIII
INTEMPERANCE – POE

We have thus far considered Intemperance with reference to its effects upon individuals and private communities; but are we not authorised to extend our view? and in doing so, can we not discern its baneful influence, not only on individuals and private communities, but upon the sacred institutions of our country?

Does not the history of that great and glorious nation, whose poetry and eloquence have dazzled whilst they instructed us, and whose prowess in arms has been surpassed by no nation on earth, teach us this salutary lesson, that luxury and effeminacy will paralyse the best institutions, and open a door to the entrance of tyranny so wide, that no human effort can prevent its encroachment? The luxury of the Roman nation consisted not in the extravagancy of her citizens, the costliness of her shows, and the magnificence of her palaces alone; but in the excesses of the table, and her bacchanalian indulgencies, producing a state of morals indicated by scenes of lewdness and debauchery, the details of which, no one possessed of one feeling of delicacy, could peruse without sensations of the most unqualified disgust.

That proud and independent nation who, having by her military discipline, her capacity to endure fatigue and hardship, and above all, her high sense of the value of freedom – not only drove back the armies of the foreign invader, but extended her conquests so far as to be denominated the mistress of the world. After accomplishing all this, and in effecting it, enduring without a murmur, the scorching heat of the torrid, and the chilling cold of the frigid zones – by the withering influence of luxury and excess became the willing dupe of the designing and ambitious, and tamely submitted to the yoke of tyranny.

In a government like our own, in which all power resides in the people, and where those who govern and legislate, do so by the will and permission of their constituents, it will ever be found that the representatives of the people not only maintain the political principles, but likewise personate the moral character of the majority they represent. Show me a profligate and intemperate representative, and I will guide you to a licentious and drunken community. It cannot be otherwise, the one follows the other as certainly as the effect follows the cause.

While this discovery destroys the hypothesis of the speech to the Washingtonians, it by no means simplifies the problem of authenticity. The appearance of the item in print during Poe's lifetime, and the absence of any known denial of authorship by Poe, is on its face a strong argument for authenticity. It is by no means impossible that the compiler may have bought the contribution from Poe, and although it is obviously an extract, it may be that he cut it down. It is also possible that he had found the paragraphs in some place which he thought made it clear that Poe was the author. But whether he was correctly informed or not is problematical, for Mason is not known to have had dealings with Poe, and unhappily the book appeared in a remote part of the country, and is just the kind of volume Poe himself may never have laid eyes on. The argument from lack of repudiation therefore is weakened. Hypotheses to be considered are that this was the work of some other man named Poe, whose name became confused by Mason with Edgar Poe. That the thing was a joke, alas, is by no means impossible. Poe did not drink so much before 1842 for it to have been a very apparent joke, and incidentally, he never approved, though he often practised the use of too much liquor. The attack on politicians falls in with his usual feelings, to some extent, and of course, if requested to write for a schoolbook Poe might well have modelled his style partly with a view to the readers. Still, the second paragraph seems to me rather bombastic for Poe. In the absence of further evidence, I am not willing to condemn the article at present. But on the whole I am inclined to classify it as one to be 'doubtfully rejected from the canon of Poe's works' or at best only to be referred to with a caveat that no real certainty of the authorship can yet be had.

18 July 1942

THE BALLOON HOAX

POE WAS a great lover of practical jokes and, shortly after he arrived in New York in April 1844, he perpetrated one of the greatest newspaper hoaxes of all time. Drawing on the current interest in ballooning, he wrote a report that the great contemporary balloonist Monck Mason had succeeded in flying the Atlantic. Despite the virtual impossibility of the flight – it still remains to be achieved today – for some hours after the appearance of the story in the *New York Sun* of 13 April many readers believed it to be true. Later, on 25 May, Poe himself described the impact of his imaginary narrative in a letter to the *Columbia Spy* magazine.

THE 'BALLOON HOAX' made a far more intense sensation than anything of that character since the 'Moon Story' of Locke. On the morning (Saturday) of its announcement, the whole square surrounding the *Sun* building was literally besieged, blocked up – ingress and egress being alike impossible, from a period soon after sunrise until about two o'clock pm. In Saturday's regular issue, it was stated that the news had been just received, and that an 'Extra' was then in preparation, which would be ready at ten. It was not delivered, however, until nearly noon. In the meantime I never witnessed more intense excitement to get possession of a newspaper. As soon as the few first copies made their way into the streets, they were bought up, at almost any price, from the newsboys, who made a profitable speculation beyond doubt. I saw a halfdollar given, in one instance, for a single paper, and a shilling was a frequent price. I tried, in vain, during the whole day, to get possession of a copy. It was excessively amusing, however, to hear the comments of those who had read the 'Extra'.

SATURDAY, APRIL 13th, 1844

Astounding News by Express via Norfolk!

◆

THE ATLANTIC CROSSED IN THREE DAYS

SIGNAL TRIUMPH OF MR. MONCK MASON'S FLYING MACHINE!

◆

ARRIVAL AT SULLIVAN'S ISLAND, NEAR CHARLESTON, S.C., OF MR. MASON, MR. ROBERT HOLLAND, MR. HENSON, MR. HARRISON AINSWORTH AND FOUR OTHERS IN THE STEERING BALLOON "VICTORIA," AFTER A PASSAGE OF SEVENTY-FIVE HOURS FROM LAND TO LAND!

FULL PARTICULARS OF THE VOYAGE!

◆

The great problem is at length solved! The air, as well as the earth and the ocean, has been subdued by science, and will become a common and convenient highway for mankind. The Atlantic has been actually

---

Newspaper cutting of Poe's famous Balloon Hoax and (below) an illustration of his 'fantastic' tale 'Mellonta Tauta' by C. A. Stoddard

A Worthless Writer

AS HAS already been stated in the Introduction, Edgar Allan Poe was the first real American literary critic, and he demanded standards which made him many enemies. During the period of his critical writings – 1835 to the time of his death – he was often engaged in fierce literary battles with writers in rival journals, each attacking the other with articles of such fierceness and so much slander that they would have certainly led to libel suits if published today. Perhaps not surprisingly in the light of this, Poe found his own work usually harshly criticised (the attacks often being based on his unstable life rather than on his ability), and saw very few favourable notices during his lifetime. Even after his death, the tirades against him continued, reaching 'the climax of detraction', as his biographer Arthur Hobson Quinn has said, in the following anonymous article from the *Edinburgh Review* of April 1858. Poor Poe, long since dead, had to leave it to other hands to restate his true worth.

EDGAR ALLAN POE was incontestibly one of the most worthless persons of whom we have any record in the world of letters. Many authors may have been as idle; many as improvident; some as drunken and dissipated; and a few, perhaps, as treacherous and ungrateful; but *he* seems to have succeeded in attracting and combining, in his own person, all the floating vices which genius had hitherto shown itself capable of grasping in its widest and most eccentric orbit. As the faults of this writer present themselves more upon a level with the ordinary gaze than the loftier qualities which his friends ascribe to him, we shall venture to introduce him to the reader, in the first instance, by his humbler everyday actions; satisfied that it is not of much moment how a picture has been commenced, if the proportions prove correct at last. Fuseli, as we know, preferred beginning his sketch of the human figure at the lowest point, and worked from the foot upwards. In like manner, we shall begin with the defects – or, to give them their true title, with the substantial vices, of Edgar Poe – proposing to ourselves to ascend ultimately to his virtues, should we discover any; at all events, to those rare qualities and endowments, the demonstration of which has entitled him to no mean place on the rolls of the Temple of Fame.

He was, as we have said, a blackguard of undeniable mark. Yet his chances of success at the outset of life were great and manifold. Nature was bountiful to him; bestowing upon him a pleasing person and excellent talents. Fortune favoured him; education and society expanded and polished his intellect, and improved his manner into an insinuating and almost irresistible address. Upon these foundations he took his stand; became early very popular amongst his associates; and might have erected a laudable reputation, had he possessed ordinary prudence. But he defied his good Genius. There was a perpetual strife between him and virtue, in which virtue was never triumphant. His moral stamen was weak, and demanded resolute treatment; but instead of seeking a bracing and healthy atmosphere, he

One of a series of outstanding paintings based on Poe stories which appeared in *The Century* magazine in 1903. This one depicted 'The Masque of the Red Death'

Ernest Wallcousins portrays a grim bedside scene from 'The Facts in the Case of M Valdemar' (1935)

THE EDGAR ALLAN POE SCRAPBOOK

preferred the impurer airs, and gave way readily to those low and vulgar appetites, which infallibly relax and press down the victim to the lowest state of social abasement.

He arrived at the end of his descent, after many alarms, many warnings, that might have deterred him, and induced him to try another course. For the most instructive teaching of Edgar Poe was in the roughest school of life. He had, indeed, for a brief period the advantage of some grave counsel at Charlottesville. But he left that place early, when his intellect was merely in its adolescent state. It was in his subsequent transit through poverty and degradation, when he had to battle not only with the world, but also with those compunctious visitors that force their way into the most obstinate bosom, that he received his most valuable lessons. The natural soil, however, was barren of good. The seed was sown upon a rock; or, if the reader prefer it, upon one of those shifting unprofitable sands which no culture will bring into fertility.

It seems impossible to have kept him upright. His tendency was decidedly downwards. He was, time after time, cautioned, forgiven, punished. All tender expostulation, all severe measures, were alike unavailable. The usual prizes of life – reputation, competency, friendship, love – presented themselves in turn; but they were all in turn neglected or forfeited – repeatedly, in fact, abandoned, under the detestable passion for drink. He outraged his benefactor, he deceived his friends, he sacrificed his love – he became a beggar – a vagabond – the slanderer of a woman – the delirious drunken pauper of a common hospital – hated by some – despised by others – and avoided by all respectable men. The weakness of human nature has, we imagine, its limit; but the biography of Poe has satisfied us that the lowest abyss of moral imbecility and disrepute was never attained until he came, and stood forth a warning to the times to come.

We say all this very unwillingly; for we admire sincerely many things that Mr Poe has produced. We are willing to believe that there may have been, as Mrs Osgood has stated, an amiable side to his character; and that his mother-in-law had cause to lament his loss. We learn, moreover, from Mr Willis, that at one time, in the later portion of his life, 'he was invariably punctual and industrious'. The testimony of that gentleman and of Mr Lowell (both men of eminence in literature) tempted us at first to suspend our opinion of the author; but the weight of evidence on the darker side proved overwhelming, and left us no choice but to admit the fact upon record, and to stigmatise with our most decided reprobation those misdeeds that seem to have constituted almost the only history of his short career.

And, here, let it not be surmised that Poe was an 'enemy only to himself'. His was, as Mr Griswold states, a 'shrewd and naturally unamiable character'. We refuse our assent to the argument of one of his advocates, that 'his whole nature was reversed by a single glass of wine'; and that 'his insulting arrogance and bad heartedness' had no deeper origin than a modicum of that agreeable liquid. We lean rather to the ancient proverb, which asserts that Truth is made manifest upon convivial occasions. Morever, his ingratitude and insults towards Mr Allan, Mr White, Mr Burton, and his affianced wife – his harsh and dishonest criticisms upon Mr Osborn and Mr Jones (each, in fact, contradicted by himself) and others, were not momentary flashes of ill humour; while his long and elaborate depreciation of Mr Longfellow (one part of it meriting particular condemnation), and finally his deliberate threats of publicly slandering a lady merely because she claimed the return of a loan of money, cannot by possibility be referred

The Angel of Death hovers over 'Ligeia'. Another picture from *The Century* **magazine, 1903**

to so feeble and temporary an impetus as 'a single glass of wine'. They sprang undoubtedly from what Mr Griswold calls 'his naturally unamiable character'.

To this and to his moral weakness must be ascribed the melancholy and poverty which we are told overshadowed his life. That he was very often unhappy we have no doubt; but that condition of mind was obviously referable to his excesses. It was the collapse after the high-strained revel. That he was frequently poor enough is also very probable; and yet, what is that but saying that he shared the ordinary fortunes of authors, many of whom too readily barter for the pleasures of writing and popularity, or the remote chances of future fame, those material comforts which are found to spring generally from regular mechanical industry, or other unexciting employments of common life. Some of these men, however, endure poverty very bravely; some with little help and no sympathy; some for years – some for all their humble and laborious days. They begin life with bright hopes and resolute hearts. They see above them Parnassus or Helicon, quite accessible. There is El Dorado also, in the misty distance. Yet they work on, from hour to hour, from week to week, without much repining. And, at the end of many years, perhaps, they discover that their only reward has been in the shape of a vulgar payment – a loaf of bread, a pot of beer, and an empty garret. Finally, they die without an historian to chronicle their labours, or even to notice their having once existed. Their very comrades content themselves with looking out for better fare tomorrow, and pass on to another friend.

THE LITERARY MOHAWK

PERHAPS THE most ingenious of the hundreds of attacks launched at Poe was the following piece of poetry which compared him to an Indian seeking scalps! It appeared in *Holden's Dollar Magazine*, January 1849, and once again the author has remained anonymous.

> With tomahawk upraised for deadly blow,
> Behold our literary Mohawk, Poe!
> Sworn tyrant he O'er all who sin in verse –
> His own the standard, damns he all that's worse;
> And surely not for this shall he be blamed –
> For worse than his deserves that it be damned!
>
> Who can so well detect the plagiary's flaw?
> 'Set thief to catch thief' is an ancient saw:
> Who can so scourge a fool to shreds and slivers?
> Promoted slaves oft make the best slave drivers!
> Iambic Poe! of tyro bards the terror –
> Ego is he – the world his pocket-mirror!

For *The Fall of the House of Usher*, **also from** *The Century*, **1903**

PRAISE FOR MR POE

POE RECEIVED very few good reviews of his work during his lifetime, and of these perhaps just two gave him any real pleasure. The first, from the *Yankee and Boston Literary Gazette* of September 1829 was written by the editor, a poet named John Neal, and was, according to Poe, 'the very first words of encouragement I ever remember to have heard'. The second, which is a review of *Tales of the Grotesque and Arabesque*, was written for the *New York Mirror* of 28 December 1839, by L. F. Tasistro.

IF E. A. P. of Baltimore – whose lines about 'Heaven', though he professes to regard them as altogether superior to anything in the whole range of American poetry, save two or three trifles referred to, are, though nonsense, rather exquisite nonsense – would but do himself justice he might make a beautiful, perhaps a magnificent poem. There is a good deal here to justify such a hope.

HAD MR POE written nothing else but 'Morella', 'William Wilson', 'The Fall of the House of Usher' and the 'MS Found in a Bottle', he would deserve a high place among imaginative writers, for there is fine poetic feeling, much brightness of fancy, an excellent taste, a ready eye for the picturesque, much quickness of observation, and great truth of sentiment and character in all of these works. But there is scarcely one of the tales published in the two volumes before us, in which we do not find the development of great intellectual capacity, with a power for vivid description, an opulence of imagination, a fecundity of invention, and a command over the elegances of diction which have seldom been displayed, even by writers who have acquired the greatest distinction in the republic of letters.

A Russian engraving of Poe

POE THE RUSSIAN FAVOURITE!

FYODOR DOSTOEVSKY

THOUGH FOR so long reviled in his own country, Poe rapidly built up an appreciative readership abroad – and he was as quickly adopted and praised in Russia as anywhere else. Casual translations of Poe – 'mad Edgar' as he was called – began to appear in leading Russian periodicals as early as the late 1830s and by 1860 his 'fantastic realism' was being discussed in magazines of all shades of opinion. As Abraham Yarmolinsky wrote in an article in 1916, 'The Slav has taken him to heart with all his unearthliness and morbidity, his fantastic rationalism and super-excited aestheticism, with all his dreams and nightmares. Poe's popularity in Russia is hard to over-rate.' One of the great champions of Poe in Russia was Fyodor Dostoevsky, the famous novelist and writer of short stories, who introduced the American to readers of his magazine *Wremia* in 1861, with the following preamble to translations of three stories, 'The Tell-Tale Heart', 'The Black Cat' and 'The Devil in the Belfry'. Today the whole body of Poe's work is translated into Russian and sells steadily year after year.

TWO OR THREE stories by Edgar Poe have already been translated and published in Russian magazines. Here we present to our readers three more. What a strange, though enormously talented writer, that Edgar Poe! His work can hardly be labelled as purely fantastic, and in so far as it falls into this category, its fantasticalness is a merely external one, if one may say so. He admits, for instance, that an Egyptian mummy that had lain five thousand years in a pyramid, was recalled into life with the help of galvanism. Or he presumes that a dead man, again by means of galvanism, tells the state of his mind, and so on, and so on. Yet such an assumption alone does not make a story really fantastic. Poe merely supposes the outward possibility of an unnatural event, though he always demonstrates logically that possibility and does it sometimes even with astounding skill; and this premise once granted, he in all the rest proceeds quite realistically. In this he differs essentially from the fantastic as used for example by Hoffmann. The latter personifies the forces of Nature in images, introduces in his tales sorceresses and spectres, and seeks his ideals in a far-off utterly unearthly world, and not only assumes this mysterious magical world as superior but seems to believe in its real existence – but not so Edgar Poe. Not fantastic should he be called but capricious. And how odd are the vagaries of his fancy and at the same time how audacious! He chooses as a rule the most extravagant reality, places his hero in a most extraordinary outward or psychological situation, and, then, describes the inner state of that person with marvellous acumen and amazing realism. Moreover, there exists one characteristic that is singularly peculiar to Poe and which distinguishes him from every other writer, and that is the vigour of his imagination. Not that his fancy exceeds that of all other poets, but his imagination is endowed with a quality which in such magnitude we have not met anywhere else, namely the power of details. Try, for instance, yourselves to realise in your mind anything that is very unusual or has never before occurred, and is only conceived as possible, and you will experience how vague and shadowy an image will appear before your inner eye. You will either grasp more or less general traits of the inward image or you will concentrate upon the one or the other particular, fragmentary feature. Yet Edgar Poe presents the whole fancied picture of events in all its details with such stupendous plasticity that you cannot but believe in the reality or possibility of a fact which actually never has occurred and even never could happen. Thus he describes in one of his stories a voyage to the moon, and his narrative is so full and particular, hour by hour following the imagined travel, that you involuntarily succumb to the illusion of its reality. In the same way he once told in an American newspaper the story of a balloon that crossed the ocean from Europe to the New World, and his tale was so circumstantial, so accurate, so filled with unexpected, accidental happenings, in short was so realistic and truthful that at least for a couple of hours everybody was convinced of the reported fact and only later investigation proved it to be entirely invented. The same power of imagination, or rather combining power, characterises his stories of the Purloined Letter, of the murder committed by an orang-outang, of the discovered treasure, and so on.

Poe has often been compared with Hoffmann. As we have said before, we believe such a comparison to be false. Hoffmann is a much greater poet. For he possesses an ideal, however wrong sometimes, yet an ideal full of purity and of inherent human beauty. You find this ideal embodied even oftener in Hoffmann's non-fantastic creations, such as 'Meister Martin' or the charming and delightful 'Salvator Rosa', to say nothing of his masterpiece, 'Kater Murr'. In Hoffmann, true and ripe humour, powerful realism as well as malice, are welded with a strong craving for beauty and with the shining light of the ideal. Poe's fantasticalness, as compared with that, seems strangely 'material', if such expression may be allowed. Even his most unbounded imagination betrays the true American.

THE BURIED ALIVE

ANONYMOUS

THERE HAS been much discussion over the years about the possible sources of Poe's stories, and as the quote at the front of the book indicates, he was a voracious reader and collector of newspaper cuttings which certainly gave him many ideas. One source that does seem to have played an important part was the Scottish magazine, *Blackwood's*.

There can be little doubt that from an early stage in his career, Poe was anxious to contribute to foreign publications, particularly British ones, and indeed this is supported by the fact that he arranged a meeting with Charles Dickens during the Englishman's visit to Philadelphia to enlist his aid in finding a British publisher. Poe also claimed in a letter in September 1839 that he had 'made a profitable engagement with *Blackwood's* Mag and my forthcoming tales are promised a very commendatory Review in that journal from the pen of Professor Wilson'.

While it has never been possible to substantiate this claim (indeed it seems very unlikely) it is now clear that Poe found the inspiration for several of his tales from stories published in *Blackwood's* during the ten year period from 1827 to 1837. Indeed, he penned an appreciative essay 'How To Write A *Blackwood* Article' in 1838. Critics elsewhere have written of the magazine stories which Poe allegedly drew on, but of all these the one which impresses me as being the most strongly influential on a tale is 'The Buried Alive' from the October 1821 issue, which contains some of the style and atmosphere to be found in the famous 'The Premature Burial'.

In writing of this story (which he mistitles) in his article on *Blackwood's*, Poe comments, '"The Dead Alive" a capital thing! The record of a gentleman's sensations when entombed before the breath was out of his body – full of taste, terror, sentiment, metaphysics and erudition. You would have sworn that the writer had been born and brought up in a coffin.' Poe's praise for the magazine was in some degree returned in a review of his 'Tales' published in November 1847 and also reprinted here. (It is interesting to note that one of Poe's correspondents, believing him to have a strong connection with *Blackwood's*, actually accused him of having written the review himself!)

I HAD been for some time ill of a low and lingering fever. My strength gradually wasted, but the sense of life seemed to become more and more acute as my corporeal powers became weaker. I could see by the looks of the doctor that he despaired of my recovery; and the soft and whispering sorrow of my friends taught me that I had nothing to hope.

One day towards the evening, the crisis took place – I was seized with a strange and indescribable quivering, – a rushing sound was in my ears – I saw around my couch innumerable strange faces; they were bright and visionary, and without bodies. There was light, and solemnity, and I tried to move, but could not. – For a short time a terrible confusion overwhelmed me – and when it passed off, all my recollection returned with the most perfect distinctness, but the power of motion had departed. – I heard the sound of weeping at my pillow – and the voice of the nurse say, 'He is dead.' – I cannot describe what I felt at these words. – I exerted my utmost power of volition to stir myself, but I could not move even an eyelid. After a short pause my friend drew near; and sobbing, and convulsed with grief,

Above: **A picture by Frederick Simpson Coburn, 1902, based on 'The Premature Burial'**

The Edgar Allan Poe Scrapbook

I TRIED TO REMAIN *CALM*... TO REMEMBER THESE *FINAL* MOMENTS BEFORE *BLACKNESS* OVERTOOK ME....!

BUT ONLY ONE *THOUGHT* COULD I RETAIN.

EVEN *KNOWING* THE CURSE I LIVED UNDER, THEY WENT AHEAD AND *BURIED* ME *ALIVE*!

THE GODDAMN *FOOLS*!

THE ROPE! WHERE WAS THE *ROPE* THAT ROGERS HAD *MADE* FOR ME? MY FINGERS SEARCHED THE DARKNESS, BUT NO *TRACE* OF IT COULD I *FIND*.

VAGUELY I *REMEMBERED* WALKING THROUGH A DISTANT PART OF TOWN JUST BEFORE THE *SEIZURE* WRACKED MY BODY...!

AND WITH THAT REMEMBRANCE, CAME THE *KNOWLEDGE*... THE *TERRIFYING* KNOWLEDGE...

...THAT I WAS *NOT* BURIED IN MY OWN COFFIN!

THE HORROR OF IT *OVERWHELMED* ME. I SCREAMED!

AND FROM SOMEWHERE *ABOVE* ME, THE SCREAM WAS *ANSWERED* BY A RAY OF *LIGHT*!

drew his hand over my face, and closed my eyes. The world was then darkened, but I still could hear, and feel, and suffer.

When my eyes were closed, I heard by the attendants that my friend had left the room, and I soon after found, the undertakers were preparing to habit me in the garments of the grave. Their thoughtlessness was more awful than the grief of my friends. They laughed at one another as they turned me from side to side, and treated what they believed a corpse, with the most appalling ribaldry.

When they had laid me out, these wretches retired, and the degrading formality of affected mourning commenced. For three days, a number of friends called to see me. – I heard them, in low accents, speak of what I was; and more than one touched me with his finger. On the third day, some of them talked of the smell of corruption in the room.

The coffin was procured – I was lifted and laid in – My friend placed my head on what was deemed its last pillow, and I felt his tears drop on my face.

When all who had any peculiar interest in me, had for a short time looked at me in the coffin, I heard them retire; and the undertaker's men placed the lid on the coffin, and screwed it down. There were two of them present – one had occasion to go away before the task was done. I heard the fellow who was left begin to whistle as he turned the screw-nails; but he checked himself, and completed the work in silence.

I was then left alone – every one shunned the room. – I knew, however, that I was not yet buried; and though darkened and motionless, I had still hope – but this was not permitted long. The day of interment arrived – I felt the coffin lifted and borne away – I heard and felt it placed in the hearse. – There was a crowd of people around; some of them spoke sorrowfully of me. The hearse began to move – I knew that it carried me to the grave. It halted, and the coffin was taken out – I felt myself carried on shoulders of men, by the inequality of the motion – A pause ensued – I heard the cords of the coffin moved – I felt it swing as dependent by them – It was lowered, and rested on the bottom of the grave – The cords were dropped upon the lid – I heard them fall. – Dreadful was the effort I then made to exert the power of action, but my whole frame was immoveable.

Soon after, a few handfuls of earth were thrown upon the coffin – Then there was another pause – after which the shovel was employed, and the sound of the rattling mould, as it covered me, was far more tremendous than thunder. But I could make no effort. The sound gradually became less and less, and by a surging reverberation in the coffin, I knew that the grave was filled up, and that the sexton was treading in the earth, slapping the grave with the flat of his spade. This too ceased, and then all was silent.

I had no means of knowing the lapse of time; and the silence continued. This is death, thought I, and I am doomed to remain in the earth till the resurrection. Presently the body will fall into corruption, and the epicurean worm, that is only satisfied with the flesh of man, will come to partake of the banquet that has been prepared for him with so much solicitude and care. In the contemplation of this hideous thought, I heard a low and undersound in the earth over me, and I fancied that the worms and the reptiles of death were coming – that the mole and the rat of the grave would soon be upon me. The sound continued to grow louder and nearer. Can it be possible, I thought, that my friends suspect they have buried me too soon? The hope was truly like light bursting through the gloom of death.

The sound ceased, and presently I felt the hands of some

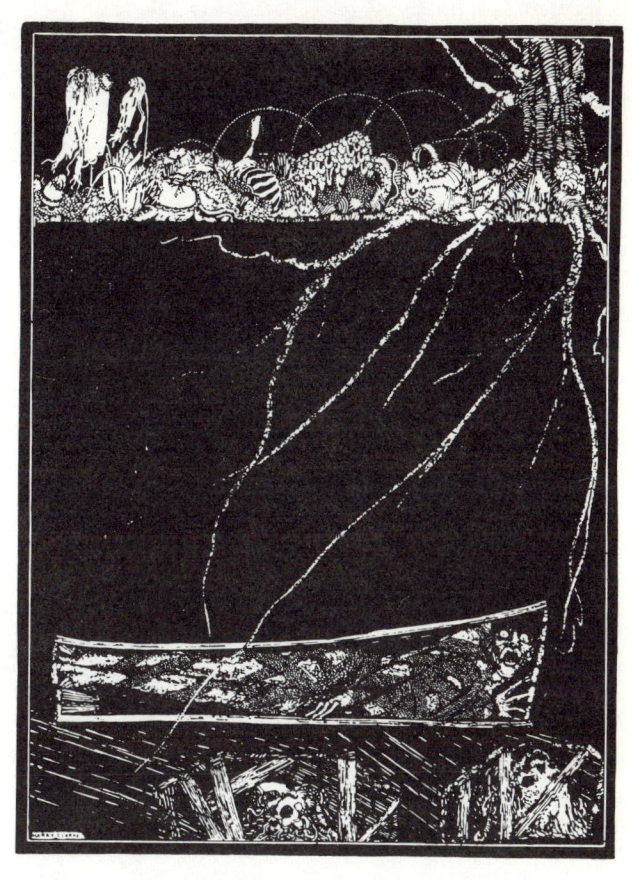

Three more illustrations based on 'The Premature Burial'. (Facing page) **A picture-strip version by Vincente Alcazar from** *Creepy* **magazine, 1975.** (Above,) **A Harry Clarke picture from 1919.** (Below) **Arthur Rackham using a rather unusual style, 1930**

Ray Milland in the film version of *The Premature Burial* made by Roger Corman in 1962

dreadful being working about my throat. They dragged me out of the coffin by the head. I felt again the living air, but it was piercingly cold; and I was carried swiftly away – I thought to judgement, perhaps perdition.

When borne to some distance, I was then thrown down like a clod – it was not upon the ground. A moment after I found myself on a carriage; and, by the interchange of two or three brief sentences, I discovered that I was in the hands of two of those robbers who live by plundering the grave, and selling the bodies of parents, and children, and friends. One of the men sung snatches and scraps of obscene songs, as the cart rattled over the pavement of the streets.

When it halted, I was lifted out, and I soon perceived, by the closeness of the air, and the change of temperature, that I was carried into a room; and, being rudely stripped of my shroud, was placed naked on a table. By the conversation of the two fellows with the servant who admitted them, I learnt that I was that night to be dissected.

My eyes were still shut, I saw nothing; but in a short time I heard, by the bustle in the room, that the students of anatomy were assembling. Some of them came round the table, and examined me minutely. They were pleased to find that so good a subject had been procured. The demonstrator himself at last came in.

Previous to beginning the dissection, he proposed to try on me some galvanic experiment – and an apparatus was arranged for that purpose. The first shock vibrated through all my nerves: they rang and jangled like the strings of a harp. The students expressed their admiration at the convulsive effect. The second shock threw my eyes open, and the first person I saw was the doctor who had attended me. But still I was as dead: I could, however, discover among the students the faces of many with whom I was familiar; and when my eyes were opened, I heard my name pronounced by several of the students, with an accent of awe and compassion, and a wish that it had been some other subject.

When they had satisfied themselves with the galvanic phenomena, the demonstrator took the knife, and pierced me on the bosom with the point. I felt a dreadful crackling, as it were, throughout my whole frame – a convulsive shuddering instantly followed, and a shriek of horror rose from all present. The ice of death was broken up – my trance ended. The utmost exertions were made to restore me, and in the course of an hour I was in the full possession of all my faculties.

TALES

NO ONE can read these tales, then close the volume, as he may with a thousand other tales, and straightway forget what manner of book he has been reading. Commonplace is the last epithet that can be applied to them. They are strange – powerful – more strange then pleasing, and powerful productions without rising to the rank of genius. The author is a strongheaded man, which epithet by no means excludes the possibility of being, at times, wrongheaded also. With little taste, and much analytic power, one would rather employ such an artist on the anatomical model of the Moorish Venus, then entrust to his hands any other sort of Venus. In fine, one is not sorry to have read these tales; one has no desire to read them twice.

Lafcadio Hearn

'THE RAVEN'

An essay on Gustav Doré's illustrations for
Edgar Allan Poe's famous poem

LAFCADIO HEARN

POE'S 'THE RAVEN' is undoubtedly one of the world's best known poems, and as Arthur Hobson Quinn has written, 'It made an impression probably not surpassed by that of any single piece of American poetry.' After its first appearance in the *New York Mirror* in 1845 (see illustration) it was widely copied, parodied and studied with endless suggestions being offered as to its meaning and purpose. Arguments have been put forward that 'The Raven' was a plagiarism, that it was suggested by the raven in Charles Dickens' *Barnaby Rudge* and that it is grossly over-rated. Even Poe did not help matters by giving an 'explanation' in 'The Philosophy of Composition' as to how he wrote the poem, which seems anything but the truth. In any event, to most lovers of poetry it stands as a work of genius.

When Poe published the work in volume form in November 1845 as *The Raven and Other Poems* he dedicated the book to the English gentlewoman and writer, Elizabeth Barrett (later the wife of the poet, Robert Browning), with the words 'To the Noblest of her Sex – Miss Elizabeth Barrett'. Miss Barrett's delight and her awareness of the impact of the poem on readers is contained in the letter she wrote to Poe which is also reprinted here. Lafcadio Hearn (1850-1904), the American author of the following essay, from the *New Orleans Times-Democrat*, 2 December 1883, was another great admirer of Poe, and also lived a somewhat wayward and unsettled life as journalist and writer. It is one of the ironies of publishing that the sumptuous volume of *The Raven* with Doré's illustrations which Hearn reviews was published by Harper Brothers who, during Poe's lifetime, had more than once rejected his work. And for this book they paid Doré alone thirty thousand francs for his illustrations!

THE APPARITION of Doré's 'Raven' – just issued in a luxurious folio by Messrs Harper Bros – is something worthy of larger attention than may be excited by the ordinary newspaper review: it is both an artistic and a literary event, which we cannot dwell upon without regretting that the limits of a journalistic article do not permit full justice to be done. The artistic importance of the work is now enhanced by the fact that it is posthumous – that the Promethean brain which conceived these wonderful drawings shall never again dream those 'dreams no mortal ever dared to dream before'.

A lithograph by the French Impressionist painter, Edouard Manet, to illustrate 'The Raven'

The house near Eighty-fourth Street and Broadway in New York where Poe finished 'The Raven' in 1844. From a photograph circa 1870

Since it was first publicly announced, many months ago, that Doré had illustrated this singular and sinister poem, all who had been impressed by the methods of the French artist or the American poet, must have from time to time vainly endeavoured to divine how 'The Raven' had affected the fancy of the great Alsatian. It did not appear to critical expectancy altogether the best theme that could have been selected from among Poe's numerous creations. Its only scene is the interior of a well-furnished modern parlour on a winter evening; its weirdness is intangible as those seraphim, 'whose footfalls tinkled on the tufted floor'. Lovers of

Poe would have much preferred to hear about a forthcoming Doré edition of the poet's prose works, or (as Edmund Clarence Stedman suggests in his superb introductory article, the best beyond all question ever written upon Poe) of *Tales of the Grotesque and Arabesque*. Doré was certainly the only artist of the age who could have pictured that ghastly nightmare, 'The House of Usher' – the unearthly weirdness of 'Ligeia' – the supernatural horror of 'The Masque of the Red Death'. What magnificent illustrations might not Doré have made of 'Silence: A Fragment' – or of 'Shadow: A Parable' – what transcendent architectural splendour might not have characterised his interpretation of that mysterious Venetian story, 'The Assignation'! . . .

It has been well said of Doré's work that its unfinished character in no sense impaired its power: his pictures did not need perfecting in order to satisfy the imagination – for they invariably surpassed it. His conception of Poe's 'Raven' is, like all his other conceptions, astonishing – astonishing in a two-fold sense: first by reason of its magnification of the poet's several fancies; secondly, because of his surprising interpretation of the theme as a whole. He has solved the difficulty of translating the stanzas into pictures by treating 'The Raven' as an inconsolable mourner's revery upon the vast and eternal Enigma of Death. Maddened by grief, this solitary mourner becomes the victim of strange nervous hallucinations – he hears many voices in heaven and on Earth; he is haunted by sounds and forms inaudible and invisible to others. This is certainly a proper comprehension of the poem. But we may question whether it has been carried out as Poe himself could have wished. 'The Raven' is rather weird than ghastly. Now Doré has materialised the weirdness into palpable ghastliness – the ghastliness of Death made visible – gazing with eyeless sockets, grinning with fleshless face.

This bony grin startles one at the very first picture. High up, at the right-hand corner, the Skeleton lets fall a long scroll bearing the word NEVERMORE. Below in the foreground, the figure of a robed man makes prodigious efforts to lift or push aside a curtain impenetrable and endless as the Veil of Isis – a curtain whose enormous folds seem full of mystery and menace. Is not this the curtain of Death's mystery which no mortal may lift and look beyond?

The opening scene of the poem proper – 'Once upon a midnight dreary' etc – much more than satisfies all anticipation. The sombre and lofty room; the dim richness of upholstery and heavy mouldings; the bereaved lover slumbering with his elbow upon the table, while the 'quaint and curious' volume lies upon his knees – form a picture that, even devoid of any fantastic details whatever, would be strongly impressive. The engraver has seconded the artist splendidly – his peculiar treatment of the upward glow from the shaded lamp is realistic to a startling degree. But the weirdness of the scene is due to the presence of a beautiful female face – mistily fair – which seems to materialise out of the light below the lampshade to gaze into the dreamer's face.

Engraving of the room where 'The Raven' was written

THE EDGAR ALLAN POE SCRAPBOOK

One of the earliest pictorial representations of 'The Raven' by Henry Anelay (1875)

The next scene is perhaps the only genuine disappointment in the book – because it does not fairly illustrate the line – 'And each separate dying ember wrought its ghost upon the floor'. The poet's idea is not at all realised; there are ghosts, indeed, in every shadowy nook and corner, but no 'ghosts upon the floor'. The reason probably is that Doré did not read Poe in English, but in the French version of Baudelaire, where translation of the verse is defective. Baudelaire, although generally more or less successful in rendering Poe's prose, failed notably in translating his poetry. Moreover the peculiar model of fireplace selected by Doré – like that of an English baronial hall – renders the realisation of Poe's fancy out of the question. Poe certainly imagined a coal-fire glowing in an elevated grate – Doré shows us a log-fire in a huge recess!

In addition to the ghosts which have already made their appearance, Death enters upon the scene in the next plate – illustrating the lines beginning: 'Eagerly I wished the morrow'. The skeleton sits upon the floor beside the poet's chair – a strangely material horror! The plate illustrating 'Sorrow for the lost Lenore' is singularly impressive: A deep tomb, whose walls of cut stone are yet open to the day above, allowing the departing train of mourners to be seen. Within the recess stands an angel, shaking flowers from his robe, whose vast and voluminous folds cover all the floor of the vault, and conceal the place of the dead. There is an appalling look in the angel's upturned eyes.

It is not possible to mention in detail each of the twenty-six engravings; we will therefore confine our remarks to those plates which best exhibit the powers of the artist. Among these must be included the successive illustrations portraying the phantasmal incidents preceding the Raven's entrance. The first of these (' 'Tis some visitor entreating entrance') exhibits two huge folding doors forced ajar as by the pressure of the night wind; but in the black opening towers up the half-concealed figure of a woman – a ghost – and above the phantom-face appears the bald skull and cavernous eyes of Death. The next view illustrates the lines:

> . . . Open here I flung the door:
> Darkness there, and nothing more!

Between the folding doors flung widely back into the darkness of the lobby, the figure of the haunted listener appears in striking relief against the warm glow within; while the ghosts shrink into the dark spaces behind the open doors, or rise into the shadows of the ceiling. Next we come to the illustration of the famous 'dreams no mortal ever dared to dream before' – the world circling in the star-spaces like some cloud-robed monster ridden by Death – and the sable mantle of the skeleton trails over the globe into a pall.

Doré produced the shadow of the Raven in the only way possible – viz: by conceiving the bust of Pallas immediately before a lofty transom, through which the light of a hall-lamp could invade the apartment; and the lamp, being higher than the head of Pallas, would naturally fling the shadow downward, to broaden as it descended. The effect is very remarkable.

But the two most truly Dorésque conceptions in the volume are those suggested by the lines – 'Wandering from the Nightly Shore', and 'The Night's Plutonian Shore'. The first is the weirdest of graveyards, under a moon magnified by mists and ringed with a halo – the second represents Death conducting the ghost of a woman into the eternal darkness. Their spectral figures float high in air, above the waters of a pallid river whose shores are

The first publication of 'The Raven' in the New York *Evening Mirror*, February 1845

veiled in darkness – far in the distance appear the lighted windows of that mansion where the body doubtless lies, awaiting burial. One recognises that wan river readily; it flows about the Hell of Dante, and supports the bark of Charon. Another powerful fancy is introduced by the cry – 'On this home by Horror haunted'. The lamp has died down; the fire-glow only remains – above the bereaved man's chair bends the exquisite phantom of a woman – the face is the face of one that strives to speak and cannot – while over all, darkly looms up the figure of a Sphinx whose features are the features of a skull!

Pathos is not wanting in Doré's pictures. Very touching is his interpretation of the line – 'If within the distant Aidenn', etc – where the lover again clasps his beloved in such a fair and luminous yet phantom paradise as appears in dreams. Pathetic also is the design accompanying the

'A stately Raven of the saintly days of yore.' One of the Gustave Doré engravings for 'The Raven', published by Harper in 1884
(POE FOUNDATION INC)

'Get thee back into the tempest and the Night's Plutonian Shore!' Also by Doré for the Harper edition of 'The Raven', now a much sought-after item by collectors and Poe enthusiasts
(POE FOUNDATION INC)

story of the Raven's ruthless answer, when the misty paradise fades into hopeless blackness, and the dear ghost passes voicelessly away.

The last plate – or vignette, rather – illustrating the artist's conception as a whole, is very sinister. There is a great Sphinx gazing over a shoreless ocean; and a youth stands on the ocean's verge, looking in the face of the Sphinx, as if seeking a reply. But the eyes of the Sphinx give no answer, being only hollows, void darknesses; and her face is the face of Death. This vignette admirably ends the grand series of plates, just as the vignette representing ANANKE (*Necessity*) opens it; a female figure poised in air on black wings, but apparently ready to drift in any direction, like a ghost blown by a wind.

On the whole, it may be said that Doré has interpreted Poe in an unexpected manner – yet with such force that however reluctantly we may first receive his version of 'The Raven', we shall never be able to dissociate the pictures of the great artist from the stanzas of the great poet, after having once fairly examined the former. The pictures were not altogether conceived in the true spirit of Poe – their ghastliness is not a ghastliness of suggestion, but is visible, is palpable. But Doré was of those who, below the lowest deep, beholds a lower deep; and above the loftiest heights, still loftier summits lost in glory – the one who could not but magnify human ideas to the verge of the superhuman when called upon to express them. If he transfigured the idea of the poem, he also expanded it. He comprehended the weirdness of the American brother's half-expressed thought, and completed it for him most wondrously – as the Mysterious Stranger is said to have completed that design which the first architect of Cologne Cathedral could never finish.

If Doré has intensified the horror of the poem, he has also ennobled and dignified its theme, by interpreting its relationship to the Universal Enigma – to the vain yet irresistible longing of man to lift the Veil of the Black Isis. And, however revolting to our sense of beauty the actual portrayal of death horrors must be, Doré's representation of them in this work is strictly in keeping with the artistic philosophy of his purpose. What man who, like the personage of Poe's 'Raven', has loved and lost, can think only of the dead face as it was in life – not as it *might* appear were the grave compelled to yield up its hideous secrets?

The question remains: Has Doré been well-represented by the American wood-engravers? Certainly the work before us is a veritable triumph of American art-execution; and some of the plates, at least, will rival the best Parisian work, perhaps surpass it! A few are not altogether above the possibility of criticism – there are effects which Doré might have modified had he lived to correct all his proofs. The best *set* of engravings of Doré's works are still, we think, to be found in the French plates to his Chateaubriand; but it is only fair to remind the reader that these were executed under his personal supervision. American engravers have in this case shown a capacity which even surpasses their well-deserved reputation, for the task of engraving 'The Raven' plates involved work of a unique and excessively difficult kind, and uniformity of execution could not be expected on the part of so many different artists.

THE EDGAR ALLAN POE SCRAPBOOK

Vincent Price in the 1963 film version of *The Raven*

Elizabeth Barrett Browning

5 Wimpole Street, London. April 1846

Dear Sir:

Receiving a book from you seems to authorise or at least encourage me to try to express what I have felt long before – my sense of the high honour you have done me in both your country and mine by the dedication of your poems. It is too great a distinction, conferred by a hand of too liberal a generosity. I wish for my own sake I were worthy of it. But I may endeavour, by future work, to justify a little what I cannot deserve anywise, now. For it, meanwhile, I may be grateful – because gratitude is the virtue of the humblest.

After which imperfect acknowledgement of my personal obligation may I thank you as another reader would thank you for this vivid writing, this power which is felt! Your 'Raven' has produced a sensation, a 'fit horror' here in England. Some of my friends are taken by the fear of it and some by the music. I hear of persons haunted by the 'Nevermore', and one acquaintance of mine who has the misfortune of possessing a 'bust of Pallas' never can bear to look at it in the twilight. I think you will like to be told that our great poet, Mr Browning, the author of 'Paracelsus' and the 'Bells of Pomegranates' was struck much by the rhythm of that poem.

Then there is a tale of yours ('The Case of M Valdemar') which I do not find in this volume, but which is going the rounds of the newspapers, about mesmerism, throwing us all into 'most admired disorder', and dreadful doubts as to whether 'it can be true', as the children say of ghost stories. The certain thing in the tale in question is the power of the writer, and the faculty he has of making horrible improbabilities seem near and familiar.

And now will you permit me, dear Mr Poe, as one who though a stranger is grateful to you, and has the right of esteeming you though unseen by your eyes – will you permit me to remain very truly yours always,

ELIZABETH BARRETT

AN UNPUBLISHED POEM BY EDGAR ALLAN POE

ALFRED R. WALLACE

THERE ARE quite a number of instances on record of tales and poems being 'discovered' and put forward as the work of Poe – indeed, as we have

DREAMLAND.

" There the traveller meets aghast
Sheeted Memories of the Past, —
Shrouded forms that start and sigh
As they pass the wanderer by, —
White-robed forms of friends long given,
In agony, to the Earth - and Heaven."

Henry Anelay picture for 'Dreamland' in the 1875 edition of *The Poetical Works of Edgar Allan Poe*

seen earlier, scholars like Professor Mabbott have devoted much time and effort to the study of such material. Perhaps one of the most interesting 'discoveries' was that reported by Alfred R. Wallace in the British *Fortnightly Review* in February 1904.

LEONAINE

Leonaine angels named her, and they took the light
Of the laughing stars and framed her, in a smile of white,
And they made her hair of gloomy midnight, and her eyes of bloomy
Moonshine, and they brought her to me in a solemn night.

In a solemn night of summer, when my heart of gloom,
Blossomed up to greet the comer, like a rose in bloom,
All foreboding that distressed me, I forgot as joy caressed me,
Lying joy that caught and pressed me, in the arms of doom.

Only spake the little lisper in the angel tongue,
Yet I listening heard the whisper – 'Songs are only sung
Here below that they may grieve you, tales are told you to deceive you,
So must Leonaine leave you while her love is young.'

Then God smiled – and it was morning, matchless and supreme,
Heaven's glory seemed adorning earth with its esteem;
Every heart but mine seemed gifted with a voice of prayer, and lifted,
When my Leonaine drifted from me like a dream.

E.A.P.

A MS copy of this poem came into my hands about eleven years since in the following manner. My elder brother, John Wallace, who emigrated to California in 1849, resided there till his death in March 1895. I had visited him at his home at Stockton in the summer of 1887, and from that time we corresponded about twice or thrice a year. I think it was in the last letter I received from him, nearly a year before his death, that I found an enclosure in his handwriting of the poem in question, with the following heading: 'Lines left by a wanderer at a wayside house in lieu of cash for board and lodging one night.'

At the end of the poem are the initials, E. A. P., but there is neither date nor any further particulars as to how it was obtained, neither was there any reference to it in the letter itself. Being at the time fully occupied with literary work, I gave little attention to it beyond noticing that it appeared to have all the best characteristics of Poe's style, and naturally supposing that it must be known to Poe's various editors and biographers, and that it was included in some of the recent editions of his works, none of which I had seen. I therefore put the verses away among other poetical scraps and newspaper cuttings, fully expecting to hear something about it in my brother's next letter. One peculiarity was, that it was written in pencil, as if it had been hastily copied when away from home and inserted in the letter because he knew that I was an admirer of Poe. Soon after I heard of his illness, and I do not think I received another letter from him.

The verses remained almost forgotten till Mr Marriott's letter (in the *Fortnightly* of September last) about Poe's essay on the Universe led me to inquire of him if this poem had appeared in any edition of Poe's works, and finding that

Two of Poe's famous poems are ingeniously combined to make a single picture story in the April 1974 issue of *Scream* magazine

it was, apparently, quite unknown, I wrote to my brother's widow, asking for any information as to where my brother obtained the poem. The reply received a few weeks back was unsatisfactory. None of the family had seen the verses, or remembered anything about them, and no copy of them was to be found in any of my brother's papers. I can, therefore, only suppose that the occupier of the 'wayside house' referred to had emigrated to California shortly afterwards, and that the original poem, or a copy of it, had been preserved, perhaps in an album, and perhaps even without any knowledge of the poet's name as indicated by the initials. It is not improbable that during one of my brother's journeys on surveying or engineering work he may have stayed at the house of the possessors of the MS, and have made a copy of it for me, and enclosed it in the letter, intending to give me further information about it when he wrote again, an intention frustrated by the extremely painful circumstances attending his fatal illness.

Coming now to the poem itself, if, as I have not the shadow of a doubt, it was written by Poe, why did he not acknowledge it or communicate it to any of his friends, or leave any copy of it among his papers? Here, again, we can find, I think, a very natural and sufficient, though of course purely hypothetical, explanation. It appears to me that this little poem must have been written under the influence of genuine poetical inspiration, at a time when the author was comparatively free from worry, and in a state of good bodily health and mental tranquillity. While possessing all the characteristics of his best style, it is in some respects superior to most, perhaps to all his similar productions. Its subject matter is unusually simple, the birth and early death of a child; and it is treated in a most simple but highly poetical manner, in which, though the morbid gloom of his nature appears, it is relieved by passages of such rare descriptive beauty and pathos as to give an exceptional charm to the whole. In the perfection of rhyme and rhythm, and the easy flow of the verse, the lines will bear comparison with his very best efforts, while in two points they seem to me to indicate the culmination of his genius: the first being the almost complete absence of alliteration as an adjunct to the general effect – though I often greatly admire the use of this artifice – the second, that a new and very beautiful form of versification is here used not to be found in any of his other poems. Each verse possesses eight rhyming words, one pair and two triplets, five of these being two-syllable words, and their somewhat peculiar arrangement is so carefully followed in each verse as to be evidently the result of a well thought-out plan which this little poem was composed to illustrate. In his essay on the Philosophy of Composition he had referred to the absence of originality in versification, declaring his belief that the possible varieties of metre and stanza are infinite, and that much of the possible charm and beauty of poetry are lost by the absence of invention of new forms of versification.

Turning to the Memoir prefixed to Mr J. H. Ingram's edition of the *Complete Poetical Works*, we find it stated:

> In 1849 Poe revisited the South, and, amid the scenes and friends of his early life, passed some not altogether unpleasing time. At Richmond, Virginia, he again met his early love, Elmira, now a wealthy widow, and after a short renewed acquaintance, was once more engaged to marry her.

Now this short period must have been one of intense relief from continual mental strain as well as of physical recuperation and enjoyment, and we can well imagine that

Frontispiece illustrating 'Eulalie' from the rare 1909 Pear Tree Press edition of *Some Poems of Edgar Allan Poe*

during his rambles about the country he would enjoy working out his ideas of new and beautiful poetic forms. He was also an athlete, and we may be sure that he would delight in long rambles on foot when going from one friend's house to another; and nothing is more likely than that he should have had to ask for a night's lodging at some farm-house or cottage, and, either from finding his pocket empty, or because his hospitable hosts would accept no payment, left with them the latest product of his muse as a memento of his visit.

If this is what occurred, the poem may quite possibly have been written only a few days before his tragical end; and, as this was in the year 1849, at a time when the Californian gold fever was at its height, Poe's host of the 'wayside house' may have been one of the many thousands who left the Eastern States for the land of gold, and may thus have carried away into such a long obscurity this last outcome of the poet's genius. How prophetic of his own approaching fate now seem the lines:

> All foreboding that distressed me, I forgot as joy caressed me,
> Lying joy that caught and pressed me, in the arms of doom.

And how the tranquillity and beauty of nature, which so rarely find expression in his poems, seem to have produced their full effect upon him when he gave us the exquisite lines:

Then God smiled – and it was morning, matchless and supreme,
Heaven's glory seemed adorning earth with its esteem.

The long tragedy of Poe's life is intensified by the consideration of what he might have given us had the final catastrophe been averted. With the most passionate human affections and with poetic and literary genius of the highest order, almost his whole life was a desperate and often agonising struggle to support himself and these dearest to him. Just when, for the first time, there seemed to open out before him a vista of comparative affluence and tranquillity, in which his genius might have developed those forms of beauty which he considered should be the poet's truest and highest aim, he was cut off in his prime, and, if the account given by Mr Ingram is correct, not, as usually supposed, by any fault of his own.

This little poetic gem, never before published, may have been the first, and also the last fruit of that happier period that seemed to be opening upon him. It is, of course, an unpolished gem, and has some of the defects of a rough draft hastily written down after being composed in the memory only; but I think that all admirers of Poe will welcome it, even in its unfinished state, as a worthy addition to the limited number of his shorter poems of the first rank.

Edmund Dulac design for 'The Bells' and (above right) another interpretation by W. Heath Robinson

THE MYSTERIOUS POET
MISS ELISABETH ELLICOTT POE

(An extract from 'Poe, The Weird Genius, An Authentic and Intimate Account of the Personality and Life of the Most Tragic Figure in American Literary History. Written by a Member of His Own Family.')

'THE BELLS' is another of Edgar Allan Poe's poems which enjoys enormous fame and popularity – not to mention a good many legends as to how it was composed. Certainly the poem took several forms before reaching the state we know today, and doubtless Poe carried out his revisions in several places before its first full publication in *Sartain's Union Magazine* in November 1849. One of the most fascinating – though unlikely – stories as to how it was written is given in the following item by 'a member of Poe's family'. Historian Arthur Hobson Quinn believes that Poe's friend, Mrs Marie Shew, may well have suggested the idea to him when he stayed with her on one occasion in New York, and that the bells in question were those of the Grace Church near her Tenth street home. In any event, Quinn believes there is no disputing that the poem is 'one of the most successful verbal imitations of sound in the English language'.

ON ONE of his Baltimore visits, Poe wrote the world-famous poem, 'The Bells'.

Perhaps Mrs Houghton had inspired him with the germ of the poem in New York, but the house where it was written in Baltimore still stands, a mute testimony of its Baltimore birth.

Tradition treasures this story of 'The Bells': One winter night Poe had been to the public library and was walking home down Saint Paul's Street. It was snowy, and the sleigh-bells made merry music. Their lilt and swing got into his brain, and he searched his pockets for pencil and paper. He had none.

Stores were closed, and meanwhile exquisite phrases were being lost. He rushed up the steps of Judge A. E. Giles's residence and rang the bell. The Judge himself opened the door, and Poe requested paper and ink. The judge saw that he was a gentleman, invited him into the library, and courteously withdrew. After a time he looked in after his strange guest, only to find him gone.

But there, lying on the table, were the first three stanzas of 'The Bells', which the judge afterward had framed and hung in his office.

COSMOPOLITAN, February 1909

> For every sound that floats
> From the rust within their ghostly throats
>   Is a groan.
> And the people — ah, the people
> They that up in the steeple
>   All alone,
> And who, tolling, tolling, tolling,
>   In that muffled monotone,
> Feel a glory in so rolling
>   On the human heart a stone —
> They are neither man nor woman —
> They are neither brute nor human,
> But are pestilential carcases
>   disparted from their souls —
>   Called Ghouls: —
> And their king it is who tolls: —
> And he rolls, rolls, rolls, rolls
>   A Paean from the bells!
> And his merry bosom swells
>   With the Paean of the bells!
> And he dances and he yells;
> Keeping time, time, time,
> In a sort of Runic rhyme,
>   To the Paean of the bells —
>   Of the bells: —

A facsimile of the original manuscript of 'The Bells' in Poe's handwriting

Virginia Poe, Edgar's ill-fated young wife

POE'S MARY
AUGUSTUS VAN CLEEF

THIS IS A controversial article, but one that has never been reprinted in full, although much discussed at length by all Poe's major biographers. It purports to be the reminiscences of an old lady who maintains that Poe was once passionately in love with her. Although her name is not given in the article, 'Mary Deveraux's' story is probably in the main fictitious, although it is quite possible that Poe did meet her and even flirted with her. As we know Poe idolised the women in his life, and it seems that if we can draw anything from this following article he was in turn attractive to them – dark moods and all. The piece appeared in Harper's New Monthly Magazine **of December 1888.**

SHE WAS a lively, handsome old lady of seventy-one. I call her an old lady not because she looked one, but because she was. She looked rather sixty than seventy; and though her hair, once auburn, was white, her step was brisk, and her figure was as erect, round, and trim apparently as it was fifty years ago. Her bright dark brown eyes had a kindly sparkle, and her frequent laugh was contagious. She was charming still, and it is easy to believe that, when a young girl, she was loved by and loved a man so strange and fascinating in many ways as Edgar Allan Poe. That she knew the poet and that he had been in love with her had been in later years known only in a vague, general way among her family, of which I am fortunate to count myself one, and friends. During the life of Poe she naturally said

The trouble-worn features of Poe in 1845

little about his early love for her, and since its close she has said but little more, except in general terms. Though for a year, when he lived in Baltimore with Mrs Clemm and Virginia, they were engaged in fact, if not in name, though she remained to the end his friend and the friend of his wife and Mrs Clemm, she is mentioned in none of the biographies of the poet. She died in the West in 1887.

Naturally I was curious to hear her story. Finding, after she had told it to me, during a number of conversations, that it gave an intimate insight on certain traits of his character, described him with the minuteness of observation of a loving woman, corrected some statements and threw new light on others, I told her that it ought to be published. I had also prefaced my original inquiries by stating my purpose in making them. She gave her consent, stipulating that her identity should not be revealed. And so the grandmother who was loved in many households in New York and other cities told me the story of what was the chief romance of her life. On that of Poe, those who read it will see it cannot fail to have had a strong influence. If he had not been finally rejected by the heroine of the present story he would never have married Virginia, his child cousin, who acted as go-between during what was probably the first robust passion of his manhood. It also interferes somewhat with the romantic story of the gradual growth of his love for Virginia, in Mr Eugene L. Didier's life of the poet.

Occasionally, as the old lady told her story, her eyes would become moistened as she spoke of him she called 'Eddie' with something of the tenderness of old days, read again, half to me and half to herself, some of her early lover's poems, and lingered over the lines she thought referred to herself, or looked at the portrait reproduced in several books which she declared was the best one she had ever seen, and had his expression. She recalled, as being like one which was in a volume of his poems Poe gave her in after-years. She pronounced those in later biographies caricatures, making an exception in favour of the steel engraving which accompanies the life by Mr George E. Woodberry, in the 'American Men of Letters' series. I give her recollections as much in her own words as possible, as I took them down at the time, while she sat by my side, and occasionally remarked that I could put what she said in my own words. This I only did when I had to, for sometimes statements in one conversation were amplified in another. In all but dates the old lady's memory was remarkably good, considering the lapse of years.

'When I first met Mr Poe', she said, 'I was about seventeen, and lived in Essex Street, I think it was, in the "old town" of Baltimore. It was about 1835 (1832?), I think. Our house adjoined that of a Mr Newman, who was our landlord. He had a daughter about my own age, whose name was also Mary. Mr Poe had at that time recently come to live with his aunt, Mrs Clemm, after leaving West Point, and while his relations with Mr Allan, whom he always called father, were not pleasant. Mrs Clemm lived around the corner from us, in a street which crossed ours. She lived in the upper part of a house, and supported herself by sewing, dressmaking, or some similar work. They were all very poor, but everything was wax neat. Mr Poe was then quite a young man, and Virginia Clemm, who afterward became his wife, was a delicate schoolgirl of about ten years of age. Her sole beauty was in the expression of her face. Her disposition was lovely. She had violet eyes, dark brown hair, and a bad complexion that spoiled her looks. She had a brother, a dissipated young man, who went West; I never knew what became of him.'

Mrs Clemm, Edgar Allan Poe's devoted mother-in-law

Poe's residence in Carmine Street, New York in 1837

When I asked if Virginia was fond of Poe, Mary answered: 'Oh my, yes! She was fond of her cousin, as any child would be of anybody that paid her attention.'

'The stoops of Mr Newman's house and ours', she continued, 'were adjoining, and each had an inner balustrade. One summer afternoon Miss Newman and I were seated, talking, each on her own stoop, when Mr Poe passed, as usual, on the other side of the street, on his way home. We were neither of us acquainted with him, but I knew him very well by sight, as we had flirted with each other for some time from the garret windows of our houses. We used to wave handkerchiefs and throw kisses to each other. My mother used to ask me, "What takes you upstairs so much, Mary?" Mr Poe once during that time sent Virginia around for a lock of my hair, and I sent it to him. Well, in passing, on the afternoon I have just spoken of, Mr Poe bowed. My companion asked me if I knew him. I said no. She said he was Edgar Poe, who had recently come from West Point. She also said he wrote poetry. After Mr Poe bowed he started across the street and Miss Newman said: "Why, I declare! there comes Mr Poe across the street. Oh! isn't he handsome? He is coming to see you, not me." He was handsome, but intellectually so, not a pretty man. He had the way and the power to draw any one to him. He was very fascinating, and any young girl would have fallen in love with him.

'Mr Poe, having crossed the street, came up the Newman's stoop. As he did so, I turned my back, as I was then young and bashful. He said, "How do you do, Miss Newman?" She then turned and introduced him to me, and then happened to be called into the house. Mr Poe immediately jumped across the balustrades separating the stoops, and sat down by me. He told me I had the most beautiful head of hair he ever saw, the hair that poets always raved about. It was auburn, and worn with frizzed puffs on the sides, as was then the style. From that time on he visited me every evening for a year, and during that time, until the night of our final lovers' quarrel, he never drank a drop, as far as I knew.

'Mr Poe was about five feet eight inches tall, and had dark, almost black hair, which he wore long and brushed back in student style over his ears. It was as fine as silk. His eyes were large and full, gray and piercing. He was then, I think, entirely clean-shaven. His nose was long and straight, and his features finely cut. The expression about his mouth was beautiful. He was pale, and had no colour. His skin was of a clear, beautiful olive. He had a sad, melancholy look. He was very slender when I first knew him, but had a fine figure, an erect military carriage, and a quick step. But it was his manner that most charmed. It was elegant. When he looked at you it seemed as if he could read your very thoughts. His voice was pleasant and musical, but not deep.

'He always wore a black frock-coat buttoned up, with a cadet or military collar, a low turned-over shirt collar, and a black cravat tied in a loose knot. He did not follow the fashions, but had a style of his own. His was a loose way of dressing, as if he didn't care. You would know that he was very different from the ordinary run of young men. Affectionate! I should think he was; he was passionate in his love.

'My intimacy with Mr Poe isolated me a good deal. In fact my girlfriends were many of them afraid of him, and forsook me on that account. I knew none of his male friends. He despised ignorant people, and didn't like trifling and small-talk. He didn't like dark-skinned people. When he loved, he loved desperately. Though tender and very

A sketch of the Poe cottage at Fordham with vignettes based on his works (1903)

affectionate, he had a quick, passionate temper, and was very jealous. His feelings were intense, and he had but little control of them. He was not well balanced; he had too much brain. He scoffed at everything sacred, and never went to church. If he had had religion to guide him, he would have been a better man. He said often that there was a mystery hanging over him he never could fathom. He believed he was born to suffer, and this embittered his whole life. Mrs Clemm also spoke vaguely of some family mystery, of some disgrace.

'Eddie's life was embittered, and it was a great disappointment to him when Mr Allan married again. He had no business to treat Eddie as he did, to educate him as he did, and then throw him over. Eddie was never educated to work. He was very proud and very sensitive. Mr Poe once gave me a letter to read from Mr Allan, in which the latter said, referring to me, that if he married any such person he would cut him off without a shilling. I think that Eddie told me that Mr Allan's second wife (Miss Patterson) had been his housekeeper. She said she could not take care of him unless she was his wife. He could do nothing afterward without her approval.

'Eddie and I never talked of his poetry then or in later years. He would not have done that; he would have considered it conceited. We were young, and only thought [of] our love. Virginia always carried his notes to me. I never kept any of his letters. Do you suppose I would, after I had married? Eddie's favourite name was Mary, he said. He used often to quote Burns, for whom he had a great admiration. We used to go out walking together in the evenings. We often walked out of the city and sat down on the hills.

'One moonlight summer night we were walking across the bridge, which was not far from our house. At the other end of the bridge was a minister's house. Eddie took my arm and pulled me, saying, "Come, Mary, let us go and get married; we might as well get married now as any other time." We were then but two blocks from home. I was taken by surprise and frightened, and ran from him toward home. He followed, and came in after me.

'We had no definite engagement, but we understood each other. He was then not in circumstances to marry. When my brother found that Mr Poe was coming so often, he said to me: "You are not going to marry that man, Mary? I would rather see you in your grave than that man's wife. He can't support himself, let alone you." I replied, being as romantic as Eddie was, that "I would sooner live on a crust of bread with him than in a palace with any other man."

'The only thing I had against him,' she continued, 'was that he held his head so high. He was proud, and looked down on my uncle, whose business did not suit him. He always liked my father, and talked with him a good deal.

biting the nails of the other hand to the quick, as he always did when excited. He then walked over to the piano, and snatched the music and threw it on the floor. I said that it made no matter, that I could sing the song without the music, and did so. Mr Morris, knowing me well, called me always "Mary". That also made Eddie jealous. He stayed after Mr Morris left, and we had a little quarrel.

'Our final lovers' quarrel came about in this way: One night I was waiting in the parlour for Eddie, and he didn't come. My mother came into the room about ten o'clock and said, "Come, Mary, it's bedtime". The parlour windows were open, and I lay with my head on my arms on one of the window sills. I had been crying. Eddie arrived shortly after my mother spoke to me, and had been drinking. It was the only time during that year that I ever knew him to take anything. He found the front door locked. He then came to the window where I was, and opened the shutters, which were nearly closed. He raised my head, and told me where he had been. He said he had met some cadets from West Point when on his way across the bridge. They were old friends, and took him to Barnum's Hotel, where

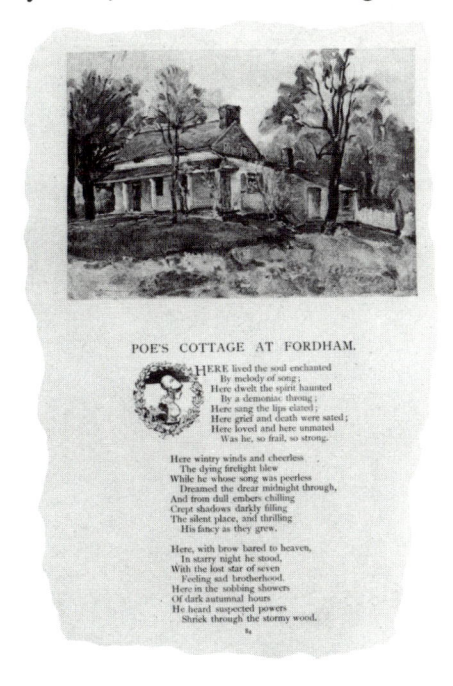

Engraving and poem based on Poe's life at Fordham from *The Century* **magazine (1909)**

'The following little story will show you how much Mr Poe was a creature of sudden impulse: One day in Baltimore, after some very heavy rains, the streets were flooded and almost impassable. A young lady stood at a corner wondering how she should get across. The first thing she knew, Eddie came up behind her, picked her up in his arms, and carried her across the street. His feet were wet when he came to our house and told me about it. The young lady was the daughter of a rich man living "on the Point". She asked Mr Poe to whom she was indebted. He took out his card and gave it to her, and she fell in love with him, though she had never seen him before. He said she was a beautiful girl, and "I guess I will have to go and see her."

'To show you how jealous he was, I will tell you of the cause of one of our quarrels. One evening a friend of my brother's, a Mr Morris, was visiting us. He knew that Mr Poe's favourite song, which I often sang him, was "Come rest in this bosom". He asked me to sing it, in order to tease Mr Poe. I went to the piano and began to sing. Mr Morris stood by me and turned the leaves. Mr Poe walked, with one hand behind his back, up and down the room,

they had a supper and champagne. He had gotten away as quickly as possible to come and explain matters to me. A glass made him tipsy. He had more than a glass that night. As to his being a habitual drunkard, he never was as long as I knew him.

'I went and opened the door and sat on the stoop with him in the moonlight. We then had a quarrel, about whose cause I do not care to speak. The result was that I jumped past him off the stoop, ran around through an alleyway to the back of the house, and into the room where my mother was.

'She said, "Mary! Mary! what's the matter?"

'Mr Poe had followed me, and came into the room. I was much frightened, and my mother told me to go upstairs. I did so.

'Mr Poe said: "I want to talk to your daughter. If you don't tell her to come downstairs, I will go after her. I have a right to."

'My mother was a tall woman, and she placed her back against the door of the stairs, and said, "You have no right to; you cannot go upstairs."

'Mr Poe answered: "I have a right. She is my wife now in the sight of Heaven."

'My mother then told him he had better go home and to bed, and he went away.' (This is evidently the second of the occasions which Poe's friend Mr L. A. Wilmer spoke of in his recollections published on 23 May 1866, in the Baltimore *Daily Commercial*, as when Mrs Clemm scolded her nephew 'for coming home intoxicated the night before from a tavern, but as if it were a rare occurrence'.)

'He didn't value the laws of God', she continued, 'or man. He was an atheist. He would just as lief have lived with a woman without being married to her as not. Well, I made a narrow escape in not marrying him. I don't think he was a man of much principle.

'After the quarrel I have just told you about I broke off all intercourse with Mr Poe, and returned his letters unopened. My mother also forbade him the house. He sent me a letter by Virginia. I sent it back unopened. He wrote again, and I opened the letter. He addressed me formally as Miss ——, and upbraided me in satiric terms for my heartless, unforgiving disposition. I showed the letter to my mother, and she in turn showed it to my grandmother, who was then visiting us. My grandmother read it, and took it to my uncle James. My uncle was very indignant, and resented Mr Poe's letter so much that he wrote him a very severe, cutting letter, without my knowledge. Mr Poe also published at the same time in a Baltimore paper a poem of six or eight verses, addressed 'To Mary ——'. There was an initial for my last name. The poem was very severe, and spoke of fickleness and inconstancy. All my friends and his knew whom he meant. This also added to my uncle's indignation. Mr Poe was so incensed at the letter he received that he bought a cowhide, and went to my uncle's store one afternoon and cowhided him. My uncle was a man of over fifty at the time. My aunt and her two sons rushed into the store, and in the struggle to defend my uncle tore his assailant's black frock-coat at the back from the skirts to the collar. Mr Poe then put the cowhide up his sleeve and went up the street to our house as he was, with his torn coat, and followed by a crowd of boys. When he arrived at our house he asked to see my father. He told him he had been up to see his brother, pulled out my uncle's letter, said he resented the insult, and had cowhided him. I had been called downstairs, and when Mr Poe saw me he pulled the cowhide out of his sleeve and threw it down at my feet, saying, "There, I make you a present of that!"

'He then asked to see me alone, and upbraided me for telling about his letter, and being the cause of all the trouble. I told him I would have nothing to say to him, and did not wish to see him again. At the same time it was breaking my heart. My uncle had no business to take it up. I could have done so myself. We soon after this moved from Baltimore and back to Philadelphia, where I was born. I was so much disturbed by the quarrel with Mr Poe that I was sick for a long time. I never saw him again until after he was married to Virginia. I married, and settled in New York city. When on a visit to Philadelphia, several years after, I met Mr Poe on the street with his wife and Mrs Clemm. I stopped and talked with them. They asked me to come to see them. I went, with a young lady cousin of mine. They lived in Seventh Street, in the back part of a little house. Eddie asked me to sing one of my old songs. I asked him what song. He said, "Come rest in this bosom." I sang it, and he thanked me. We spent a pleasant evening, and Mr Poe accompanied my cousin and myself back to her house.

'A few years afterward, when living in Jersey City, I saw Mr Poe again. He was still living in Philadelphia. He came

A beautiful interpretation of 'Bridal Ballad' by Edmund Dulac

to New York, and went to my husband's place of business to find out where we lived. He was on a spree, however, and forgot the address before he got across the river. He made several trips backward and forward on the ferry-boat. He asked different people on board if they knew where I lived, and finally found a deck hand who happened to know, and told him. Mr Poe said he was determined to find me, if he "had to go to hell" to do it. When my husband returned home he was told on the boat that a crazy man had been looking for his wife!

'When Mr Poe reached our house I was out with my sister, and he opened the door for us when we got back. We saw he was on one of his sprees, and he had been away from home for several days. He said to me: "So you have married that cursed —— [referring to her husband's business]. Do you love him truly? Did you marry him for love?" I answered, "That's nobody's business; that is between my husband and myself." He then said: "You don't love him. You do love me. You know you do."

'Mr Poe stayed to tea with us, but ate nothing; only drank a cup of tea. He got excited in conversation, and taking up a table-knife, began to chop at some radishes on a dish in front of him. He cut them all up, and the pieces flew over the table, to everybody's amusement. After tea he asked me if I would not play and sing for him, and I sang his favourite song again. He then went away. A few days afterward Mrs Clemm came to see me, much worried about "Eddie dear", as she always addressed him. She did not know where he was, and his wife was almost crazy with anxiety. I told Mrs Clemm that he had been to see me. A search was made, and he was finally found in the woods on the outskirts of Jersey City, wandering about like a crazy man. Mrs Clemm took him back with her to Philadelphia. This was in the spring of 1842.' (This was evidently the time that he was away for a short time from his desk as editor of *Graham's Magazine*, and on coming back found Dr Griswold temporarily in his place, and left the office with wounded feelings, not to return again.)

'I visited them afterward', Mary went on, 'in New York

city, in Amity Street, and at the cottage at Fordham. The cottage was very humble, you know – you wouldn't have thought decent people could have lived in it; but there was an air of refinement about everything. There were vines growing all over the house, which had been fixed up for them by the owner; and Virginia loved flowers, so there was a bed in front of the porch. Over a door in the parlour stood on a bracket a plaster cast of a bird. I suppose it was a raven, but it might have been a parrot. It was the only piece of sculpture in the room.

'When Eddie was composing a poem he walked up and down the floor of the little parlour, with one hand behind his back in his usual way, biting the fingernails of his other hand till the blood came. When he got what he wanted he would sit down and write the lines, and then begin walking again. I have heard it said that at times, after Virginia's death, when he could not sell a poem, he would say to the person to whom he offered it, "Then give me a glass of brandy, and take it."

'The day before Virginia died I found her in the parlour. I said to her, "Do you feel any better today?" and sat down by the big armchair in which she was placed. Mr Poe sat on the other side of her. I had my hand in hers, and she took it and placed it in Mr Poe's, saying, "Mary, be a friend to Eddie, and don't forsake him; he always loved you – didn't you, Eddie?" We three were alone, Mrs Clemm being in the kitchen. On the day Virginia died I came down from the cottage to the city in the same stage with Mrs and Dr Shew. She was a great friend of theirs, and we talked about Virginia. On the day of the funeral I remember meeting at the cottage Mrs Ann S. Stephens, Mrs Shew, N. P. Willis and his partner Morris, and some of the neighbours. It was very cold, and I did not go to the grave, but stayed at the house.

'They were so very poor that Mrs Clemm told me that, in order to get money to live, she picked manuscripts out of Mr Poe's wastepaper-basket which he had rejected, and sold them without his knowledge. When my daughter was to be married I wanted Eddie and Mrs Clemm to come to the wedding. She said they could not, as neither she nor he had any clothes. She wanted me to buy Virginia's gold thimble for ten dollars for a wedding present, but I could not afford it, as I had many things to buy. Mrs Clemm however, did sell the thimble.'

In talking of Poe's intended marriage to Mrs Shelton, whom he had known as a young man while she was Miss Sarah Elmira Royster, Mary said that Mr Allan had originally intended them for each other, and spoke of the lady as being a protégée or adopted daughter of that gentleman. As Mr Woodberry speaks of this affair as coming to naught on account of Mr Allan's opposition, and Mr Gill says it was strongly opposed by that gentleman, and the cause of a violent quarrel between him and his adopted son, perhaps the statement of the lady who followed Miss Royster in Poe's affections should have some weight. It is evident that with the natural disposition of a man to make light of a previous affair he intimated to his new love that it was Mr Allan who wanted the match, and not he. In this there was, it is likely, also considerable truth. My informant having been perhaps naturally inclined to laugh at much of the story of the love of Poe for his child cousin Virginia, which his biographers speak of as if it made up, with the motherly love of Mrs Clemm, the whole sum of his experience in female affection during his stay at the latter's home in Baltimore, was also at variance with these gentlemen on another point. She insisted, contrary to all accounts, that Mrs Shelton, who was the widow, she said, of a rich Southerner, old enough to have been her father, sent first for Mrs Clemm, and that the latter then sent for Poe. There were some details given about this matter which gave the statement a strong air of probability, but are not worth relating here.

Edmund Dulac's graceful tribute to 'To One in Paradise'

Thomas Holley Chivers

POE'S MAGAZINE SCHEME

THOMAS HOLLEY CHIVERS

THROUGHOUT HIS life, Poe nursed the ambition to run his own magazine as both proprietor and editor. In 1840 he actually prepared a prospectus of his idea, entitled *The Penn Magazine*, which he circulated among his friends and acquaintances to try and raise money to finance the publication. His scheme was greeted with a certain amount of support, but circumstances prevented his going ahead just then. A while later he revised the project on a broader basis, retitled it *The Stylus* and tried once more to revive interest. Despite the fact that he was already a formidable critic, accomplished short-story writer and poet, and hoped to be able to recruit some of the most important American writers of the day to contribute, his plans came to nought.

On these pages is the prospectus that he prepared for *The Penn Magazine* plus some intimate details of the scheme by his friend, Thomas Holley Chivers, who he hoped would be one of his supporters in the venture. Chivers, who has been described by the historian Edward Wagenknecht as 'one of the most incredible characters in American literary history' was an eccentric poet who gave the impression during Poe's lifetime of being a sincere admirer and friend, yet after the unfortunate Edgar's death made some strong accusations of plagiarism against him. In this extract, drawing on Chivers's papers, from *The Century* of February 1903, the poet describes a meeting which takes place at the Poes' cottage at Fordham, with both Virginia Poe and her mother, Mrs Clemm, in attendance.

NOT LONG after this – even while we were talking about the state of his health – his wife entered the room, to whom he very politely introduced me. Presently Mrs Clemm, his mother-in-law, came in, to whom he also introduced me. I was very much pleased with his wife. She appeared to me to be a very tender-hearted and affectionate woman – particularly so to him – whom she addressed with the endearing appellation of *My Dear*! But she was not a healthy woman, as I perceived after a little acquaintance with her – as, at irregular intervals – even while we were talking – she was attacked with a terrible paroxysm of coughing whose spasmodic convulsions seemed to me almost to rend asunder her very body. This was so severe at times as to threaten her with strangulation. I then asked him if Mrs Poe had been long ill? He replied, 'Yes, she has always been sick, never having been well since I first knew her!'

Poe's design for the cover of his proposed magazine *The Stylus*

An early twentieth-century charcoal portrait of Poe by Edmund Sullivan

'Has she caught cold? or is it a consumption under which she is labouring?' I then asked.

'No – it is not a cold – Dr Mitchell of Philadelphia, says that she has the bronchitis. She ruptured a blood vessel while singing, in Philadelphia, and had never been well since. Do you know Dr Mitchell? He is a Poet.'

I then said, 'No, I am not acquainted with him; but have often seen his pieces in the papers.'

Mrs Poe then got up and left the room – Mrs Clemm, her mother, following her. Presently she returned with a glass of lemonade, which she handed to me. Then turning to Poe, she asked, 'My dear! will you have a glass?'

'No – I do not want any at present,' said he, with an indifferent look.

Handing her the empty glass, she then left the room. Poe then turning to me, said 'I have long wished to see you upon a subject in which I am vitally interested. It is the publication of a magazine about which I wrote you first from Philadelphia, to be called *The Stylus*. When I first wrote you from Philadelphia in the letter containing the prospectus, it was my intention then to call it *The Penn Magazine*; but after having received your letter in which you suggested that such a title would render it too local, I then came to the conclusion to give it the name of the pen with which the Greeks used to write, called *The Stylus*. This would not only be more significant, but determine in some sense – in fact, as far as any title whatsoever could – the precise nature of the work.'

By this time Mrs Poe had returned into the room again with her bonnet on.

Turning to her, he then said, 'My Dear, hand me the bundle of letters there in the bureau drawer touching upon the publication of *The Stylus*.'

She then went to the bureau, took out a large bundle of letters – perhaps a hundred – and laid them down on a small table near the window where I was sitting. Then passing around the bed towards the door, she said: 'My Dear, I am going out with mother to take a small walk. I think it will do me good.'

'Very well', said he, then turning towards me – 'I am very willing. But you had, perhaps, better not walk too far. You know that Dr Mitchell said too much exercise was not good for you.'

A sinister assembly. Members of the Inquisition sit in judgement in this illustration by Arthur Rackham for 'The Pit and the Pendulum'

She then said, while adjusting her bonnet-strings, 'Shall I tell the servant girl should any persons call to see you, not to admit them?'

'Yes, tell her to tell them that I am sick and cannot see them,' said he.

She then left the room.

'If you will glance at those letters there', said he to me, 'you will perceive in what estimation my proposal to publish *The Stylus* is held by the most influential men in the Union. But those are not the tenth part of what I have received during the present year. I have many strong friends in the South and West who have promised me their aid in the procuring of subscribers. If you will open that letter which you now hold in your hand you will perceive that Mr John Tomlin of Jackson, Tennessee, who has written some pretty little things, has already obtained me thirty good paying subscribers. This, you will perceive, is strong evidence in favour of our establishing the magazine immediately.'

I then asked him in what form it should be published.

'Just hand me that book yonder on the bureau', said he, 'and I will show you.'

I got up and handed it to him.

'This', said he, 'is part of a fine London edition of *The Arabian Nights Entertainments*, translated by Lane. It is beautifully printed – in just such a style as we ought to get up the magazine. I saw it at Wiley & Putnam's Book Store, and bought it on purpose to show to you.'

I then asked him how many papers ought each number to contain.

He then said, 'About the number of Colton's *Whig Review* – but no less. If you say that you will join me, I will publish a new prospectus in which I will announce our-

THE EDGAR ALLAN POE SCRAPBOOK

selves to the public as the editors. But as I am not very well at present, we will talk more about it at our leisure. But if we intend to do anything, we ought to go to work immediately – for there is no time to be lost.'

Prospectus
of
THE PENN MAGAZINE
A Monthly Literary Journal

To be edited and published in the city of Philadelphia
By EDGAR A. POE

TO THE public: Since resigning the conduct of the *Southern Literary Messenger*, at the commencement of its third year, I have always had in view the establishment of a Magazine which should retain some of the chief features of that journal, abandoning or greatly modifying the rest. Delay, however, has been occasioned by a variety of causes, and not until now have I found myself at liberty to attempt the execution of the design.

I will be pardoned for speaking more directly of the *Messenger*. Having in it no proprietary right, my objects too being at variance in many respects with those of its very worthy owner, I found difficulty in stamping upon its pages that *individuality* which I believe essential to the full success of all similar publications. In regard to their permanent influence, it appears to me that a continuous definite

Facsimile of a letter from Poe to his relative, Washington Poe, seeking support for his magazine project

ART

Poe, Artist

Most U. S. citizens think of Edgar Allan Poe as a morose genius who wrote horrible stories magnificently and died of drink. Many remember that he was one of New York's most dogmatic literary critics, that he helped invent the detective story. A few know that he was a soldier for three years, for three months a West Point cadet. Three small pencil portraits in battered gilt frames arrived in New York last week to remind people that Edgar Allan Poe was also an artist and a draughtsman.

The portraits arrived in custody of astute Gabriel Wells, who vies for newspaper space with Dr. A. S. W. Rosenbach as premier U. S. rare-book seller. One was a self-portrait, one was of Mrs. Sarah E. Shelton, traditionally Poe's inspiration for "Annabel Lee." The third was of his tragic child-wife, Virginia Clemm, who died in a garret of misery and malnutrition, with a purring cat on her stomach to keep her warm. All three were signed, but Poe who wrote with the careful legible hand of a pretypewriter newspaper man, had one of the easiest signatures to forge. Careful Bookman Wells took his pictures to the leading Poe authority in the U. S., Dr. Thomas O. Mabbott of Hunter College. Dr. Mabbott was enthusiastic, authenticated the signatures, referred to a landscape by Poe in the Poe cottage at Richmond, quoted a letter from Poe to his mother to prove the existence of the picture of Sarah Elmira Shelton:

"I told Elmira when I first came here, that I had one of the pencil-sketches of her that I took a long while ago in Richmond; and I told her that I would write to you about it."

Said Dr. Mabbott:

"The self portrait of Poe is in one way the greatest find of all, the date is probably late 1845. It not only represents him in his prime, but the self portrait is probably the most satisfactory picture we have of him at this period. In this he has given us with surprising skill for an amateur what the author of 'The Raven' thought he looked like....

"But the picture one rejoices most in seeing is the lovely head of Virginia Clemm Poe. It is said that the only other picture that is accessible was made after her death. But here we have her as her husband saw her—a most romantic and tragic lady, the poet's best love."

Bookseller Wells explained last week that the three sketches had been given by Poe to Henry O'Reilly, a well-to-do Irish American journalist who often entertained morose Edgar at his Washington Heights home. They remained in the O'Reilly family until a few weeks ago when Mr. Wells discovered them in Italy.

VIRGINIA CLEMM — POET POE — MRS. SHELTON
He gave them to his friend in Washington Heights.

Reproduction of an article from *Time* magazine in 1936 on Poe's alleged talents as an artist

character, and a marked certainty of purpose, are requisites of vital importance; and I cannot help believing that these requisites are only attainable when one mind alone has the general direction of the undertaking. Experience has rendered obvious – what might indeed have been demonstrated *a priori* – that in founding a Magazine of my own lies my sole chance of carrying out to completion whatever peculiar intentions I may have entertained.

To those who remember the early days of the Southern periodical in question, it will be scarcely necessary to say that its main feature was a somewhat overdone causticity in its department of Critical Notices of new books. The *Penn Magazine* will retain this trait of severity insomuch only as the calmest yet sternest sense of justice will permit. Some years since elapsed may have mellowed down the petulance without interfering with the vigour of the critic. Most surely they have not yet taught him to read through the medium of a publisher's will, nor convinced him that the interests of letters are unallied with the interests of truth. It shall be the first and the chief purpose of the Magazine now proposed to become known as one where may be found at all times, and upon all subjects, an honest and a fearless opinion. It shall be a leading object to assert in precept, and to maintain in practice, the rights, while in effect it demonstrates the advantages, of an absolutely independent criticism; a criticism self-sustained; guiding itself only by the purest rules of Art; analysing and urging these rules as it applies therein; holding itself aloof from all personal bias; acknowledging no fear save that of outraging the right; yielding no point either to the vanity of the author, or to the assumptions of critical prejudice, or to the involute and anonymous cant of the Quarterlies, or to the arrogance of those organised cliques which, hanging like nightmares upon American literature, manufacture, at the nod of our principal booksellers, a pseudo-public opinion by wholesale. These are objects of which no man need be ashamed. They are purposes, moreover, whose novelty at least will give them interest. For assurance that I will fulfil them in the best spirit and to the very letter, I appeal with confidence to those friends, and especially to those Southern friends, who sustained me in the *Messenger*, where I had a very partial opportunity of completing my own plans.

In respect to the other characteristics of the *Penn Magazine* a few words here will suffice.

It will endeavour to support the general interests of the republic of letters, without reference to particular regions – regarding the world at large as the true audience of the author. Beyond the precincts of literature, properly so called, it will leave in better hands the task of instruction upon all matters of *very* grave moment. Its aim chiefly shall be *to please* – and this through means of versatility, originality, and pungency. It may be as well here to observe that nothing said in this Prospectus should be construed into a design of sullying the Magazine with any tincture of the buffoonery, scrurrility, or profanity, which are the blemish of some of the most vigorous of the European prints. In all branches of the literary department, the best aid, from the highest and purest sources, is secured.

To the mechanical execution of the work the greatest attention will be given which such a matter can require. In this respect it is proposed to surpass, by very much, the ordinary Magazine style. The form will somewhat resemble that of the *Knickerbocker*; the paper will be equal to that of the *North American Review*; pictorial embellishments are promised only in the necessary illustration of the text.

The *Penn Magazine* will be published in Philadelphia, on the first of each month; and will form, half-yearly, a volume of about 500 pages. The price will be $5 per annum, payable in advance, or upon receipt of the first number, which will be issued on the first of March 1841. Letters addressed to the Editor and Proprietor,

EDGAR A. POE
Philadelphia, 1 January 1841

LAST DAYS OF EDGAR A. POE

SUSAN ARCHER WEISS

THIS IS perhaps the most accurate and certainly the kindest account of the end of Poe's life by a contemporary. It is also an essay that, although frequently quoted in biographies and studies of Poe, has not been reprinted in full since its original appearance in the major American publication, *Scribner's* magazine of March 1878. Mrs Weiss gives us intimate details of herself and her involvements with Poe in her engrossing and informative narrative.

Mrs Susan Archer Weiss

WHEN I was about seven years of age, it was my habit to peruse eagerly every scrap of literature that fell in my way. In this manner I had read *The Children of the Abbey*, *Pike's Expeditions*, *Buck's Theology*, *Castle of Otranto*, and *The Spectator*, with other prose works of equally dissimilar character, but as yet the world of poetry was an unknown world to me.

One day I came across an old number of the *Southern Literary Messenger*, containing the well-known ballad beginning:

> Lo, the ring is on my hand,
> And the wreath is on my brow.

Whatever may be my present opinion of this poem, no words can describe the charm which it exercised over my childish fancy. The music of it was a keen delight, the mystery of it, which I could in no wise fathom, was a subtle fascination, and its sadness a pain which 'touched my soul with pity'; for that it was an authentic history, an actual experience of Edgar A. Poe, it never occurred to me to doubt.

Who was Edgar A. Poe? My idea of him was then, and for years after, as other productions of his pen met my eye, that of a mysterious being in human shape, yet gifted with a power more than human; a something of weird beauty and despairing sadness, touched with a vague suspicion of evil which inspired in me a sense of dread, mingled with compassion. To this feeling was added in time one akin to horror, upon my reading the sketch of the 'Pest' family, every word of which I received as truth; and the picture of the awful Pests seated in their coffins around the festal board, and of their subsequent wild flight with their winding-sheets streaming behind them, long haunted me with an unspeakable horror.

Who was Edgar A. Poe? I at length inquired of my mother. With wondering interest I learned that he was a gentleman of Richmond, and that he had resided in the very house which I had visited the day before. Thenceforth this house with its massive portico, in which Edgar Poe had played when a child, and the trees on the lawn which he had climbed, were to me objects of solemn and mysterious interest.

This house was that of Mr Allan, who had adopted Poe when a child. It is still to be seen at the corner of Main and Fifth streets, unchanged, with the exception of a modern addition. Opposite, in old times, stood the large frame mansion, surrounded by piazzas, of Mrs Jane Mackenzie, who adopted Poe's sister, Rosalie. On the right of Mr Allan's there yet stands a tall brick house (now occupied by the Rev Moses Hoge) which was at the time of which I speak the residence of Major James Gibbon. These three families occupied a first social position, and were on terms of mutual intimacy, and from them and others I have heard many anecdotes of Edgar Poe's youth and childhood. Passing over these for the present, I will proceed to speak of the time when I myself became acquainted with him.

In 1849 I was residing at our suburban home near Richmond, Virginia, in the immediate neighbourhood of Duncan's Lodge, then the residence of Mrs Mackenzie. Being intimate with the family (of which Mr Poe's sister was a member), we had been for years accustomed to hear him constantly and familiarly spoken of. Mrs Mackenzie had always been fond of him, and he, like his sister, was accustomed to call her 'Ma', and to confide in her as in a mother.

I remember Miss Poe describing to us her visits to her brother at Fordham, then informing us of the death of his wife, and, afterward, mentioning a vague rumour of his engagement to Mrs Whitman, and finally announcing with great delight that Edgar was coming on a visit to his friends in Richmond.

The Swan Tavern, Richmond, where Poe stayed in 1849

103

Duncan Lodge, Richmond, one of Poe's favourite places

It was in July that he arrived. He first took a room at the American Hotel, but soon changed his quarters to the Old Swan Tavern – a long, low, antiquated building which had been in its day the fashionable hotel of Richmond. Poe remarked that he had a quadruple motive in choosing it – it was cheap, well kept in 'the old Virginia style', associated with many pleasant memories of his youth, and, lastly and chiefly, nearest Duncan's Lodge, where most of his time was passed.

It was a day or two after his arrival that Poe, accompanied by his sister, called on us. He had, some time previous, in a critique on Griswold's *American Female Poets*, taken flattering notice of my early poems, which had recently appeared in the *Southern Literary Messenger*; and now, on learning from Mrs Mackenzie that I resided in the neighbourhood, he had desired an introduction. The remembrance of that first meeting with the poet is still as vividly impressed upon my mind as though it had been but yesterday. A shy and dreamy girl, scarcely more than a child, I had all my life taken an interest in those strange stories and poems of Edgar Poe; and now, with my old childish impression of their author scarcely worn off, I regarded the meeting with an eager, yet shrinking anticipation. As I entered the parlour, Poe was seated near an open window, quietly conversing. His attitude was easy and graceful, with one arm lightly resting upon the back of his chair. His dark curling hair was thrown back from his broad forehead – a style in which he habitually wore it. At sight of him, the impression produced upon me was of a refined, high-bred, and chivalrous gentleman. I use this word 'chivalrous' as exactly descriptive of something in his whole *personnel*, distinct from either polish or high-breeding, and which, though instantly apparent, was yet an effect too subtle to be described. He rose on my entrance, and, other visitors being present, stood with one hand resting on the back of his chair, awaiting my greeting. So dignified was his manner, so reserved his expression, that I experienced an involuntary recoil, until I turned to him and saw his eyes suddenly brighten as I offered my hand; a barrier seemed to melt between us, and I felt that we were no longer strangers.

I am thus minute in my account of my first meeting with Poe, because I would illustrate, if possible, the manner peculiar to him, and also the indescribable charm, I might almost say magnetism, which his eyes possessed above any others that I have ever seen. It was this mysterious influence, I am inclined to think, which often, so powerfully at first sight, attracted strangers to him (*vide* Mr Kennedy's account); and this it was, undoubtedly, which Mrs Osgood on her first interview with him experienced, but scarcely understood.

From this time I saw Poe constantly – especially during the last weeks of his stay in Richmond. From his sister also, and from intimate common friends, we knew all concerning him – so that about this portion of his life there is no reserve and no mystery.

It would be better, indeed, for his fair name, could a veil be drawn over certain dark spots which disfigure this otherwise unusually pure and happy phase of his life. On these, I prefer to touch as lightly as possible. I know that he strove against the evil; but his will was weak; and having once yielded, in however slight a degree, said his friends, he seemed to lose all control over himself; and twice during his visit to Richmond, his life was thus seriously endangered. Yet, though I heard something of these things, I did not then, nor until long after, fully understand them. It was his own request that I should not be informed of his weakness; and he was scrupulously careful never to appear in our presence, except when he was, as he expressed it, 'entirely himself'.

And as himself – that is, as he appeared to me in my own home and in society – Poe was pre-eminently a gentleman. This was apparent in everything about him, even to the least detail. He dressed always in black, and with faultless taste and simplicity. An indescribable refinement pervaded all that he did and said. His general bearing in society, especially toward strangers, was quiet, dignified and somewhat reserved, even at times unconsciously approaching *hauteur*. He rarely smiled and never laughed. When pleased, nothing could exceed the charm of his manner – to his own sex cordial, to ladies, marked by a sort of chivalrous, respectful courtesy.

I was surprised to find that the poet was not the melancholy person I had unconsciously pictured. On the contrary, he appeared, except on one occasion, invariably cheerful, and frequently playful in mood. He seemed quietly amused by the light-hearted chat of the young people about him, and often joined them in humorous repartee, sometimes tinged with a playful sarcasm. Yet he preferred to sit quietly, and listen and observe. Nothing escaped his keen observation. He was extremely fastidious in his idea of feminine requirements, and himself lamented that at slight things in women he was apt to be repelled and disgusted, even against his better judgement. Though in the social evenings with us or at Duncan's Lodge, Poe would join in the light conversation or amusement of the hour, I observed that it had not power to interest him for any length of time. He preferred a seat on the portico, or a stroll about the lawn or garden, in company with a friend.

In his conversations with me Poe expressed himself with a freedom and unreserve which gave me a clearer insight into his personal history and character than, I think, was possessed by many persons. Indeed, I may say that from the moment of our meeting he was never to me the 'inexplicable' character that he was pronounced by others. Young as I was, I had yet by some intuitive instinct of perception, as it were, comprehended the finer and more elevated nature of the man, and it was probably to his own consciousness of this that I owed his confidence. I remember his saying, near the beginning of our acquaintance, and in reply to a remark of my own, 'I cannot express the pleasure – the more than pleasure – of finding myself so entirely understood by you,' adding, 'It is not often that I am so understood.' Again, he said of Mrs Osgood, 'She is the only one of my friends who *understands* me.' His own insight into personal character was quick and intuitive, but not deep; and it struck me even then, with all my youthful inexperience, that in knowledge of human nature he was, for a man of his genius, strangely deficient.

Among other things, Poe spoke to me freely of his future plans and prospects. He was at this time absorbed in his cherished scheme of establishing his projected journal, *The Stylus*. Nearly all his old friends in Virginia had promised to aid him with the necessary funds, and he was sanguine of success. He intended to spare no pains, no effort, to establish this as the leading literary journal of the country. The plan of it, which he explained in detail, but of which I retain little recollection, was to be something entirely original; and the highest 'genius, distinctive from talent,' of the country was to be represented in its pages. To secure this result, he would offer a more liberal price for contributions than any other publisher. This would, of course, demand capital to begin with, which was all that he required; and of that he had the promise. To establish this journal had been, he said, the cherished dream of his life, and now at last he felt assured of success. And in thus speaking he held his head erect, and his eyes glowed with enthusiasm. 'I must and will succeed!' he said.

Much curiosity has been expressed and many and various statements have been made in regard to the poet's relations at this time with Mrs Sarah Shelton of Richmond. So far as I am certainly informed upon the subject, the story is simply this:

The two had been schoolmates, and, as such, a childish flirtation had existed between them. When, some years previous to this time, Poe made a brief visit to Richmond, Mrs Shelton, then a wealthy widow, had invited him to her house and treated him with special attention. Shortly after the death of his wife, an intimate friend wrote to him that Mrs Shelton often inquired after him, and suggested the plan which he somewhat later, when so much in need of money, came seriously to consider. Certain it is that a correspondence existed between the poet and Mrs Shelton almost from the time of Mrs Poe's death, and that for months before his appearance in Richmond it was understood by his friends that an engagement of marriage existed between them. His attentions to the lady immediately upon his arrival tended to confirm the report. Some friend of hers, however, represented to her that Poe's motives were of a mercenary nature; and of this she accused him, at the same time declaring her intention of so securing her property as to prevent his having any command of it. A rupture ensued, and thenceforth no further communication took place between them.

It will be seen from the above account of the affair with Mrs Shelton that Poe did not, as is stated by his biographers, leave Richmond for New York with the intention of preparing for his marriage with that lady. Yet that he had entered into an engagement of marriage with her even previous to his appearance in Richmond, I am assured. It was at a time when, as he himself declared, he stood more in need of money than at any previous period of his life. It was, to his own view, the turning-point of his fortunes, depending upon his cherished scheme of establishing *The Stylus*, through which he was to secure fame and fortune. This could not be done without money. Money was the one thing needful, upon which all else depended; and money he must have, at whatever cost or sacrifice. Hence the affair with Mrs Shelton. She was a lady of respectability, but of plain manners and practical disposition; older than Poe, and not gifted with those traits which might be supposed capable of attracting one of his peculiar taste and temperament.

While upon this subject, I venture, though with great hesitation, to say a word in relation to Poe's own marriage with his cousin, Virginia Clemm. I am aware that there exists with the public but one view of this union, and that so lovely and touching in itself, that to mar the picture with even a shadow inspires almost a feeling of remorse. Yet since in the biography of a distinguished man of genius truth is above all things desirable, and since in this instance the facts do not redound to the discredit of any party concerned, I may be allowed to state what I have been assured is truth.

Poets are proverbial for uncongenial marriages, and to this Poe can scarcely be classed as an exception. From the time when as a youth of nineteen he became a tutor to his sweet and gentle little cousin of six years old, he loved her with the tender and protective fondness of an elder brother. As years passed he became the subject of successive fancies or passions for various charming women; but she, gradually budding into early womanhood, experienced but one attachment – an absorbing devotion to her handsome, talented, and fascinating cousin. So intense was this passion that her health and spirits became seriously affected, and her mother, aroused to painful solicitude, spoke to Edgar about it. This was just as he was preparing to leave her house, which had been for some years his home, and enter the world of business. The idea of this separation was insupportable to Virginia. The result was that Poe, at that time a young man of twenty-eight, married his little, penniless, and delicate child-cousin of fourteen or fifteen, and thus unselfishly secured her own and her mother's happiness. In his wife he had ever the most tender and devoted of companions; but it was his own declaration that he ever missed in her a certain intellectual and spiritual sympathy necessary to perfect happiness in such an union. It was this need which so often impelled him to 'those many romantic little episodes' of which Mrs Osgood speaks, and which were well known to Poe's acquaintance. He was never a deliberately unkind husband, and toward the close of Mrs Poe's life he was assiduous in his tender care and attention. Yet his own declaration to an intimate friend of his youth was that his marriage 'had not been a congenial one'; and I repeatedly heard the match ascribed to Mrs Clemm, by those who were well acquainted with the family and the circumstances. In thus alluding to a subject so delicate, I have not lightly done so, or unadvisedly made a statement which seems refuted by the testimony of so many who have written of 'the passionate idolatry' with which the poet regarded his wife. I have heard the subject often and freely discussed by Poe's most intimate friends, including his sisters [sic], and upon this authority I speak. Lovely in person, sweet and gentle in disposition, his young wife deserved, doubtless, all the love that it was in his nature to bestow. Of his unvarying filial affection for Mrs Clemm, and of her almost angelic devotion to himself and his interests, there can be no question.

Mr Poe, among other plans for raising the funds so sorely needed, decided to give a series of lectures in Richmond. The first of these ('The Poetic Principle') brought him at once into prominent notice with the Richmond public. The press discussed him, and the elite of society fêted him. With the attention and kindness thus shown him he was much gratified. Yet he did not appear to care for the formal parties, and declared that he found more enjoyment with his friends in the country.

I can vividly recall him as he appeared on his visits to us. He always carried a cane, and upon entering the shade of the avenue would remove his hat, throw back his hair, and walk lingeringly, as if enjoying the coolness, carrying his hat in his hand, generally behind him. Sometimes he would pause to examine some rare flower, or to pluck a grape from the laden trellises. He met us always with an expression of pleasure illuminating his countenance and lighting his fine eyes.

Poe's eyes, indeed, were his most striking feature, and it was to these that his face owed its peculiar attraction. I have never seen other eyes at all resembling them. They were large, with long, jet-black lashes – the iris dark steel-gray, possessing a crystalline clearness and transparency, through which the jet-black pupil was seen to expand and contract with every shade of thought or emotion. I observed that the lids never contracted, as is so usual in most persons, especially when talking; but his gaze was ever full, open, and unshrinking. His usual expression was dreamy and sad. He had a way of sometimes turning a slightly askance look upon some person who was not observing him, and, with a quiet, steady gaze, appear to be mentally taking the calibre of the unsuspecting subject. 'What *awful* eyes Mr Poe has!' said a lady to me. 'It makes my blood run cold to see him slowly turn and fix them upon me when I am talking.'

Apart from the wonderful beauty of his eyes, I would not have called Poe a very handsome man. He was, in my opinion, rather distinguished-looking than handsome. What he had been when younger I had heard, but at the period of my acquaintance with him he had a pallid and careworn look – somewhat haggard, indeed – very apparent except in his moments of animation. He wore a dark moustache, scrupulously kept, but not entirely concealing a slightly contracted expression of the mouth and an occasional twitching of the upper lip, resembling a sneer. This sneer, indeed, was easily excited – a motion of the lip, scarcely perceptible, and yet intensely expressive. There was in it nothing of ill-nature, but much of sarcasm, as when he remarked of a certain pretentious editor, 'He can make bold plunges in shallow water'; and again, in reference to an editor presenting a costly book to a lady whose poems he had for years published while yet refusing to pay for them, Poe observed, 'He could afford it', with that almost imperceptible curl of the lip, more expressive of contempt than words could have been. The shape of his head struck me, even on first sight, as peculiar. There was a massive projection of the broad brow and temples, with the organ of casualty very conspicuously developed, a marked flatness of the top of the head, and an unusual fullness at the back. I had at this time no knowledge of phrenology; but now, in recalling this peculiar shape, I cannot deny that in Poe what are called the intellectual and animal portions of the head were remarkably developed, while in the moral regions there was as marked a deficiency. Especially there was a slight depression instead of fullness of outline where the organs of veneration and firmness are located by phrenologists. This peculiarity detracted so much from the symmetrical proportions of the head that he sought to remedy the defect by wearing his hair tossed back, thus producing more apparent height of the cranium.

Young lovers meet in Byam Shaw's illustration for Poe's 'The Assignation' (1909)

I am convinced that this time of which I speak must have been what Poe himself declared it – one of the brightest, happiest, and most promising of his maturer life. Had he but possessed a will sufficiently strong to preserve him from the temptation which was his greatest bane, how fair and happy might have been his future career!

As I have said, the knowledge of this weakness was by his own request concealed from me. All that I knew of the matter was when a friend informed me that 'Mr Poe was too unwell to see us that evening.' A day or two after this he sent a message by his sister requesting some flowers, in return for which came a dainty note of thanks, written in a tremulous hand. He again wrote, enclosing a little anonymous poem which he had found in some newspaper and admired; and on the day following he made his appearance among us, but so pale, tremulous and apparently subdued as to convince me that he had been seriously ill. On this occasion he had been at his rooms at the Old Swan where he was carefully tended by Mrs Mackenzie's family, but on a second and more serious relapse he was taken by Dr Mackenzie and Dr Gibbon Carter to Duncan's Lodge, where during some days his life was in imminent danger. Assiduous attention saved him, but it was the opinion of the physicians that another such attack would prove fatal. This they told him, warning him seriously of the danger. His reply was that if people would not tempt him, he would not fall. Dr Carter relates how, on this occasion, he had a long conversation with him, in which Poe expressed the most earnest desire to break from the thraldom of his besetting sin, and told of his many unavailing struggles to do so. He was moved even to tears, and finally declared, in the most solemn manner, that this time he *would* restrain himself – *would* withstand any temptation. He kept his word as long as he remained in Richmond; but for those who thereafter placed the stumbling-block in the way of the unsteady feet, what shall be said?

Among the warmest of his personal friends at this time, and those whom he most frequently visited, were Dr Robert G. Cabell, Mrs Julia Mayo Cabell, Mrs Chevalie, and Mr Robert Sully, and his venerable mother and accomplished sisters. These had all known him in his boyhood, and he expressed to me with earnestness the pleasure of the hours spent with them in their own homes. Especially did he enjoy his visits to the Sullys, 'where' said he, 'I always find pictures, flowers, delightful music and conversation, and a kindness more refreshing than all.'

The only occasion on which I saw Poe really sad or depressed, was on a walk to the Hermitage, the old deserted seat of the Mayo family, where he had, in his youth, been a frequent visitor. On reaching the place, our party separated, and Poe and myself strolled slowly about the grounds. I observed that he was unusually silent and preoccupied, and, attributing it to the influence of memories associated with the place, forbore to interrupt him. He passed slowly by the mossy bench called the 'lovers' seat,' beneath two aged trees, and remarked, as we turned toward the garden, 'There used to be white violets here.' Searching amid the tangled wilderness of shrubs, we found a few late blossoms, some of which he placed carefully between the leaves of a notebook. Entering the deserted house, he passed from room to room with a grave, abstracted look, and removed his hat, as if involuntarily, on entering the saloon, where in old times many a brilliant company had assembled. Seated in one of the deep windows, over which now grew masses of ivy, his memory must have borne him back to former scenes, for he repeated the familiar lines of Moore:

> I feel like one who treads alone,
> Some banquet hall deserted . . .

and paused, with the first expression of real sadness that I had ever seen on his face. The light of the setting sun shone through the drooping ivy-boughs into the ghostly room, and the tattered and mildewed paper-hangings, with their faded tracery of rose garlands, waved fitfully in the autumn breeze. An inexpressibly eerie feeling came over me, which I can even now recall, and, as I stood there, my old childish idea of the poet as a spirit of mingled light and darkness, recurred strongly to my imagination. I have never forgotten that scene, or the impression of the moment.

Once, in discussing 'The Raven', Poe observed that he had never heard it correctly delivered by even the best readers – that is, not as he desired that it should be read. That evening, a number of visitors being present, he was requested to recite the poem, and complied. His impressive delivery held the company spellbound, but in the midst of it, I, happening to glance toward the open window above the level roof of the greenhouse, beheld a group of sable faces the whites of whose eyes shone in strong relief against the surrounding darkness. These were a number of our family servants, who having heard much talk about 'Mr Poe, the poet', and having but an imperfect idea of what a poet was, had requested permission of my brother to witness the recital. As the speaker became more impassioned and excited, more conspicuous grew the circle of white eyes, until when at length he turned suddenly toward the window, and, extending his arm, cried, with awful vehemence:

> Get thee back into the tempest, and the night's Plutonian shore!

there was a sudden disappearance of the sable visages, a scuttling of feet, and the gallery audience was gone. Ludicrous as was the incident, the final touch was given when at that moment Miss Poe, who was an extraordinary character in her way, sleepily entered the room, and with a dull and drowsy deliberation seated herself on her brother's knee. He had subsided from his excitement into a gloomy despair, and now, fixing his eyes upon his sister, he concluded:

> And the raven, never flitting, still is sitting,
>   *still* is sitting,
> On the pallid bust of Pallas, just above my
>   chamber door;
> And its eyes have all the seeming of a demon
>   that is dreaming . . .

The effect was irresistible; and as the final 'nevermore' was solemnly uttered the half-suppressed titter of two very young persons in a corner was responded to by a general laugh. Poe remarked quietly that on his next delivery of a public lecture he would 'take Rose along, to act the part of the raven, in which she seemed born to excel'.

He was in the habit of teasing his sister, in a half-vexed, half-playful way, about her peculiarities of dress and manner. She was a very plain person, and he with his fastidious idea could not tolerate her want of feminine tact and taste. 'Rose, why do you wear your hair in that absurd style?' 'Where *did* you get that extraordinary dress pattern?' 'Why don't you try to behave like other people?' And once, when she presented herself in a particularly old-fashioned garb and coiffure, observing that she had been asleep, he replied: 'Yes, and with Rip Van Winkle, evidently.' She took all with an easy indifference. She was very proud of

The fiendish revenge of Montresor in 'The Cask of Amontillado'.
Illustration by Byam Shaw

her brother, and nothing that Edgar did or said could possibly be amiss.

It is with feelings of deep sadness, even after the lapse of so many years, that I approach the close of these reminiscences.

Poe one day told me that it was necessary that he should go to New York. He must make certain preparations for establishing his magazine, *The Stylus*, but he should in less than two weeks return to Richmond, where he proposed henceforth to reside. He looked forward to this arrangement with great pleasure. 'I mean to turn over a new leaf; I shall begin to lead a new life,' he said confidently. He had often spoken to me of his books – 'few, but recherché' – and he now proposed to send certain of these by express, for my perusal. 'You must annotate them extensively,' he said. 'A book wherein the minds of the author and the reader are thus brought in contact is to me a hundred-fold increased in interest. It is like flint and steel.' One of the books which he thus desired me to read was Mrs Browning's poems, and another one of Hawthorne's works. I remember his saying of the latter that he was 'indisputably the best prose writer in America'; that 'Irving and the rest were mere commonplace beside him'; and that 'there was more inspiration of true genius in Hawthorne's prose than in all Longfellow's poetry'. This may serve to give an idea of his own opinion of what constitutes genius, though some of Longfellow's poems he pronounced 'perfect of their kind'.

The evening of the day previous to that appointed for his departure from Richmond, Poe spent at my mother's. He declined to enter the parlours, where a number of visitors were assembled, saying he preferred the more quiet sitting-room; and here I had a long and almost uninterrupted conversation with him. He spoke of his future, seeming to anticipate it with an eager delight, like that of youth. He declared that the last few weeks in the society of his old and new friends had been the happiest that he had known for many years, and that when he again left New York he should there leave behind all the trouble and vexation of his past life. On no occasion had I seen him so cheerful and hopeful as on this evening. 'Do you know', he inquired, 'how I spent most of this morning? In writing a critique of your poems to be accompanied by a biographical sketch. I intend it to be one of my best, and that it shall appear in the second number of *The Stylus*' – so confident was he in regard to this magazine. In the course of the evening he showed me a letter just received from his 'friend, Dr Griswold', in reply to one but recently written by Poe, wherein the latter had requested Dr Griswold in case of his sudden death to become his literary executor. In this reply, Dr Griswold accepted the proposal, expressing himself as much flattered thereby, and writing in terms of friendly warmth and interest. It will be observed that this incident is a contradiction of his statement that previous to Poe's death he had had no intimation of the latter's intention of appointing him his literary executor.

In speaking of his own writings Poe expressed his conviction that he had written his best poems, but that in prose he might yet surpass what he had already accomplished. He admitted that much which he had said in praise of certain writers was not the genuine expression of his opinions. Before my acquaintance with him I had read his critique on Mrs Osgood, in the *Southern Literary Messenger*, and had in my turn criticised the article, writing my remarks freely on the margin of the magazine. I especially disagreed with him in his estimate of the lines on Fanny Elsler and 'Fanny's Error', – ridiculing his suggested amendment of the latter. This copy of the magazine Mrs Mackenzie afterward showed to Poe, and upon my expressing consternation thereat, she remarked laughingly, 'Don't be frightened; Edgar was delighted.' On this evening he alluded to the subject saying, 'I am delighted to find you so truly critical; your opinions are really the counterpart of my own.' I was naturally surprised, when he added, 'You must not judge of me by what you find me saying in the magazines. Such expressions of opinion are necessarily modified by a thousand circumstances – the wishes of editors, personal friendship, etc.' When I expressed surprise at his high estimate of a certain lady writer, he said, 'It is true, she is really commonplace, but her husband was kind to me,' and added, 'I cannot point an arrow against any woman.'

Poe expressed great regret in being compelled to leave Richmond, on even so brief an absence. He would certainly, he said, he back in two weeks. He thanked my mother with graceful courtesy and warmth for her kindness and hospitality; and begged that we would write to him in New York, saying it would do him good.

He was the last of the party to leave the house. We were standing on the portico, and after going a few steps he paused, turned, and again lifted his hat, in a last adieu. At the moment, a brilliant meteor appeared in the sky directly over his head, and vanished in the east. We commented laughingly upon the incident; but I remembered it sadly afterward.

That night he spent at Duncan's Lodge; and as his friend said, sat late at his window, meditatively smoking, and seemingly disinclined for conversation. On the following morning he went into the city, accompanied by his friends, Dr Gibbon Carter and Dr Mackenzie. The day was passed with them and others of his intimate friends. Late in the

Frederick Pickersgill illustration for the poem, 'For Annie'

evening he entered the office of Dr John Carter, and spent an hour in looking over the day's papers; then taking Dr Carter's cane he went out, remarking that he would step across to Saddler's (a fashionable restaurant) and get supper. From the circumstance of his taking the cane, leaving his own in its place, it is probable that he had intended to return; but at the restaurant he met with some acquaintances who detained him until late, and then accompanied him to the Baltimore boat. According to their account he was quite sober and cheerful to the last, remarking, as he took leave of them, that he would soon be in Richmond again.

On this evening I had been summoned to see a friend who was dangerously ill. On the way I was met by Miss Poe, who delivered a note left for me by her brother, containing a MS copy of 'Annie' – a poem then almost unknown, and which I had expressed a wish to see. These strange prophetic lines I read at midnight, while the lifeless body of my friend lay in an adjoining chamber, and the awful shadow of death weighed almost forebodingly upon my spirit. Three days after, a friend came to me with the day's issue of the *Richmond Dispatch*. Without a word she pointed to a particular paragraph, where I read – 'Death of Edgar A. Poe, in Baltimore'.

Poe had made himself popular in Richmond. People had become interested in him, and his death cast a universal gloom over the city. His old friends, and even those more recently formed, and whom he had strangely attached to himself, deeply regretted him. Mr Sully came to consult with me about a picture of 'The Raven' which he intended to make; and in the course of conversation expressed himself in regard to his lost friend with a warmth of feeling and appreciation not usual to him. The two had been schoolmates; and the artist said, 'Poe was one of the most warmhearted and generous of men. In his youth and prosperity, when admired and looked up to by all his companions, he invariably stood by me and took my part. I was a dull boy at learning, and Edgar never grudged time or pains in assisting me.' In further speaking he said, with a decision and earnestness which impressed me, 'It was Mr Allan's cruelty in casting him upon the world, a beggar, which ruined Poe. Some who had envied him took advantage of his change of fortune to slight and insult him. He was sensitive and proud, and felt the change keenly. It was this which embittered him. By nature no person was less inclined to reserve or bitterness, and as a boy he was frank and generous to a fault.' In speaking of his poems, Mr Sully remarked: 'He has an eye for dramatic, but not for scenic or artistic effect. Except in 'The Raven' I can nowhere in his poems find a subject for a picture.'

On some future occasion I may speak further of Poe, and give some details which will clear up certain obscurities of his life. At present, there is one point connected with his history which I feel that I cannot in justice pass over, because upon it has hung the darkest and most undeserved calumny which has overshadowed his name. I allude to the cause of the estrangement and separation between himself and Mr Allan.

All the horror of the victims of the dwarf 'Hop Frog' is captured in this 1903 illustration by H. Church

For obvious reasons, I prefer, at present, not to speak in detail upon this subject. It will be sufficient to state that the affair was simply a 'family quarrel', which was not in the first instance the fault of Poe; that he received extreme provocation and insult, and that of all the parties concerned, it appears that he was the least culpable and the most wronged. Mr Allan, though a kind-hearted and benevolent man, was quick-tempered and irascible, and in the heat of sudden anger treated Poe with a severity which he afterward regretted. In any event, his conduct in utterly casting off one whom he had brought up as a son, and had by education and mode of life made dependent on him, must ever, in the opinion of just-minded persons, detract from if not wholly outweigh the merit of former kindness. But the saddest part of the story is, that long after this, Poe, who, never cherished resentments, being informed that his former guardian was ill and had spoken kindly of and had expressed a wish to see him, went to Mr Allan's house, and there vainly sought an interview with him – and that of this the latter was never informed, but died without seeing him; and as Dr Griswold with unwitting significance observes, 'without leaving Poe a mill of his money'.

This is the simple truth of the story to which Dr Griswold has attached a 'blackness of horror' before the unrevealed mystery of which the mind shrinks aghast. As to my authority in making this statement, I will only say that I have heard the facts asserted by venerable ladies of

Richmond, who were fully acquainted with the circumstances at the time of their occurrence.

In closing these reminiscences, I may be allowed to make a few remarks founded upon my actual personal knowledge of Poe, in at least the phase of character in which he appeared to me. What he may have been to his ordinary associates, or to the world at large, I do not know; and in the picture presented us by Dr Griswold – half maniac, half demon – I confess, I cannot recognise a trait of the gentle, grateful, warm-hearted man whom I saw amid his friends – his careworn face all aglow with generous feeling in the kindness and appreciation to which he was so little accustomed. His faults were sufficiently apparent; but for these a more than ordinary allowance should be made, in consideration of the unfavourable influences surrounding him from his very birth. He was ever the sport of an adverse fortune. Born in penury, reared in affluence, treated at one time with pernicious indulgence and then literally turned into the streets, a beggar and an outcast, deserted by those who had formerly courted him, maliciously calumniated, smarting always under a sense of wrong and injustice – what wonder that his bright, warm, and naturally generous and genial nature should have become embittered? What wonder that his keenly sensitive and susceptible poetic temperament should have become jarred, out of tune, and into harsh discord with himself and mankind? Let the just and the generous pause before they judge; and upon their lips the breath of condemnation will soften into a sigh of sympathy and regret.

An Arthur Rackham illustration for 'William Wilson'

A DUEL TO THE DEATH!

Edgar A. Poe throws out a challenge

WHILE IN Richmond during the summer of 1848, Poe spent most of his time in the company of newspaper writers or about resorts frequented by them. He roomed most of this time with a Richmond newspaper editor. Among others he had met John M. Daniel, of the *Examiner*, and bad blood was shown between them from the start. They had talked about literary matters and did not agree. There also had been a debt transaction, which was a disputed matter. Daniel was also acquainted with some member of the Whitman family and made disparaging allusions to Poe and his intentions toward Mrs Whitman, which came to the poet's ears.

He became infuriated and at once sent a challenge to Daniel to fight a duel. Judge Robert W. Hughes, who wrote for the *Examiner* and had a personal acquaintance with Poe, remembered the affair well and told the particulars. The newspaper friends of Poe did not regard the affair as serious, and knew that it would soon blow over. Poe's challenge, written on the letterhead of a sheet of one of the Richmond newspaper offices, was taken to Daniel, who also regarded the matter lightly. An arrangement was effected by which Poe was to seek satisfaction from the fiery editor in his sanctum. Poe was informed that Daniel would not meet him on the outside in the usual way, but preferred to settle matters between them alone in the *Examiner* office. While Poe was hardly in any condition to fight a duel, he was induced to go to the *Examiner* office, where Daniel awaited him alone by appointment.

When he entered and saw Daniel he drew himself up to full height and demanded, in his haughty manner, why he had sent for him. Daniel was sitting near a table on which was displayed two very large, old-fashioned pistols, which the quick glance of Poe soon espied. Daniel in a cool and quiet manner asked Poe to be seated. Then he told him that he did not care to have the matter get to the police authorities, and suggested that instead of the usual formalities of the code they settle the dispute between them then and there. They were alone, the room was large and he pointed to the pistols ready for use. The quietude of the place, Daniel's demeanour, and this strange request tinged something of the grotesque. Poe began to sober up. He asked some questions about their difficulty and soon became convinced that matters were exaggerated.

Then he told Daniel, in his characteristic way, of the challenge sent by the Maryland poet, Edward Coate Pinkney, to his former early benefactor, John Neal, editor of the *Boston Yankee*, and how the young poet had walked for a week before Neal's office in order to meet him. Daniel evinced much interest in the story, and Poe remarked to him that he hoped that he would not turn matters into ridicule in the next issue of the *Examiner*, like Neal did in his journal.

Friends who had stood not far away, knowing there was little likelihood of any bloodshed, then broke in upon the scene. Matters were explained in a friendly way, and Poe was called upon by Daniel to finish his story about Pinkney which he did, and recited as he only could:

> I fill this cup to one made up
> Of loveliness alone;
> A woman, of her gentle sex,
> The seeming paragon;
> To whom the better elements
> And kindly stars have given
> A form so fair that like the air,
> 'T is less of earth than heaven.

After this they all repaired to a nearby popular resort, where there were more 'healths'.

J. H. WHITTY
Richmond Times-Despatch, January 1909

Jasper Crospsey's graphic picture for the poem 'City in the Sea' (1901)

POE'S LAST TALE – 'THE LIGHTHOUSE'

SURPRISINGLY LITTLE attention seems to have been given to what is probably the last story Poe wrote. This is an untitled and unfinished fragment which was called 'The Lighthouse' by Professor Woodberry. It survives in the original manuscript, which consists of four leaves, and is written in the very neat hand characteristic of Poe's last years. On the first leaf the story begins well down on the page, space being left for a title and the name of the author. And on the last page the writing ceases a good way above the bottom of the page. The text joins together perfectly and there is no doubt that we have a complete text of what Poe wrote in this particular manuscript. The style is one that is common toward the end of Poe's career, almost without ornament, clear and direct. And we know that the manuscript was at one time in the hands of Poe's literary executor, Griswold, who obtained papers chiefly from Mrs Clemm and from Poe's trunk at Baltimore, after his death. For these reasons I am convinced of the very late date of the piece, and am of the opinion that it is unfinished, not because Poe gave it up, but because he was at work upon it and was prevented from completing it by his sudden death.

The four leaves of manuscript became separated long ago; the first going into the collection of Stephen Wakeman. At the sale of his collection, in 1919, the text of this leaf was printed, not too accurately. The other three leaves remained in the Griswold family, and were printed by Woodberry as an appendix to his *Life of Poe* in 1909. I saw the first leaf at the sale, and later through the courtesy of Dr Rosenbach; and I examined the other three leaves at the opening of the Poe Foundation at Richmond, Va, in 1922. As was recently pointed out by Mr John Cook Wyllie (*Humanistic Studies in Honour of John Calvin Metcalf*, Charlottesville, 1941, p 329) no printing of the story as a unit seems to have been made, although all of it has been published, for over twenty years. The text which follows is based on my own reading of the MSS, and is complete. Poe himself used the three dots to indicate breaks or imagined omissions in several places; they do not indicate cuts by editors, only the title and last two words in brackets are additions.

THE LIGHTHOUSE

Jan. 1 – 1796. This day – my first on the lighthouse – I make this entry in my Diary, as agreed on with DeGrät. As regularly as I *can* keep this journal, I will – but there is no telling what may happen to a man all alone as I am – I may get sick or worse... So far well! The cutter had a narrow escape – but why dwell on that, since I am *here*, all safe? My spirits are beginning to revive already, at the mere thought of being – for once in my life at least – thoroughly *alone*; for, of course, Neptune, large as he is, is not to be taken into consideration as 'society'. Would to Heaven I had ever found in 'society' one half as much *faith* as in this poor dog: – in such case I and 'society' might never have parted – even for a year... What more surprises me, is the difficulty DeGrät had in getting me the appointment – and I a noble of the realm! It could not be that the Consistory had any doubt of my ability to manage the light. *One* man has attended it before now – and got on quite as well as the three that are usually put in. The duty is a mere nothing; and the printed instructions are as plain as possible. It never would have done to let Orndoff accompany me. I never should have made any way with my book as long as he was within reach of me, with his intolerable gossip – not to mention that everlasting meerschaum. Besides, I wish to be alone... It is strange that I never observed, until this moment, how dreary a sound that word has – 'alone'! I could half fancy there was some peculiarity in the echo of these cylindrical walls – but oh, no! – this is all nonsense. I do believe I am going to get nervous about my insulation. *That* will never do. I have not forgotten DeGrät's prophecy. Now for a scramble to the lantern and a good look around to 'see what I can see'... To see what I can see indeed! – not very much. The swell is subsiding a little, I think – but the cutter will have a rough passage home, nevertheless. She will hardly get within sight of the Nordland before noon tomorrow – and yet it can hardly be more than 190 or 200 miles.

Jan. 2. I have passed this day in a species of ecstasy that I find it impossible to describe. My passion for solitude could scarcely have been more thoroughly gratified. I do not say *satisfied*; for I believe I should never be satiated with such delight as I have experienced today... The wind lulled about daybreak, and by the afternoon the sea had gone down materially... Nothing to be seen, with the telescope even, but ocean and sky, with an occasional gull.

Jan. 3. A dead calm all day. Towards evening, the sea looked very much like glass. A few seaweeds came in sight; but besides them absolutely *nothing* all day – not even the slightest speck of cloud... Occupied myself in exploring the lighthouse... It is a very lofty one – as I find to my cost when I have to ascend its interminable stairs – not quite 160 feet, I should say, from the low-water mark to the top of the lantern. From the bottom *inside* the shaft, however, the distance to the summit is 180 feet at least – thus the floor is 20 feet below the surface of the sea, even at low-tide... It seems to me that the hollow interior at the bottom should have been filled in with solid masonry. Undoubtedly the whole would have been thus rendered more *safe* – but what am I thinking about? A structure such as this is safe enough under any circumstances. I should feel myself secure in it during the fiercest hurricane that ever raged – and yet I have heard seamen say that, occasionally, with a wind at south-west, the sea has been known to run higher here than any where with the single exception of the western opening of the Straits of Magellan. No mere sea, though, could accomplish anything with this solid iron-riveted wall – which, at 50 feet from high-water mark, is four feet thick, if one inch . . . The basis on which the structure rests seems to me to be chalk . . .

Jan. 4. [Cetera desunt.]

Obviously the story is a typical one, finding a close parallel in theme to 'The Descent into the Maelström' which also concerns an adventure with perils of the sea. The inspiration no doubt came partly from Poe's own familiarity with sailing and from some encyclopaedia article on lighthouses. The theme of loneliness is one frequent in Poe's poems and tales. Even the name of the big dog, Neptune, Poe had used for a canine character before, in his 'Julius Rodman'. And the tale was obviously to be of mood, the mood of terror. The question remains however which is always asked of an unfinished story. Can we guess how it would come out? This is not an idle question in the case of Poe, for we know that he planned his tales completely before he wrote them, at least before he wrote a version that required no change of any word, and the manuscript is without corrections. I have decided that we have enough to hazard an answer.

Poe said that every word should contribute to the effect of a story, and his theory summed up his own practice. No man can read the fragment without knowing that the lighthouse is to be destroyed, and that the diary must reach safety. The suspense must lie in whether or not the hero escapes; and being a skilled artist Poe contrives that the beginning does not reveal that plainly. But here is a scrap of external evidence – Poe had already written the 'MS Found in a Bottle'; and mere rescue of the diary would have been a rather decided repetition, even for Poe. But the deciding factor is the dog. He is introduced immediately, and we are at once told of his size. This is enough to mark him as an important character. But we have also a comment on his faithfulness. I think that is to prepare us for his heroic part in the story; and believe that his master was to escape, helped by his powerful dog; and that the story, like several of Poe's tales of terror, was to have a happy ending.

THOMAS O. MABBOTT
Notes and Queries, 25 April 1942

THE FORGOTTEN CENTENARY

GEORGE BERNARD SHAW

AS HAS been said earlier, Poe was a prophet without honour in his homeland for many years – but abroad, in Britain and Europe particularly, his fame and genius were acknowledged well before the end of the nineteenth century. By the beginning of the twentieth century the situation had changed somewhat, and indeed the centenary of Poe's birth, in 1909, was marked in America with ceremony and grandiose tributes. Still, it was left to an Irishman, and a famous one at that, to provide perhaps the most deeply felt and richly textured tribute on this anniversary – George Bernard Shaw. His article is reprinted from *The Nation* of 16 January 1909.

THERE WAS a time when America, the Land of the Free,

The young George Bernard Shaw, another respected Poe supporter

and the birthplace of Washington, seemed a natural fatherland for Edgar Allan Poe. Nowadays the thing has become inconceivable: no young man can read Poe's works without asking incredulously what the devil he is doing in *that* galley. America has been found out; and Poe has not; that is the situation. How did he live there, this finest of fine artists, this born aristocrat of letters? Alas! he did not live there: he died there, and was duly explained away as a drunkard and a failure, though it remains an open question whether he really drank as much in his whole lifetime as a modern successful American drinks, without comment, in six months.

If the Judgement Day were fixed for the centenary of Poe's birth, there are among the dead only two men born since the Declaration of Independence whose plea for mercy could avert a prompt sentence of damnation on the entire nation; and it is extremely doubtful whether those two could be persuaded to pervert eternal justice by uttering it. The two are, of course, Poe and Whitman; and there is between them the remarkable difference that Whitman is still credibly an American, whereas even the Americans themselves, though rather short of men of genius, omit Poe's name from their Pantheon, either from a sense that it is hopeless for them to claim so foreign a figure, or from simple Monroeism. One asks, has the America of Poe's day passed away, or did it ever exist?

Probably it never existed. It was an illusion, like the respectable Whig Victorian England of Macaulay. Karl Marx stripped the whitewash from that sepulchre; and we have ever since been struggling with a conviction of social sin which makes every country in which industrial capitalism is rampant a hell to us. For let no American fear that America, on that hypothetic Judgement Day, would perish alone. America would be damned in very good European company, and would feel proud and happy, and contemptuous of the saved. She would not even plead the influence of the mother from whom she has inherited all

A special centenary engraving of Poe. Unfortunately the publishers spelt Poe's middle name wrongly!

phonies of Beethoven, the paintings of Giotto and Mantegna, Velazquez and Rembrandt. Instead of being heir to all the ages, he came into a comparatively small and smutty literary property bequeathed by Smollett and Fielding. His criticism of Fechter's Hamlet, and his use of a speech of Macbeth's to illustrate the character of Mrs Macstinger, show how little Shakespeare meant to him. Thackeray is even worse: the notions of painting he picked up at Heatherley's school were further from the mark than Dickens's ignorance; he is equally in the dark as to music; and though he did not, when he wished to be enormously pleasant and jolly, begin, like Dickens, to describe the gorgings and guzzlings which make Christmas our annual national disgrace, that is rather because he never does want to be enormously pleasant and jolly than because he has any higher notions of personal enjoyment. The truth is that neither Dickens nor Thackeray would be tolerable were it not that life is an end in itself and a means to nothing but its own perfection; consequently any man who describes life vividly will entertain us, however uncultivated the life he describes may be. Mark Twain has lived long enough to become a much better philosopher than either Dickens or Thackeray: for instance, when he immortalised General Funston by scalping him, he did it scientifically, knowing exactly what he meant right down to the foundation in the natural history of human character. Also, he got from the Mississippi something that Dickens could not get from Chatham and Pentonville. But he wrote *A Yankee at the Court of King Arthur* just as Dickens wrote *A Child's History of England*. For the ideal of Catholic chivalry he had nothing but derision; and he exhibited it, not in conflict with reality, as Cervantes did, but in conflict with the prejudices of a Philistine compared to whom Sancho Panza is an Admirable Crichton, an Abelard, even a Plato. Also, he described Lohengrin as 'a shivaree', though he liked the wedding chorus; and this shows that Mark, like Dickens, was not properly educated; for Wagner would have been just the man for him if he had been trained to understand and use music as Mr Rockefeller was trained to understand and use money. America did not teach him the language and the great ideals, just as England did not teach it to Dickens and Thackeray. Consequently, though nobody can suspect Dickens or Mark Twain of lacking the qualities and impulses that are the soul of such grotesque makeshift bodies as Church and State, Chivalry, Classicism, Art, Gentility, and the Holy Roman Empire; and nobody blames them for seeing that these bodies were mostly so decomposed as to have become intolerable nuisances, you have only to compare them with Carlyle and Ruskin, or with Euripides and Aristophanes, to see how, for want of a language of art and a body of philosophy, they were so much more interested in the fun and pathos of personal adventure than in the comedy and tragedy of human destiny.

Whistler was a Philistine, too. Outside the corner of art in which he was a virtuoso and a propagandist, he was a Man of Derision. Important as his propaganda was, and admired as his work was, no society could assimilate him. He could not even induce a British jury to award him substantial damages against a rich critic who had 'done him out of his job'; and this is certainly the climax of social failure in England.

Edgar Allan Poe was not in the least a Philistine. He wrote always as if his native Boston was Athens, his Charlottesville University Plato's Academy, and his cottage the crown of the heights of Fiesole. He was the greatest journalistic critic of his time, placing good European work

her worst vices. If the American stands today in scandalous pre-eminence as an anarchist and a ruffian, a liar and a braggart, an idolater and a sensualist, that is only because he has thrown off the disguises of Catholicism and feudalism which still give Europe an air of decency, and sins openly, impudently, and consciously, instead of furtively, hypocritically, and muddle-headedly, as we do. Not until he acquires European manners does the American anarchist become the gentleman who assures you that people cannot be made moral by Act of Parliament (the truth being that it is only by Acts of Parliament that men in large communities can be made moral, even when they want to); or the American ruffian hand over his revolver and bowie knife to be used for him by a policeman or soldier; or the American liar and braggart adopt the tone of the newspaper, the pulpit, and the platform; or the American idolater write authorised biographies of millionaires; or the American sensualist secure the patronage of all the Muses for his pornography.

Howbeit, Poe remains homeless. There is nothing at all like him in America: nothing, at all events, visible across the Atlantic. At that distance we can see Whistler plainly enough, and Mark Twain. But Whistler was very American in some ways: so American that nobody but another American could possibly have written his adventures and gloried in them without reserve. Mark Twain, resembling Dickens in his combination of public spirit and irresistible literary power with a congenital incapacity for lying and bragging, and a congenital hatred of waste and cruelty, remains American by the local colour of his stories. There is a further difference. Both Mark Twain and Whistler are as Philistine as Dickens and Thackeray. The appalling thing about Dickens, the greatest of the Victorians, is that in his novels there is nothing personal to live for except eating, drinking, and pretending to be happily married. For him the great synthetic ideals do not exist, any more than the great preludes and toccatas of Bach, the sym-

Byam Shaw's vivid painting for 'Ligeia', published in the centenary year

at sight when the European critics were waiting for somebody to tell them what to say. His poetry is so exquisitely refined that posterity will refuse to believe that it belongs to the same civilisation as the glory of Mrs Julia Ward Howe's lilies or the honest doggerel of Whittier. Tennyson, who was nothing if not a virtuoso, never produced a success that will bear reading after Poe's failures. Poe constantly and inevitably produced magic where his greatest contemporaries produced only beauty. Tennyson's popular pieces, 'The May Queen' and 'The Charge of the Six Hundred', cannot stand hackneying: they become positively nauseous after a time. 'The Raven', 'The Bells', and 'Annabel Lee' are as fascinating at the thousandth repetition as at the first.

Poe's supremacy in this respect has cost him his reputation. This is a phenomenon which occurs when an artist achieves such perfection as to place himself *hors concours*. The greatest painter England ever produced is Hogarth, a miraculous draughtsman and an exquisite and poetic colourist. But he is never mentioned by critics. They talk copiously about Romney, the Gibson of his day; freely about Reynolds; nervously about the great Gainsborough; and not at all about Rowlandson and Hogarth, missing the inextinguishable grace of Rowlandson because they assume that all caricatures of his period are ugly, and avoiding Hogarth instinctively as critically unmanageable. In the same way, we have given up mentioning Poe: that is why the Americans forgot him when they posted up the names of their great in their Pantheon. Yet his is the first – almost the only name that the real connoisseur looks for.

But Poe, for all his virtuosity, is always a poet, and never a mere virtuoso. Poe put forward his 'Eureka', the formulation of his philosophy, as the most important thing he had done. His poems always have the universe as their background. So have the figures in his stories. Even in his tales of humour, which we shake our heads at as mistakes, they have this elemental quality. Toby Dammit himself, though his very name turns up the nose of the cultured critic, is more impressive and his end more tragic than the serious inventions of most story-tellers. The short-sighted gentleman who married his grandmother is no common butt of a common purveyor of the facetious: the grandmother has the elegance and free mind of Ninon de Lenclos, the grandson the *tenue* of a marquis. This story was sent by Poe to Horne, whose 'Orion' he had reviewed as poetry ought to be reviewed, with a request that it might be sold to an English magazine. The English magazine regretted that the deplorable immorality of the story made it for ever impossible in England!

In his stories of mystery and imagination Poe created a world-record for the English language: perhaps for all the languages. The story of the Lady Ligeia is not merely one of the wonders of literature: it is unparalleled and unapproached. There is really nothing to be said about it: we others simply take off our hats and let Mr Poe go first. It is interesting to compare Poe's stories with William Morris's. Both are not merely stories: they are complete works of art, like prayer carpets; and they are, in Poe's phrase, stories of imagination. They are masterpieces of style: what people call Macaulay's style is by comparison a

Harry Clarke also pays tribute to Poe's genius with this interpretation of the story 'King Pest'

mere method. But they are more different than it seems possible for two art works in the same kind to be. Morris will have nothing to do with mystery. 'Ghost stories', he used to say, 'have all the same explanation: the people are telling lies.' His 'Sigurd' has the beauty of mystery as it has every other sort of beauty, being, as it is, incomparably the greatest English epic; but his stories are in the open from end to end, whilst in Poe's stories the sun never shines.

Poe's limitation was his aloofness from the common people. Grotesques, negroes, madmen with delirium tremens, even gorillas, take the place of ordinary peasants and courtiers, citizens and soldiers, in his theatre. His houses are haunted houses, his woods enchanted woods; and he makes them so real that reality itself cannot sustain the comparison. His kingdom is not of this world.

Above all, Poe is great because he is independent of cheap attractions, independent of sex, of patriotism, of fighting, of sentimentality, snobbery, gluttony, and all the rest of the vulgar stock-in-trade of his profession. This is what gives him his superb distinction. One vulgarised thing, the pathos of dying children, he touched in 'Annabel Lee', and devulgarised it at once. He could not even amuse himself with detective stories without purifying the atmosphere of them until they became more edifying than most of Hymns, Ancient and Modern. His verse sometimes alarms and puzzles the reader by fainting with its own beauty; but the beauty is never the beauty of the flesh. You never say to him as you have to say uneasily to so many modern artists: 'Yes, my friend, but these are things that men and women should *live* and not write about. Literature is not a keyhole for people with starved affections to peep through at the banquets of the body.' It never became one in Poe's hands. Life cannot give you what he gives you except through fine art; and it was his instinctive observance of this distinction, and the fact that it did not beggar him, as it would beggar most writers, that makes him the most legitimate, the most classical, of modern writers.

It also explains why America does not care much for him, and why he has hardly been mentioned in England these many years. America and England are wallowing in the sensuality which their immense increase of riches has placed within their reach. I do not blame them: sensuality is a very necessary and healthy and educative element in life. Unfortunately, it is ill distributed; and our reading masses are looking on at it and thinking about it and longing for it, and having precarious little holiday treats of it, instead of sharing it temperately and continuously, and ceasing to be preoccupied with it. When the distribution is better adjusted and the preoccupation ceases, there will be a noble reaction in favour of the great writers like Poe, who begin just where the world, the flesh, and the devil leave off.

Sketch by the modern Danish artist, Arild Rosenkrantz, for 'The Murders in the Rue Morgue'

Arguably the screen's finest Sherlock Holmes, Basil Rathbone, who also starred in several films based on Poe stories

SHERLOCK HOLMES AND POE'S GREAT MURDER MYSTERY

'YOU REMIND me of Edgar Allan Poe's Dupin,' said Dr Watson to Sherlock Holmes shortly after they met in 1881.

'No doubt you think that you are complimenting me in comparing me to Dupin,' Holmes replied, lighting his pipe. 'Now, in my opinion, Dupin was a very inferior fellow . . .'

One wonders, though, what Holmes might additionally have had to say on the subject of any comparison between himself and detective C. Auguste Dupin when seventeen years later a motion picture called *Sherlock Holmes and the Great Murder Mystery* was released.

Produced by the Crescent Film Company of New York City, *Sherlock Holmes and the Great Murder Mystery* was based not only on the illustrious career of Holmes himself, but ironically cast Holmes in an adventure inspired by Edgar Allan Poe's classic Dupin story, 'The Murders in the Rue Morgue'.

But probably Sherlock Holmes never even heard of the film. By that time in 1908, of course, Holmes was comfortably situated in retirement in Sussex, far and away from the movie palaces of London.

But because Crescent Films released their unique Holmes–Dupin exploit in the final months of 1908, some have thought that *Sherlock Holmes and the Great Murder Mystery* was especially produced with Poe's Centennial Celebration in mind: 19 January 1909. That Crescent Films chose to substitute Holmes for Dupin, though, make the studio's Poesque intentions something more than only slightly debatable.

Regardless, *Sherlock Holmes and the Great Murder Mystery* proved an interesting blending of the two sources, with Watson here becoming interested in a series of horrible murders and then getting Holmes to start working on the case. Ultimately Holmes cracks the baffling mystery, and proves to the satisfaction of the police and all others concerned that the brutal crimes are not those of a suspected young man, but actually the work of an escaped gorilla.

While Holmes himself had generally a low opinion of what he considered the 'showy and superficial quality' of C. Auguste Dupin's deductive abilities, Sir Arthur Conan Doyle, the creator of Holmes, or literary agent of Watson – depending on which side of Baker Street you live – always held nothing but high esteem for Poe and his tales. Speaking before the Poe Centennial Celebration Dinner of the Authors' Society, at the Hotel Metropole in March 1909, Conan Doyle, in fact, even pointed out, 'Where was the detective story until Poe breathed the breath of life into it?'

Conan Doyle always acknowledged his own personal debt to Poe as well; to Poe, whose stories of mystery and detection had so fascinated Conan Doyle that years later they proved a major influence in Conan Doyle's creating his own private detective, Sherlock Holmes. The filming, then, of *Sherlock Holmes and the Great Murder Mystery* ironically brought the Baker Street sleuth right back to his creator's own literary inspirations.

But while it does seem doubtful that Crescent's Holmes–Dupin mystery adventure picture was released with Poe's

115

Centennial in mind, *Edgar Allan Poe*, a film produced by Thomas Alva Edison and released on 8 February 1909 – three weeks after Poe's hundredth birthday, and a month before Conan Doyle spoke about Poe at the Hotel Metropole – actually was a special Poe Centennial film. Interestingly enough, it was Edison and his American Mutoscope & Biograph Company in New York City who also produced the first of all Holmes movies, *Sherlock Holmes Baffled* in 1900.

Edison's commemorative *Edgar Allan Poe* starred Herbert Yost as Poe, Linda Arvidson as Virginia, Poe's sick wife to whom he was so devoted, and Biograph's trade announcements proclaimed that here was a film about 'the most original poetical genius ever produced by America'; a much-maligned man who 'might be regarded the literary lion of the universe, to which fact the public are becoming alive'. While not necessarily biographical, the film was based on incidents in Poe's life, and in that season of Poe's Centennial Celebration was a picture – 'one of the most artistic films ever produced' – that showed Poe to be 'a man of heart, and not as his enemies have painted him'.

Sherlock Holmes's creator, Sir Arthur Conan Doyle, and Lady Conan Doyle on a Hollywood film set with Mary Pickford and Douglas Fairbanks in 1924

Dramatic illustration for 'The Raven' by the American artist, James W. Carling, circa 1883 (POE FOUNDATION INC)

Edgar Allan Poe purported to show how Poe came to write 'The Raven', and had him suffering great financial woes while his beloved Virginia lay dying in a bed across the room from him. But then, suddenly, Poe looks up and sees a raven perched atop a bust of Pallas above the door of their dismal, squalid apartment. Inspired by the raven now, Poe quickly, feverishly begins writing a poem about the raven, and when he completes it rushes off to sell the poem to a publisher for the money he so desperately needs for his wife's care. After initial rejection, though, he finally sells 'The Raven' and then hurries back to Virginia with the good news. But, alas, it's too late.

Virginia is dead.

And screaming out in great despair, Edgar Allan Poe crumbles helpless and forlorn over her beautiful corpse.

RON HAYDOCK

EUREKA POE

The Father of the Detective Story

ELLERY QUEEN

WHO MORE suitable to pay tribute to the man who invented the detective story than one of the greatest modern practitioners of the art and a fellow American, Ellery Queen. In this brief essay, Mr Queen acknowledges the debt all writers of crime fiction owe to Poe and explains how, in just four stories, he 'laid down for all time the major principles of the detective story, even as we know its basic technique and boundaries today'. The article appeared in the May 1965 issue of *Ellery Queen's Mystery Magazine*.

EDGAR A. POE, the acknowledged Father of the Detective Story, wrote three tales about C. Auguste Dupin, the world's first fictional detective in a modern sense.

The first of the first three detective stories was, of course, 'The Murders in the Rue Morgue,' which appeared in *Graham's Magazine*, Philadelphia, issue of April 1841. This tale of ratiocination (Poe's own word) was not a mere pioneering effort, or an experimental incunable; it was, and still is, a technical and artistic masterpiece, so influential that it spawned literally hundreds and hundreds of thousands of short stories – which might be called 'detective descendants'. Of 'The Murders in the Rue Morgue', Dorothy L. Sayers, creator of Lord Peter Wimsey, once wrote: 'it constitutes in itself almost a complete manual of detective theory . . .'

The second Dupin story was 'The Mystery of Marie Rogêt', published as a three-part serial in Snowden's *The Ladies' Companion*, New York, issues of November and December 1842, and February 1843.

The third and final Dupin story – and artistically Poe's finest achievement in the genre he himself invented – was 'The Purloined Letter', in *The Gift*: 1845, Philadelphia, published late in 1844.

All three Dupin stories were included in Poe's *Tales*, New York, 1845 – the most important book of detective short stories ever published, from all possible viewpoints – historically, qualitatively, and bibliophilically (the rarity and value of the first edition). Howard Haycraft, the world's

Poe is called upon to solve another mystery in 'The Gold Hunters of '49' a picture strip from *The Atom* comic, 1964

The methods of Poe still hold good one hundred years after his death in this picture story from *Detective Comics*, 1971

foremost historian of the detective story, wrote: 'Thus in the brief compass of only three slight narratives, Poe foretold the entire evolution of the detective romance as a literary form'.

If we add Poe's fourth and last tale of detection (a non-Dupin story) – 'Thou Art the Man', in *Godey's Lady's Book*, Philadelphia, issue of November 1844 – it can be said, without the slightest fear of critical contradiction, that Poe laid down, for all time, the major principles of the detective story, even as we know its basic technique and boundaries today. Let us refresh your memory.

In 'The Murders in the Rue Morgue', Poe created the 'pure' classical pattern: the eccentric amateur criminologist and his worshipful assistant, amanuensis, and/or sounding board; the crime that baffles the police; the wrongly suspected person; the motif of the locked room; and (oh, how it has challenged Poe's disciples!) the surprise solution.

In 'The Mystery of Marie Rogêt', Poe applied his almost fully developed technique to the solution of a real-life case.

In 'The Purloined Letter', Poe added the use of psychological deduction; and double bluff – surprise by means of the obvious rather than the unexpected, the simple rather than the subtle.

In 'Thou Art the Man', Poe rounded out and completed the now immutable principles – to the point where the myriad of detective-story writers who have followed in Poe's footsteps are left, as Sir Arthur Conan Doyle, creator of Sherlock Holmes, has said, 'with no fresh ground they can confidently call their own'. In 'Thou Art the Man', Poe invented the least-likely-person dénouement; the laying of a false trail by the real criminal; psychological third degree to extort a confession; the anonymous sleuth; and in a truly magnificent anticipation of real life, the use of ballistics as a method of crime detection.

No wonder G. K. Chesterton, creator of Father Brown, wrote: 'I do not think that America has ever lost that great Challenge Cup won long ago by one of the first literary champions; or rather designed by him with a craftsmanship that was entirely original . . .'

Three Dupin stories – no more, no less. 'That's all there is, there isn't any more' . . . We remember that many years ago, when we were preparing to edit the first Ellery Queen anthology, we spent two weeks in the stacks of the Library of Congress in Washington, DC, searching desperately for a 'lost' Dupin story, searching in vain for even a hint or fragment of an unknown or unpublished Dupin story . . .

POE FORETELLS THE MURDER MYSTERY OF 'BARNABY RUDGE'

A Controversy discussed in
The Dickensian 1913

AN ARTICLE on Charles Dickens written by Edgar Allan Poe dealing chiefly with *Barnaby Rudge* appeared in *Graham's Magazine*, for February 1842, and is included in Poe's collected writings. In it there is a reference to a former review of the same book to the following effect: 'We are not prepared to say, so positively as we could wish, whether by the public at large the whole *mystery* of the murder committed by Rudge, with the identity of the Maypole ruffian with Rudge himself, was fathomed at any period previous to the period intended, or, if so, whether at a period so early as materially to interfere with the interest designed; but we are forced through sheer modesty to suppose this the case, since by ourselves individually the secret was distinctly understood immediately upon the perusal of

Charles Dickens. Did Poe solve his 'Barnaby Rudge' serial before it was all published?

the story of Solomon Daisy, which occurs at the seventh page of this volume of 323. In the number of the *Philadelphia Saturday Evening Post* for 1 May, 1841 (the tale having then only begun) will be found a *prospective notice* of some length in which we made use of the following words.

That Barnaby is the son of the murderer may not appear evident to our readers – but we will explain. The person murdered is Mr Reuben Haredale. He was found assassinated in his bedchamber. His steward (Mr Rudge, senior), and his gardener (name not mentioned), are missing. At first both are suspected. "Some months afterwards", here, we use the words of the story, "the steward's body, scarcely to be recognised but by his clothes, and the watch and ring he wore – was found at the bottom of a piece of water in the grounds, with a deep gash in the breast where he had been stabbed by a knife. He was only partly dressed; and all people agreed that he had been sitting up reading in his own room, where there were many traces of blood, and was suddenly fallen upon and killed, before his master".'

Poe further inferred in the *Graham's Magazine* article that he discovered that 'Rudge . . . was interrupted by his (Rudge's) wife, whom he seized by the wrist, to prevent her giving the alarm.'

This article, from which this extract is taken, has never been reprinted in any edition of Poe's writings, and Sir W. Robertson Nicoll in his book, *The Problem of Edwin Drood*, argued that Poe's claim to have anticipated the plot of *Barnaby Rudge* to the extent he states was largely a piece of mystification, and suggested that the article Poe claimed to have written should be found and reprinted as evidence of Poe's achievement.

Sir W. Robertson Nicoll is of opinion that 'to claim that the seizing of the wrist could have been deduced from Solomon Daisy's story by itself is to affirm an impossibility'. On this point he is correct as the review itself now proves that Poe had read as far as chapter eleven, and the three significant words 'by the wrist' appear in chapter five.

The comments in Sir W. Robertson Nicoll's book on the subject have caused a controversy in the *New York Times Book Review Supplement* with the result that the article in question has been unearthed and republished in the *New York Times* for 1 June, with a carefully reasoned and elaborate introductory commentary.

We reprint the article here and no doubt our readers, before reading it, will turn again to *The Problem of Edwin Drood*, and to Poe's article 'Charles Dickens' in his collection of Essays.

BARNABY RUDGE
THE ORIGINAL REVIEW
From *Philadelphia Saturday Post*, 1 May 1841
By EDGAR ALLAN POE

Barnaby Rudge. *By 'Boz' Author of* Nicholas Nickleby, Oliver Twist, *etc. With Illustrations by G. Cattermole and H. K. Browne. Nos. 1, 2 and 3. Philadelphia: Lea and Blanchard.*

We presume our readers all know that *Barnaby Rudge*, now 'in course of publication' periodically, is a story supposed to be narrated by one of the members of Master Humphrey's society; and is in fact a continuation of the 'Clock', although complete within itself. From the concluding words of *The Curiosity Shop* – or rather of the volume which contained that tale – we gather that the present narrative will be occupied with matters tending to develop the spirit, or, in the language of Mr Dickens himself, the 'heart' of the mighty London, toward the conclusion of the eighteenth century. This thesis affords the most ample scope for the great powers of the writer. His opening chapters assure us that he has at length discovered the secret of his true strength, and that *Barnaby Rudge* will appeal principally to the *imagination*. Of this faculty we have many striking instances in the few numbers already issued. We see it where the belfry-man in the lonely church at midnight, about to toll the 'passing-bell', is struck with horror at hearing the solitary note of another, and awaits, aghast, a repetition of the sound. We recognise it more fully when this single note is discovered, in the morning, to have been that of an alarm pulled by the hand of one in the death-struggle with a murderer – also in the expression of countenance which is so strikingly attributed to Mrs Rudge – 'the capacity for expressing terror' – something only dimly seen, but never absent for a moment – 'the shadow of some look to which an instant of intense and most unutterable horror only could have given rise'. This is a conception admirably adapted to whet curiosity in respect of the character of that event which is hinted at as forming the groundwork of the novel; and so far is well suited to the purposes of a periodical story. But this observation should not fail to be made – that the anticipation must surpass the reality; that no matter how terrific be the circumstances which, in the dénouement, shall appear to have occasioned the expression of countenance worn habitually by Mrs Rudge, still they will not be able to satisfy the mind of the reader. He will surely be disappointed. The skilful intimation of horror held out by the artist produces an effect which will deprive his conclusion of all. These intimations – these dark hints of some uncertain evil – are often rhetorically praised as effective – but are only justly so praised where there is *no* dénouement whatever – where the reader's imagination is left to clear up the mystery for itself – and this, we suppose, is not the design of Mr Dickens.

But the chief points in which the ideality of this story is

Barnaby Rudge and his pet raven, Grip, illustrated by Hablot K. Browne ('Phiz') from the first edition of Dickens's book, 1840

Barnaby comes across the victim of a murderous attack. Again from 'Barnaby Rudge', by the other illustrator of the first edition, George Cattermole

apparent are the creation of the hero Barnaby Rudge, and the commingling with his character, as accessory, that of the human-looking raven. Barnaby we regard as an original idea altogether, so far as novel writing is concerned. He is peculiar, inasmuch as he is an idiot endowed with the fantastic qualities of the madman, and has been born possessed with a maniacal horror of blood – the result of some terrible spectacle seen by his mother during pregnancy. The design of Mr Dickens is here twofold – first that of increasing our anticipation in regard to the deed committed – exaggerating our impression of its atrocity – and, secondly, that of causing this horror of blood on the part of the idiot, to bring about, in consistence with poetical justice, the condemnation of the murderer – for it is a murder that has been committed. We say in accordance with poetical justice – and, in fact, it will be seen hereafter that Barnaby, the idiot, is the murderer's own son. The horror of blood which he feels is the immediate result of the atrocity, since this atrocity it was which impressed the imagination of the pregnant mother; and poetical justice will therefore be well fulfilled when this horror shall urge on the son to the conviction of the father in the perpetrator of the deed. That Barnaby is the son of the murderer may not appear evident to our readers – but we will explain. The person murdered is Mr Reuben Haredale. He was found assassinated in his bedchamber. His steward (Mr Rudge, senior), and his gardener (name not mentioned), are missing. At first both are suspected. 'Some months afterward', here, we use the words of the story, 'the steward's body, scarcely to be recognised but by his clothes, and the watch and ring he wore – was found at the bottom of a piece of water in the grounds, with a deep gash in the breast where he had been stabbed by a knife. He was only partly dressed; and all people agreed that he had been sitting up reading in his own room, where there were many traces of blood, and was suddenly fallen upon and killed, before his master.'

Now, be it observed, it is not the author himself who asserts that *the steward's body was found*; he has put the words in the mouth of one of his characters. His design is to make it appear, in the dénouement, that the steward, Rudge, first murdered the gardener, then went to his master's chamber, murdered *him*, was interrupted by his (Rudge's) wife, whom he seized and held *by the wrist*, to prevent her giving the alarm – that he then, after possessing himself of the booty desired, returned to the gardener's room, exchanged clothes with him, put upon the corpse his own watch and ring, and secreted it where it was afterwards discovered at so late a period that the features could not be identified. It will appear that Rudge himself, through his wife, gave indication to the police, after due time had elapsed, of the proper spot to be searched – so that when the decomposed body was found, it might be regarded as his own. We say that Rudge, in perpetrating the murder, seized his wife *by the wrist*; and we draw this inference from the fact that Barnaby is said to have upon his wrist the appearance of a smear of blood.

The ruffian who, at the Maypole, listens so attentively to the story told by Solomon Daisy, and who subsequently forces himself into Mrs Rudge's house, holding with her so mysterious a connection – this ruffian is Rudge himself, the murderer. Twenty-two years having elapsed, he has ventured to return. To bring about the conviction of the assassin, after the lapse of so long a time, though his son's mysterious *awe of blood – an awe created in the unborn by the assassination itself* – is most probably, we repeat, the design of Mr Dickens, and is no doubt one of the finest possible embodiments of the idea we are accustomed to attach to 'poetical justice'. Joe, John Willett's son, who has received a blow from Rudge, will be made to supply in the idiot the want of precision of thought – a precision without which there would be some difficulty in working out the catastrophe; but the main agency in the conviction will be that of the hero, Barnaby Rudge.

The elder Rudge himself has probably been only a tool in the hands of Geoffrey Haredale, the brother of the murdered man and the present incumbent of the Warren estate, which he has inherited upon Reuben's decease. This idea is corroborated by the fact that, the families of Chester and Haredale being at variance, an attempt is made by Rudge upon the life of young Chester, who is in love with Miss Haredale, the daughter of Reuben. She resides at the Warren estate; is no doubt the ward of her uncle; her fortune is in his possession, and, that he may not have to part with it, especially to the son of this enemy, he is anxious to get the young man out of the way.

We may as well here observe that the reader should note carefully the ravings of Barnaby, which are not put into his mouth at random, as might be supposed, but are intended to convey indistinct glimmerings of the events to be evolved – and in this evident design of Mr Dickens his ideality is strongly evinced. It would be difficult to impress upon the mind of a merely general reader how vast a degree of interest may be given to the story by such means; for in truth that interest, great as it may be made, will not be, strictly speaking, of a popular cast.

But an example will be necessary to convey our meaning fully upon this head, and one may be found where the idiot draws Mr Chester to the windows and directs his attention to the clothes hanging upon the lines in the yard.

'Look down', he said, softly; 'do you mark how they

The mysterious murderer of 'Barnaby Rudge' leaves one of his victims: an illustration by Hablot K. Browne

whisper in each other's ears, then dance and leap to make believe they are in sport? Do you see how they stop for a moment, when they think there is no one looking, and mutter among themselves again? And then how they roll and gambol, delighted with the mischief they've been plotting? Look at 'em now! See how they whirl and plunge. And now they stop again and whisper cautiously together – little thinking, mind, how often I have laid upon the ground and watched them. I say – what is it they plot and hatch? Do you know?'

Now these incoherences are regarded by Mr Chester simply as such, and no attention is paid them; but they have reference, *indistinctly*, to the counsellings together of Rudge and Geoffrey Haredale upon the topic of the bloody deeds committed; which counsellings have been watched by the idiot. In the same manner almost every word spoken by him will be found to have an undercurrent of meaning, by paying strict attention to which the enjoyment of the imaginative reader will be infinitely heightened.

A confirmation of our idea in regard to the perpetrators of the murder will be seen in the words of Mrs Rudge addressed to the locksmith, when the latter attempted to prevent the egress of the ruffian from her house. 'Come back, come back!' she exclaimed – 'do not touch him on your life. I charge you, come back. He carries other lives besides his own!' – meaning that, if arrested and recognised, Rudge would involve in his fate not only Geoffrey Haredale, but herself, as an accessory after the fact.

The young Chester, it will be remembered, when found lying wounded in the road by the locksmith and Barnaby, was taken, as if by accident, to the house of Mrs Rudge. Upon this circumstance will be made to turn some of the most exciting incidents of the story. Many difficulties, we apprehend, will occur before the sick man makes his escape from this house – in which, for several reasons, we are inclined to think that much of the main action of the drama is to come to pass. These reasons are, that it is the home of the murderer Rudge, of Mrs Rudge so emphatically described, and especially of Barnaby, the hero, and of his raven, whose croakings are to be frequently, appropriately and prophetically heard in the course of the narrative, and whose whole character will perform, in regard to that of the idiot, much the same part as does, in music, the accompaniment in respect to the air. Each is distinct. Each differs remarkably from the other. Yet between them there is a strong analogical resemblance; and, although each may exist apart, they form together a whole which would be imperfect wanting either. This is clearly the design of Mr Dickens – although he himself may not at present perceive

it. In fact, beautiful as it is, and strikingly original with him, it cannot be questioned that he has been led to it less by artistical knowledge and reflection than by that intuitive feeling for the forcible and the true which is the *sixth sense* of the man of genius.

Of the other characters introduced we must be content to speak *in petto*. The locksmith and his wife are drawn with that boldness and vigour in which our author is never deficient; but, as far as we yet comprehend them, having nothing distinctive. Miss Miggs, Simon Tappertit, and his society of 'Prentice Knights, cannot be properly called caricatures – for there is a well-sustained exaggeration of all their traits, which has the effect of *keeping* – but they are obviously burlesques. For this reason, we feel sure that they will have no very active agency in the plot. They will form an amusing by-play – much as Swiveller and the Marchionees do in *The Curiosity Shop*. Hugh, on the contrary, who is carefully and truthfully drawn, with no very decided peculiarities as yet appearing – Hugh will be a main instrument in the action. Of Joe Willet we have already spoken. John is an attempt at character for its own sake solely. He is an original, in the sense that, while really existing in nature, he has never as yet been depicted – and such originals are very rare indeed. The features of the ruffian, Rudge, are not yet developed; neither are those of the young Chester, nor of the locksmith's daughter. The

Justice is at last done: the murderer is arrested in the closing sequence of 'Barnaby Rudge'. Illustration by George Cattermole

manner in which the portraiture of the very gentlemanly and self-composed elder Chester is elaborated assures us that here we are to look for one of the best efforts of the author.

The *designs* are, for the most part, utterly unworthy the narrative, and, very often, are not even in accordance with it. The thoughts of the writer are sometimes not conveyed at all. The hostelry upon the first page, for instance, is far from Mr Dickens's conception, and gives the idea of a portion of a street, rather than of an insulated and sequestered inn. In the interior of the taproom the figures are all crowded into close juxtaposition, while the text places Rudge and the young Chester in situations secluded from the rest of the Company. The third design, where Rudge strikes Joe Willet, is well enough executed, but has no force of subject in itself – and we can only regard it as good when we take a prospective view, and consider that the blow given will have important results. In the fourth plate, where the young Chester is found wounded, there is great vigour of conception. The *abandon* of the prostrate figure is richly ideal; and the author's intention in *Barnaby Rudge* fully made out. Plate fourth is good – Tappertit,

Frederick Coburn's painting of the murderer dragging away the girl's body in 'The Mystery of Marie Roget' (1902)

the locksmith and his daughter, are all finely portrayed. Plate the fifth, introducing Tappertit *solus*, and plate the sixth, where Barnaby plays at thread-puzzles in the sick room, are also sufficiently well done; although in the latter, the form and character of the locksmith undergo an inexcusable alteration. The tail-piece at the end of the second number (with the exception of the countenance of the dreaming Barnaby), is extravagant and ineffective – fully embodying our notion of the *false ideal*. The meeting of the 'Prentice Knights is unworthy of notice. Miss Miggs *sola* is fine, and the expression of her countenance, as described in the text (a mixture of mischief, cunning, malice, triumph, and patient expectation), is singularly well embodied. Mr Chester, Senior, seated by the fire in the large room of the inn, forms the subject of a forcibly conceived picture.

The figure of Hugh, in the concluding design of the third number, is true to the description of the author, except in the matter of position. In the plate he sits nearly erect; in the text he reclines. Upon the whole it is much to be lamented that competent artists cannot be found for the embellishments of a work so rich in material as *Barnaby Rudge*. At all events it is much to be regretted that books such as those of Mr Dickens – books which have formed an era in the reading of every man of genius – should be thought less worthy of adequate illustration than the woefully inferior compositions which are so popular under the titles of *Confessions of Harry Lorrequer*, and *Adventures of Charles O'Malley*.

ANOTHER POE MYSTERY

I

WE TAKE it for granted that our readers remember, in a general way at least, 'The Mystery of Marie Rogêt' and the conditions under which it was written. Briefly they were these.

Some time in the forties of the last century, a certain Mary Rogers, known as 'the beautiful cigar girl', dis-

The shop girl, Mary Rogers, who became the central character of Poe's 'The Mystery of Marie Roget'

appeared from the shop on Broadway, New York, in which she was employed. Several days later her body, bearing marks of extreme violence, was found in the Hudson River, at a place near Weehawken, New Jersey, known as the Sybil's Cave. It was the celebrated case of the hour.

Poe made it the basis of his story, brought in the famous Dupin whom he had used in 'The Murders in the Rue Morgue' and 'The Purloined Letter', shifted the scene from New York to Paris, substituted the Seine for the Hudson, and Gallicised the heroine's name to Marie Rogêt. In the form which the tale has come down to us it ends abruptly with an editorial note to the effect that for obvious reasons only so much of Mr Poe's story could be printed.

Now the inevitable questions are, was this merely a trick of the author's, or had he actually carried the narrative to a conclusion which could not be printed at a time when justice was still on the scent of the murderer or murderers of Mary Rogers? In support of the latter theory there was the vague impression that we had read somewhere that Mr Poe in the continuation of the narrative had fastened the guilt upon a United States naval officer.

121

The Edgar Allan Poe Scrapbook

It was a number of years ago that we first became interested in this question. Indeed we had hoped that some day we could print in this magazine the full story of 'The Mystery of Marie Rogêt' at a time when, through the lapse of years, such publication would be perfectly permissible.

Quite recently we fell to discussing the matter again with Mr Burton Egbert Stevenson. Now Mr Stevenson is himself the inventor of very intricate mysteries and a librarian of many years' standing as well. Yet he could throw no light whatever upon the subject.

So we referred the matter to that very distinguished Poe authority, George E. Woodberry, whose answer in part is as follows:

> I think the form of the story has never varied in successive editions, and I know of no manuscript. I supposed the ending was only one of Poe's hoaxes. I have seen the statement about the naval officer, but in the confused mass of my newspaper clippings I cannot now find it without a long search; and it is probably only another of the innumerable Poe legends. I got a copy of the evidence of the trial, but it contained nothing of interest, merely hallucinations of a spiritualist sort as I recall it.
>
> PS In favour of my view it is to be observed that Poe reprinted and revised the tale (1845), and retained with slight changes the editorial note in brackets. Had the editor and not he himself suppressed any portion, he had the opportunity to restore any omitted passage, and did not.

Chronicle & Comment
The Bookman, December 1912

The discovery of the body of Marie Roget, an early twentieth-century illustration by H. Meyer

II

Mr J. H. Whitty of Richmond, Virginia, a gentleman who has contributed materially to the literature about Edgar Allan Poe, throws a little more light on the problem of the 'naval officer' in 'The Mystery of Marie Rogêt'. He writes:

> I have been reading your comments about Poe's 'Mystery of Marie Rogêt'. I cannot help thinking that Professor Woodberry and yourself are a little astray in this matter.
>
> Poe himself traces the crime by his inferences most directly to the 'naval officer'. I never saw it mentioned elsewhere. See the Virginia edition of Poe's works and turn to pages 42-3: 'And here let me call your attention to the fact that the time elapsing between the first ascertained and the second elopement, is a few months more than the general period of the cruises of our men-of-war. Had the lover been interrupted in his first villainy by the necessity of departure to sea, and had he seized the first moment of his return to renew the base designs not yet accomplished – or not yet altogether accomplished *by him*? Who is that secret lover, I ask, of whom at least most of the relatives know nothing?'
>
> Then turn to pages 60-3: 'This associate is of a swarthy complexion, the "hitch" in the bandage and the "sailor's knot" with which the bonnet ribbon is tied, point to a seaman. His companionship with the deceased, a gay, but not abject, young girl, designate him as above the grade of a common sailor.'

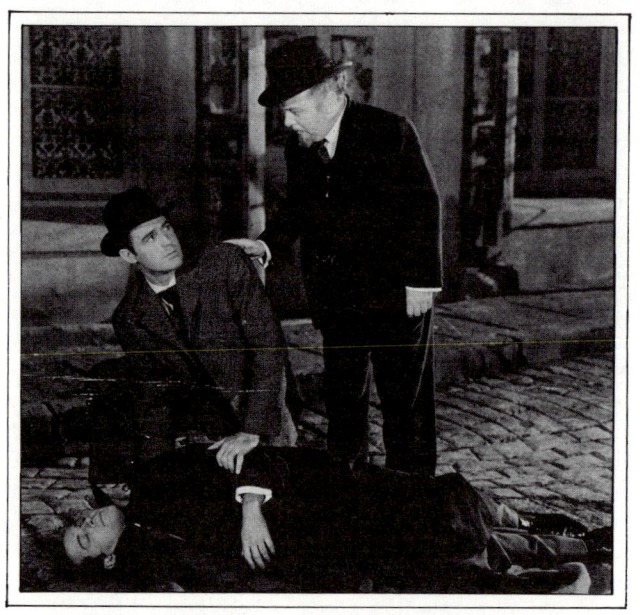

C. Auguste Dupin (Patric Knowles) and his assistant (Lloyd Corrigan) discover a corpse in the streets of Paris while investigating *The Mystery of Marie Roget,* **made by Universal in 1942**

The circumstances of the first elopement, as mentioned by *Le Mercure*, tend to blend the idea of the seaman with the 'naval officer', who is first known to have led the unfortunate into crime. Let us sift to the bottom this affair of the first elopement. Let us know the full history of this officer, with his present circumstances and his whereabouts at the precise period of the murder. Let us compare the various communications with the known MSS of this officer. Also let us trace the boat. And then, what shall we find? The murderer of Mary Rogers/Marie Rogêt?

Chronicle & Comment
The Bookman, February 1913

Patric Knowles as Dupin in a dramatic moment from *The Mystery of Marie Roget*. This film is sometimes known as *Phantom of Paris*

THE MOST AMAZING THING

(In the Style of Edgar Allan Poe)

HUGO GERNSBACK

APART FROM his vastly influential role in the development of the detective story, Poe has also been hailed as 'The Father of Science Fiction'. The leading historian of the genre, Sam Moskowitz, has written, 'The literature of science fiction owes to his influence an enduring debt, quite on a par with the recognition accorded him for his contributions to detective and mystery fiction and to the art of the short story.' Moskowitz lists the following as Poe's science fiction stories, 'Ms Found in a Bottle', 'A Descent into the Maelström', 'A Tale of the Ragged Mountains', 'Mellonta Tauta', 'The Unparalleled Adventures of One Hans Pfaall', **and** 'The Thousand-and-Second Tale of Scheherazade'.

The earliest date at which Poe's contribution to the genre appears to have been recognised was in 1905 by an anonymous reviewer in the British *Saturday Review*. It was, though, Hugo Gernsback, the man who produced the world's first science fiction magazine, *Amazing Stories*, in 1926, who really accorded the fullest credit to Poe. Gernsback, who coined the word 'scientifiction' (which later evolved into science fiction) to describe the theme of his magazine, defined the term thus, 'By "scientifiction" I mean the Jules Verne, H. G. Wells and Edgar Allan Poe type of story – a charming romance intermingled with scientific fact and prophetic vision.' And to show his admiration for Poe, Gernsback not only included one of his tales in the very first issue of *Amazing Stories*, but wrote in his editorial, 'Edgar Allan Poe may well be called the father of "scientifiction".' In a later number, the first issue of volume 2 for April 1927, he actually adopted the style of Poe for his editorial column, and this ingenious little article is reprinted here.

SEATED ON his throne, cut out of a pure crystal of carborundum, rested the all-powerful Supremental – who, in other universes, would perhaps be called the King. Before him appeared one of his distinguished explorers, who had just returned from an excursion through other worlds. The explorer's antennae touched those of the Supremental, upon which the following discourse took place:

Frank Paul illustration for one of the Poe stories reprinted by Hugo Gernsback in his magazine, *Amazing Stories*, April 1927

'It will probably interest your Highness to know that on our visit to the Third Planet of the Sixth Universe we encountered a race of most amazing creatures. An exploration of the planet showed that they were not fashioned of the natural products of their own soil, or, indeed of their geology, as for instance we are. Instead these creatures are made of a rubber-like, soft substance. In shape they are most grotesque and they have a jerky, mechanical motion similar to that of certain of our own machinery. Instead of floating in space as we do, they move around with a sort of hop-motion. Their shapeless bodies, if such they may be called, are crowned with an oval appendage, totally out of keeping with the rest of their bodies.'

'Most astonishing!' said the King.

'In this oval appendage, we found two remarkable television mechanisms, with a unique optical system. The light gathered through the two lenses is focused on a red sort of net, which is connected by literally millions of fine strands to a central exchange system, where the light is translated into pictures. A most roundabout system.'

'Extraordinary!' ejaculated the Supremental.

'In the inside of their elliptical appendages is a vast electrical sort of exchange, from which centre the entire machine is navigated and made to go through its various movements. In the inside of the creature, we found an extraordinary, but rather clumsy motor, which incessantly pumps a coloured liquid through a tube system and which I think lubricates the various part of the machine. There is also a sort of double bellows which purifies the liquid and acts in a manner similar to our own filters.'

'Most astounding!' wheezed the King. 'I don't believe a

EDGAR ALLAN POE
THE FATHER OF SCIENTIFICTION

COMPLETE WORKS $2.75

GREATEST OFFER EVER MADE

Never before has it been possible to obtain the complete works of America's greatest author and genius, Edgar Allan Poe, for the amazingly low price that we now offer them to you.

Edgar Allan Poe has come to be looked upon as the greatest literary genius that America has ever produced. **He is the originator of the first "Scientifiction" stories**—fiction with a plausible scientific background. Jules Verne and H. G. Wells freely acknowledge him as the originator of modern scientifiction.* In addition, there is little doubt but that the well known SHERLOCK HOLMES is the product of the inspiration that Sir Arthur Conan Doyle found in the works of Poe. Take advantage of this special introductory offer. There is just a limited number of copies in this edition.

........Like a razor also, the pendulum was massy and heavy, it was appended to a weighty rod of brass, and the whole *hissed* as it swung through the air. I saw that the crescent was designed to cross the region of the heart. Down—steadily down it crept. The rats were wild, bold, ravenous, their red eyes glaring upon me. And then......
From "The Pit and the Pendulum."

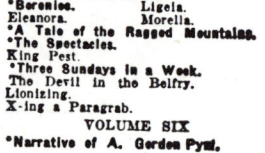

10 Volumes Cloth Bound
OVER 2000 PAGES

The complete works of Edgar Allan Poe are published in **10 beautiful volumes.** Handsome red cloth cover. Special egg-shell paper, made to order for this set. Printed from plates made for the well-known Richmond Edition. Each volume contains an average of **200 pages.** Size of type is long primer, which is easy reading and restful to the eyes. The volumes are handy in size, 4 x 6¼ inches. The greatest offer ever made. This is the chance of a lifetime. Take advantage of this astounding low price offer. Fill in the coupon now. Send no money—pay the postman $2.75 on delivery. We pay the mailing charges in U. S.

*All Scientifiction Stories in list of contents are identified with a star and printed bold face.

CONTENTS OF THE SET

VOLUME ONE
Memoir of Wm. H. Rogers.
Eulogy by James Russell Lowell.
Notice by N. P. Willis.
*Adventures of Hans Pfall.
*The Gold Bug.
Four Beasts in One.

VOLUME TWO
Murders in Rue Morgue.
Mystery of Marie Roget.
*The Balloon Hoax
*MS. Found in a Bottle.
*The Oval Portrait.

VOLUME THREE
*The Purloined Letter.
*One Thousand and Second Tale of Scheherazade.
*A Descent into the Maelstrom.
*Von Kempelen and His Discovery.
*Mesmeric Revelation.
*Facts in Case M. Valdemar.
*The Black Cat.

Fall of the House of Usher.
Silence—A Fable.

VOLUME FOUR
The Masque of the Red Death.
The Cask of Amontillado.
*The Imp of the Perverse.
The Island of the Fay.
The Assignation.
*The Pit and the Pendulum.
The Premature Burial.
The Domain of Arnheim.
Landor's Cottage.
William Wilson.

VOLUME SEVEN
Metzengerstein.
The System of Dr. Tarr and Prof. Fether.
The Literary Life of Thingumbob, Esq.
How to Write a Blackwood Article.
Predicament.
Mystification.
Diddling.

VOLUME EIGHT
The Oblong Box.
*Loss of Breath.
*The Man That Was Used Up.
The Business Man.
The Landscape Garden.
*Maelzel's Chess Player.
Poems of Words.
The Colloquy of Monas and Una.
The Conversation of Eros and Charmian.
Shadow—A Parable.
Philosophy of Furniture.
A Tale of Jerusalem.
*The Sphinx.

VOLUME NINE
Hop Frog.
The Man of the Crowd.
Never Bet the Devil Your Head.
Thou Art the Man.
Why the Little Frenchman Wears His Hand in a Sling.
Bon Bon.
*Some Words with a Mummy.
The Poetic Principle.
The Philosophy of Composition.
Old English Poetry.

VOLUME FIVE
*The Tell-Tale Heart.
*Berenice.   Ligeia.
Eleanora.   Morella.
*A Tale of the Ragged Mountains.
*The Spectacles.
King Pest.
*Three Sundays in a Week.
The Devil in the Belfry.
Lionizing.
X-ing a Paragrab.

VOLUME SIX
*Narrative of A. Gordon Pym.

The Angel of the Odd.
*Mellonta Tauta.
The Duc de L'Omelette.

VOLUME TEN
Complete Poems.
The Raven.
The Bells.
*Sonnet to Science.
*Al Aaraaf.
Tamerlane.
Etc.

SEND NO MONEY!

Popular Book Corporation,
102 Park Place, New York City.

Gentlemen:—

Please send me at once, the complete works of Edgar Allan Poe, comprising of 10 volumes, as per your advertisement. I will pay the postman $2.75 upon arrival of the books. There are no extra charges of any kind, whatsoever. If the books are not as represented, I will return them to you within three days and you are then to return me my money.

(Free delivery only in U. S. Extra postage for foreign countries.)

Name ....

Address ....

City .... State ....

POPULAR BOOK CORPORATION, 102 PARK PLACE NEW YORK

word of it. But tell me what fuel is used in these machines?'

'This is another amazing thing, which must surely tax your credulity, but it is true nevertheless. Instead of using reconverted light-rays, as we do, these creatures go through the intricate process of using the strangest fuels, which they obtain from their flora and fauna. They never use the same fuel twice in succession, but keep on varying to an astonishing degree, which, however, does not seem to affect their machinery.'

'Incredible!' snorted the King. 'And how do they communicate with each other?'

'This is the most amazing part of all,' continued the explorer. 'We were much puzzled at first by their strange methods. They use a sort of radio communication, if such I may call it. Certainly no antennae touch when communication takes place, neither do they touch each other. In the elliptical appendage of which I spoke, there is, in the centre, a large hole, which opens and closes. When these beings communicate, this hole opens and closes more or less rapidly, although no substance comes forth, and nothing is perceived. It is thought that the communication is effected by some wave motion, but inasmuch as we have no organs to interpret it, we accidentally discovered by electrical means, that when the hole is opened and closed certain vibrations issue forth which to us are unintelligible and meaningless when translated into electric vibrations.'

MASTERS of FANTASY
Edgar Allan Poe—THE PIT AND THE PEN—His Centenary

It is 100 years ago that Poe, age 40, died. But his works still live—in reprint, radio and motion picture revival—because they were masterpieces of mystery and imagination.

He dip't his pen into night's blackest pit, and wrote with it the heart-stopping classic of "The Pit and the Pendulum", the eerie account of "The Fall of the House of Usher", the feline fear tale of "The Black Cat", the resounding lines of "The Raven" and many another powerful poem and prose piece.

His mind was a maelstrom of the macabre.

His legacy to literature, a treasury of terrifying tales of the dark recesses of the human mind—and the darker recesses of the inhuman.

This strange, doomed man. This craftsman of the curious, crazed and corrupt. This Master of Fantasy, known the wide world over: Edgar Allan Poe.

An illustration by Neil Austin celebrating Poe as 'The Master of Fantasy' and published in *Famous Fantastic Mysteries* on the centenary of his death (December 1949)

Left: Advertisement from Hugo Gernsback's magazine, *Science and Invention*, crediting Poe with the creation of science fiction (August, 1928)

'Hi! Hi!!' chuckled the King. 'What rubbish!'

'We found, on inspection of a dead specimen, which we opened, that at the side of the elliptical appendage there are two holes, which, incredible as it may seem, are an almost exact replica of one of our own telephone-like instruments, which we use for registering low vibrations on a moving paper strip. There is a diaphragm, such as we use in our instruments, and several small ivory-like substances pressing against the centre. In a spiral tube of liquid there are fine strands, which go to the central exchange, evidently to convey the electric impulses to the exchange, by which communication is established between the various beings.'

'Impossible!' cried the King.

'That, however, is not all,' continued the explorer, unabashed. 'Extending from the top of their bodies are two folding levers, which can be bent back and forth, seemingly at will. Instead of having normal tentacle-like appendages, they have these folding rods, with which they perform their work. At the end of the rods are a number of tentacles by which various things may be grasped at the will of the creature. This is also most strange, because nature certainly could have equipped them with our own suction apparatus, instead of using clutching appendages that have to wrap themselves around all objects in order to handle them.'

'Piffle!' exploded the King.

'Moreover,' continued the explorer, 'electrical connections seem to run through every part of their bodies, so it is possible for each part to communicate with the central station in case of need. We found, for instance, that when we touched them on any part of their bodies with our radio performers the rest of the things were sympathetic to whatever part we touched. The same seemed to be the case with changing temperatures. They seem to be able to distinguish heat from cold without using an antenna, which they do not possess. Moreover, this communication seemed to proceed at the speed of light. For instance, when we touched one of their tentacle-like appendages by means of our instruments the double lever-like appendage with its tentacles was jerked away instantly. From this we conclude that the communication taking place between the tentacle and the seat of motion must be instantaneous. Certainly that of the speed of light.'

'Stuff!' yawned the King. 'And do they float about as we do, by means of repulsion?'

'No, indeed' – this from the explorer – 'The specific gravity of their bodies is extremely high. They are eternally chained to the soil of their planet, on top of which they live. They do not live in submerged caverns, like our own polar inhabitants, but they live in strange cubicles, which they fashion themselves. These cubicles have holes cut in their sides to admit light, and other ethereal vibrations. The things themselves never leave the surface of their planet except in clumsy contraptions. They usually conglomerate in large centres, like low insects, while most of their planet is not so peopled, but is covered with flora.'

'Preposterous,' commented the King.

'But what will interest your Highness most is that during part of the rotation of the planet, it becomes immersed in darkness. Then these incredible creatures fall down prone on their backs and relapse into a state of coma from which they are aroused only by sunlight, when the planet has rotated around sufficiently to come into the sunlight again. Why they should do this is a profound mystery to us. It seems a great waste of time.'

'Ha, Ha!' laughed the King, now thoroughly amused by the incredible tale.

'But the worst is yet to come,' continued the explorer.

'Every once in a while, for apparently no reason at all, they fall upon each other and exterminate thousands of themselves with the most astonishing implements, which bore holes through their bodies, or with weird machines which give out gases as some of our insects do; or they annihilate each other's cubicles by dropping destructive missiles on them. Yet, when it is all over, they appear to become good friends once more.'

'Enough of this,' roared the All Highest. 'I certainly do not believe a word of this fantastic tale. It is impossible that nature should create such foolish creatures. And where, may I ask, did you find these things, and by what name do they go?'

'Their world', continued the explorer, 'is called by them the planet Earth, and the things, we understand, call themselves human beings.'

Fantasy artist, Virgil Finlay, capturing a moment from 'The Cask of Amontillado' in *Fantastic*, 1956

THE MASTER OF THE MODERN HORROR STORY

H. P. LOVECRAFT

TO PAY tribute to Poe's contribution to horror and fantasy fiction, I have selected an article by H. P. Lovecraft, a fellow countryman, and also a strange, withdrawn figure, now the centre of a world-wide cult. The essay first appeared in an amateur fantasy publication with the appropriate title of *The Recluse* in 1927.

IN THE eighteen-thirties occurred a literary dawn directly affecting not only the history of the weird tale, but that of short fiction as a whole; and indirectly moulding the trends and fortunes of a great European aesthetic school. It is our good fortune as Americans to be able to claim that dawn as our own, for it came in the person of our most illustrious and unfortunate fellow-countryman Edgar Allan Poe. Poe's fame has been subject to curious undulations, and it is now a fashion amongst the 'advanced intelligentsia' to minimise his importance both as an artist and as an influence; but it would be hard for any mature and reflective critic to deny the tremendous value of his work and the persuasive potency of his mind as an opener of artistic vistas. True, his type of outlook may have been anticipated; but it was he who first realised its possibilities and gave it supreme form and systematic expression. True also, that subsequent writers may have produced greater single tales than his; but again we must comprehend that it was only he who taught them by example and precept the art which they, having the way cleared for them and given an explicit guide, were perhaps able to carry to greater lengths. Whatever his limitations, Poe did that which no one else ever did or could have done; and to him we owe the modern horror story in its final and perfected state.

Before Poe the bulk of weird writers had worked largely in the dark; without an understanding of the psychological basis of the horror appeal, and hampered by more or less of conformity to certain empty literary conventions such as the happy ending, virtue rewarded, and in general a hollow moral didacticism, acceptance of popular standards and values, and striving of the author to obtrude his own emotions into the story and take sides with the partisans of the majority's artificial ideas. Poe, on the other hand, perceived the essential impersonality of the real artist; and knew that the function of creative fiction is merely to express and interpret events and sensations as they are, regardless of how they tend or what they prove – good or evil, attractive or repulsive, stimulating or depressing, with the author always acting as a vivid and detached chronicler rather than as a teacher, sympathiser, or vendor of opinion. He saw clearly that all phases of life and thought are equally eligible as a subject matter for the artist, and being inclined by temperament to strangeness and gloom, decided to be the interpreter of those powerful feelings and frequent happenings which attend pain rather than pleasure, decay rather than growth, terror rather than tranquillity, and which are fundamentally either adverse or indifferent to the tastes and traditional outward sentiments of mankind, and to the health, sanity, and normal expansive welfare of the species.

Poe's spectres thus acquired a convincing malignity possessed by none of their predecessors, and established a new standard of realism in the annals of literary horror. The impersonal and artistic intent, moreover, was aided by a scientific attitude not often found before; whereby Poe studied the human mind rather than the usages of Gothic fiction, and worked with an analytical knowledge of terror's true sources which doubled the force of his narratives and emancipated him from all the absurdities inherent in merely conventional shudder-coining. This example having been set, later authors were naturally forced to conform to it in order to compete at all; so that in this way a definite change began to affect the main stream of macabre writing. Poe, too, set a fashion in consummate craftsmanship; and although today some of his own work seems slightly melodramatic and unsophisticated, we can constantly trace his influence in such things as the maintenance of a single mood and achievement of a single impression in a tale, and the rigorous paring down of incidents to such as have a direct bearing on the plot and will figure prominently in the climax. Truly may it be said that Poe invented the short story in its present form. His elevation of disease, perversity, and decay to the level of artistically expressible themes was likewise infinitely far-reaching in effect; for avidly seized, sponsored, and intensified by his eminent French admirer Charles Pierre Baudelaire, it became the nucleus of the principal aesthetic movements in France, thus making Poe in a sense the father of the Decadents and the Symbolists.

Poet and critic by nature and supreme attainment, logician and philosopher by taste and mannerism, Poe was by no means immune from defects and affectations. His pretence to profound and obscure scholarship, his blundering ventures in stilted and laboured pseudo-humour, and

Where Once Poe Walked

An Acrostic Sonnet

By H. P. LOVECRAFT

Eternal brood the shadows on this ground,
Dreaming of centuries that have gone before;
Great elms rise solemnly by slab and mound,
Arch'd high above a hidden world of yore.
Round all the scene a light of memory plays,
And dead leaves whisper of departed days,
Longing for sights and sounds that are no more.

Lonely and sad, a specter glides along
Aisles where of old his living footsteps fell;
No common glance discerns him, though his song
Peals down through time with a mysterious spell.
Only the few who sorcery's secret know,
Espy amidst these tombs the shade of Poe.

H. P. Lovecraft pays tribute to Poe in verse in the legendary horror magazine, *Weird Tales*, May 1938

his often vitriolic outbursts of critical prejudice must all be recognised and forgiven. Beyond and above them, and dwarfing them to insignificance, was a master's vision of the terror that stalks about and within us, and the worm that writhes and slavers in the hideously close abyss. Penetrating to every festering horror in the gaily painted mockery called existence, and in the solemn masquerade called human thought and feeling, that vision had power to project itself in blackly magical crystallisations and transmutations; till there bloomed in the sterile America of the thirties and forties such a moon-nourished garden of gorgeous poison fungi as not even the nether slopes of Saturn might boast. Verses and tales alike sustain the burthen of cosmic panic. The raven whose noisome beak pierces the heart, the ghouls

that toll iron bells in pestilential steeples, the vault of Ulalume in the black October night, the shocking spires and domes under the sea, the 'wild, weird clime that lieth, sublime, out of Space – out of Time' – all these things and more leer at us amidst maniacal rattlings in the seething nightmare of the poetry. And in the prose there yawn open for us the very jaws of the pit – inconceivable abnormalities slyly hinted into a horrible half-knowledge by words whose innocence we scarcely doubt till the cracked tension of the speaker's hollow voice bids us fear their nameless implications; daemoniac patterns and presences slumbering noxiously till waked for one phobic instant into a shrieking revelation that cackles itself to sudden madness or explodes in memorable and cataclysmic echoes. A Witches' Sabbath of horror flinging off decorous robes is flashed before us – a sight the more monstrous because of the scientific skill with which every particular is marshalled and brought into an easy apparent relation to the known gruesomeness of material life.

Poe's tales, of course, fall into several classes; some of which contain a purer essence of spiritual horror than others. The tales of logic and ratiocination, forerunners of the modern detective story, are not to be included at all in weird literature; whilst certain others, probably influenced considerably by Hoffmann, possess an extravagance which relegates them to the borderline of the grotesque. Still a third group deal with abnormal psychology and monomania in such a way as to express terror but not weirdness. A substantial residuum, however, represent the literature of supernatural horror in its acutest form; and give their author a permanent and unassailable place as deity and fountainhead of all modern diabolic fiction. Who can forget the terrible swollen ship poised on the billow-chasm's edge in 'MS Found in a Bottle' – the dark intimations of her unhallowed age and monstrous growth, her sinister crew of unseeing greybeards, and her frightful southward rush under full sail through the ice of the Antarctic night, sucked onward by some resistless devil-current toward a vortex of eldritch enlightenment which must end in destruction?

Then there is the unutterable 'M Valdemar', kept together by hypnotism for seven months after his death, and uttering frantic sounds but a moment before the breaking of the spell leaves him 'a nearly liquid mass of loathsome, of detestable putrescence.' In the 'Narrative of A. Gordon Pym' the voyagers reach first a strange south polar land of murderous savages where nothing is white and where vast rocky ravines have the form of titanic Egyptian letters spelling terrible primal arcana of Earth; and thereafter a still more mysterious realm where everything is white, and where shrouded giants and snowy-plumed birds guard a cryptic cataract of mist which empties from immeasurable celestial heights into a torrid milky sea. 'Metzengerstein' horrifies with its malign hints of a monstrous metempsychosis – the mad nobleman who burns the stable of his hereditary foe; the colossal unknown horse that issues from the blazing building after the owner has perished therein; the vanishing bit of ancient tapestry where was shown the giant horse of the victim's ancestor in the Crusades; the madman's wild and constant riding on the great horse, and his fear and hatred of the steed; the meaningless prophecies that brood obscurely over the warring houses; and finally, the burning of the madman's palace and the death therein of the owner, borne helpless into the flames and up the vast staircase astride the beast he had ridden so strangely. Afterward the rising smoke of the ruins take the form of a gigantic horse. 'The Man of the Crowd', telling of one who roams day and night to mingle with streams of people as if afraid to be alone, has quieter effects, but implies nothing less of cosmic fear. Poe's mind was never far from terror and decay, and we see in every tale, poem, and philosophical dialogue a tense eagerness to fathom unplumbed wells of night, to pierce the veil of death, and to reign in fancy as lord of the frightful mysteries of time and space.

Certain of Poe's tales possess an almost absolute perfection of artistic form which makes them veritable beacon-lights in the province of the short story. Poe could, when he wished, give to his prose a richly poetic cast; employing that archaic and Orientalised style with jewelled phrase, quasi-Biblical repetition, and recurrent burthen so successfully used by later writers like Oscar Wilde and Lord Dunsany; and in the cases where he has done this we have an effect of lyrical phantasy almost narcotic in essence – an opium pageant of dream in the language of dream, with every unnatural colour and grotesque image bodied forth in a symphony of corresponding sound. 'The Masque of the Red Death', 'Silence, a Fable', and 'Shadow, a Parable', are assuredly poems in every sense of the word save the metrical one, and owe as much of their power to aural cadence as to visual imagery. But it is in two of the less openly poetic tales, 'Ligeia' and 'The Fall of the House of Usher' – especially the latter – that one finds those very summits of artistry whereby Poe takes his place at the head of fictional miniaturists. Simple and straightforward in plot, both of these tales owe their supreme magic to the cunning development which appears in the selection and collocation of every least incident. 'Ligeia' tells of a first wife of lofty and mysterious origin, who after death returns through a preternatural force of will to take possession of the body of a second wife; imposing even her physical appearance on the temporary reanimated corpse of her victim at the last moment. Despite a suspicion of prolixity and top-heaviness, the narrative reaches its terrific climax with relentless power. 'Usher', whose superiority in detail and proportion is very marked, hints shudderingly of obscure life in inorganic things, and displays an abnormally linked trinity of entities at the end of a long and isolated family history – a brother, his twin sister, and their incredibly ancient house all sharing a single soul and meeting one common dissolution at the same moment.

These bizarre conceptions, so awkward in unskilful hands, become under Poe's spell living and convincing terrors to haunt our nights; and all because the author understood so perfectly the very mechanics and physiology of fear and strangeness – the essential details to emphasise, the precise incongruities and conceits to select as preliminaries or concomitants to horror, the exact incidents and allusions to throw out innocently in advance as symbols or prefigurings of each major step toward the hideous dénouement to come, the nice adjustments of cumulative force and the unerring accuracy in linkage of parts which make for faultless unity throughout and thunderous effectiveness at the climactic moment, the delicate nuances of scenic and landscape value to select in establishing and sustaining the desired mood and vitalising the desired illusion – principles of this kind, and dozens of obscurer ones too elusive to be described or even fully comprehended by any ordinary commentator. Melodrama and unsophistication there may be – we are told of one fastidious Frenchman who could not bear to read Poe except in Baudelaire's urbane and Gallically modulated translation – but all traces of such things are wholly overshadowed by a potent and inborn sense of the spectral, the morbid, and the horrible which gushed forth from every cell of the artist's creative mentality and stamped his macabre work with the ineffaceable mark of supreme genius. Poe's weird tales are *alive* in a manner that few others can ever hope to be.

Like most fantasistes, Poe excels in incidents and broad narrative effects rather than in character drawing. His typical protagonist is generally a dark, handsome, proud, melancholy, intellectual, highly sensitive, capricious, introspective, isolated, and sometimes slightly mad gentleman of ancient family and opulent circumstances; usually deeply learned in strange lore, and darkly ambitious of penetrating to forbidden secrets of the universe. Aside from a high-sounding name, this character obviously derives little from the early Gothic novel; for he is clearly neither the wooden hero nor the diabolical villain of Radcliffian or Ludovician romance. Indirectly, however, he does possess a sort of genealogical connection; since his gloomy, ambitious and anti-social qualities savour strongly of the typical Byronic hero, who in turn is definitely an off-spring of the Gothic Manfreds, Montonis, and Ambrosios. More particular qualities appear to be derived from the psychology of Poe himself, who certainly possessed much of the depression, sensitiveness, mad aspiration, loneliness, and extravagant freakishness which he attributes to his haughty and solitary victims of Fate.

The terror of the 'Murders in the Rue Morgue' marvellously suggested by John Mackay in this 1935 picture

Dust jacket for Sam Moskowitz's collection of stories about Poe published in America in 1969

PICTURES OF POE

A Survey of the Silent Film Era 1909–29

DENIS GIFFORD

POE'S STORIES and even his poems have proved a rich source of material for film-makers from the dawn of the cinema right through to the present day. Indeed, such a draw has Poe's name proved to be on a film, that later pictures have been made with only the title owing anything to the creator. In this, the first of two studies of Poe in films, the leading British film historian, Denis Gifford, considers the silent era. Even then, of course, Poe's work was out of copyright and the most blatant liberties were being taken with his characters and plots. In the subsequent article, Ron Haydock, a leading American writer on the cinema, looks at the two men who have become most closely identified with Poe on the screen – director Roger Corman and actor Vincent Price.

EDGAR ALLAN POE, source of many a sleepless night through the moody mystery of his disturbing words, created more nightmares than he knew. He died in 1849, seventy years before the cinema first took those words and shaped them into pictures: the first stumbling attempts at the Horror Film.

In 1909, the centenary of Edgar Allan Poe's birth was celebrated in a unique fashion: David Wark Griffith made him the hero of the cinema's first ever biography. Fittingly, the name of the film company was Biograph!

D. W. Griffith, staff director at the Biograph studio at 11 East Fourteenth street, New York, was a failed actor with literary leanings. Inspired by the centenary celebrations of the birth of the 'Great American Poet', the man who would so soon become the 'Great American Poet of the Cinema' whipped up an instant scenario around a handful of half-remembered incidents (and a couple of completely misremembered ones), shot them on 21 and 23 January 1909, and released the result to the nation's nickelodeons on 8 February. In his haste to cash in on the centennial, Griffith mis-spelled his hero's name: on 3 February the copyright clerk at the Library of Congress, Washington, entered the film in the official records as *Edgar Allen Poe*. Later 'sic' was added in brackets!

While Griffith handled the picture, Lee Daugherty handled the words. As scenario editor of the outfit, part of Daugherty's duties was to dash off the deathless prose that decorated the 'Biograph Bulletins', flowery affairs that purported to describe Griffith's pictures to prospective purchasers. No 212 outlined its subject thus: 'He was undoubtedly the most original poetical genius ever produced by America, and might be regarded as the literary lion of the universe, to which fact the public are becoming alive.' The film itself opened with a different kind of flourish. Into a black attic dashes a fellow flowing of hair and gesture. He waves his arms at a woman who lies pale and prone in the foreground, then sits down at his desk and does battle with his quill. Suddenly a stuffed raven flaps into view and perches precariously atop a bust on his wardrobe, by courtesy of the stop-frame camera. Inspired, if not astounded, the man puts quill to scroll with gusto. He declaims the result to his wife, then, with a final wave of his arm, rushes out of the room.

The scene changes to an office in a publishing house, where the poet once again declaims his epic. The initial response is little better than that of his ailing wife, but finally the editor relents and buys the poem. Daugherty's synopsis concludes as Poe returns home with a light heart and a heavy comforter. 'Spreading the quilt tenderly over Virginia, he takes her hand and gazes fondly into her sightless eyes, but the cold unresponsive hand tells him the awful truth. "My God, she is dead," and he falls prostrate across the cot.'

Poe was played by a Broadway actor called Herbert Yost, Mrs Poe by Linda Arvidson, and the photographer was G. W. Bitzer. Yost changed his name to Barry O'More, Miss Arvidson to Mrs D. W. Griffith, and as Billy Bitzer the cameraman became the most famous photographer in American silent movies. Of the talents involved, only Bitzer's might have been noted as promising. For the garret

Henry B. Walthall – a convincing-looking Poe

THE EDGAR ALLAN POE SCRAPBOOK

scenes he shone his lights through an angled window: for 1909, quite an innovation. But his Stop-action efforts with the stuffed raven showed no advance on Griffith's cinematic début of some time before: his famous fight with a dead bird in *Rescued from an Eagle's Nest*.

That *Edgar Allen Poe* was some small success (thanks to its timing rather than its time-span: it ran for less than ten minutes!) may be judged by Biograph's September 1909 release of *The Sealed Room*. This costume melodrama set in the Renaissance featured Henry B. Walthall as a minstrel in love with Marion Leonard as a duchess, unmasked in their perfidy by Arthur Johnson as the duke. In a plot straight from Poe, Johnson has the pair walled up in their love-nest, as if they were a 'Cask of Amontillado'. Mary Pickford looked on as a suitably shocked extra.

Boris Karloff gloats over the pinioned Bela Lugosi in *The Raven* **(1935)**

The great director, D. W. Griffiths, and his cameraman, Billy Bitzer

Unusual studio shot of Bela Lugosi at work on *The Black Cat* **(1934)**

Griffith's adaptation was not the first piece of pirated Poe. The very first, which had been released in the November of the previous year, 1908, had created some kind of double record by pirating not only Poe but Conan Doyle too! *Sherlock Holmes in the Great Murder Mystery*, a Crescent Production, had shown the great detective going into a trance to pin a particularly grisly murder on an escaped gorilla!

Poe's satirical suggestions on the treatment of the insane as expounded in 'The System of Doctor Tarr and Professor Fether' was adapted by Edison as *Lunatics in Power* (1909). Its tone may be judged by the climax in which loosened loonies literally treat a tourist to genuine tar and feathers!

The Italian production company of Ambrosio Films proved the interest in the American poet was international. In 1910 they made two Poe pictures, *The Pit and the Pendulum* and *Hop Frog the Jester*, both period pieces that suited the styles of the studio. Eclair, the French company, now opened a studio in America, and at Fort Lee New Jersey produced the first major film about Poe.

The Raven was advertised as 'A Literary Film-Play Sensation!' In a full page of the *Moving Picture World* for 20 April 1912, Eclair described their epic as 'The story of Poe's struggles and success, magnificently produced with a splendid corps of actors and scenes laid in the historic Poe Cottage at Fordham, New York.' Poe was played by Guy Oliver, who certainly looked the part; the lady who played Lenore (Mrs Poe) was not named. The plot described 'the poor writer's struggles to support his invalid wife' until a remarkable series of visions provides him with the plots of 'The Gold Bug', 'The Black Cat', 'The Murders in the Rue Morgue', 'The Descent into the Maelström', 'Buried Alive', 'The Pit and the Pendulum', and, finally, 'The Raven'. This last vision is soon pinned and penned, sold for a swift

sawbuck, and so saves the life of his wife. The unnamed director of this 'Raven' clearly preferred the factual happy ending to Griffith's fiction: Virginia Poe died two years after Poe's poem was published in the *New York Evening Mirror*.

'Three reels of Thrill and Sensation Coming!' cried a double-page spread in *Moving Picture World* on 12 July 1913. 'Adapted from the Great Edgar Allan Poe's Graphic, Lurid and Blood-curdling Description of the Inquisition!' It was, of course, 'The Pit and the Pendulum', and the Solax Film Company had clearly produced America's first full-blooded horror film – if their publicity prose is anything to go by. 'Situations permeate with Genuine Thrills!' they screamed. 'A Blood-curdling Classic! The screen story vibrates with all the virility and vitality of Poe's incomparable pen! The scenes mirror Poe's compellingly gruesome but not repellant verbal rhapsody!'

W. Stephen Bush, reviewing the film on 2 August, wrote that he was:

... indeed astonished at the effectiveness with which the fearful tortures of the story's hero have been illustrated by the Solax producer. The quiet occupants of many of the dungeons shown are skeletons, and all the mechanisms of torture, including the cell with the pit in its floor down which we see skulls and crawling serpents (the bottom of this pit is not so realistic as it might have been), have been extremely well conceived. The pendulum, massive and sharp, which swings back and forth and ever draws nearer to the bound victim, is also effective, as is the manner of his salvation from it. Rats gnaw the ropes that bind him.

Darwin Karr, Solax's all-purpose lead, headed an 'All

Goudron et du Professeur Plume: continental aliases for our old friends Tarr and Fether. But there was no satire here. George Blaisdell, reviewing for *Moving Picture World*, called it 'A powerful story and a horrible one, yet fascinating in spite of its horror. However, don't show it to your patrons without looking at it for yourself, for it is no food for infants or weaklings.' British critics were equally aghast: 'For sheer unadulterated horror and harrowing sensation this picture must stand practically unequalled.' – (*Bioscope*). Henri Gouget and Monsieur Bahier played the two lunatics who take over their asylum and perform eye-gouging operations on their innocent visitors during the screen's first great climactic thunderstorm.

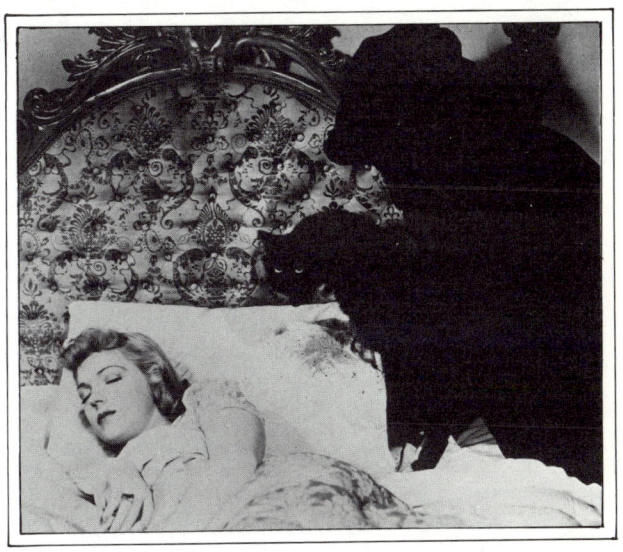

Poster for *The Black Cat* **(1934)**

The hooded Basil Rathbone menaces Anne Gwyne in the 1941 version of *The Black Cat*

Kaye Tendeter as Lord Usher about to seal up a coffin in the British-made *The Fall of the House of Usher* **(1947)**

Star Stock Company' (Blanche Cornwall and Fraunie Fraunholz).

In the same month came the release of *The Bells*, Poe's onomatopœiac poem, done up as a one-reeler by director George Lessey of the Edison Studio. Lucy, forced to marry a miser by her stern old father, is saved by her true love when the church catches fire, burning down her bridegroom in the nick of time. The critic was critical: 'Few Edisons have been weaker. Poe's famous poem is dragged in (it has nothing to do with the story), perhaps to make it seem poetical.' Or perhaps to sell the picture? It was the first time; it would not be the last. Yet the next Poe picture, curiously enough, did its best to hide its original inspiration.

The Lunatics was the American release title for *Dr Goudron's System*, produced by the French Eclair company in late 1913. Director Robert Saidreon based his two-reeler on a play by André de Lorde called *Le Système du Docteur*

D. W. Griffith returned to E. A. Poe in July 1914 and more than made amends for his mis-spellings with *The Avenging Conscience: or, Thou Shalt Not Kill*. In the five short years since the ten-minute *Edgar Allen Poe*, the cinema had grown up, thanks largely to the artistic efforts of Griffith himself. His new Poe picture ran for two hours.

Henry B. Walthall played an aspiring author for whom life turned sour when his guardian uncle stamped his sweetheart, Blanche Sweet, as a Common Woman. Where nature had once bloomed fair, Walthall now saw it as a series of systematic murders: a spider devouring a fly, an ant eating its neighbour. Brooding over Poe's 'The Tell-Tale Heart' the young man notes the physical resemblance between his uncle (Spottiswoode Aiken) and the old man in the story: both have only one eye. Inspired by Poe, the nephew kills his uncle and walls him up. Enter Ralph Lewis, detective, whose tapping pencil and tapping foot, coupled with a swinging pendulum and hooting owl, break the man down. It is perhaps the first visually rhythmic sequence in silent cinema, and hardly needed the explanatory subtitle: 'Conscience overburdened by the Tell-tale Heart'. Griffith contrived a happy ending by having the whole thing turn out to be a dream: no common cliché at the time.

Henry B. Walthall, a perfect Poe, played him again in 1915. This time it was Charles J. Brabin, of Essanay who reworked 'The Raven' as a full-blown six-reel biography, using as his basis a play by George C. Hazleton. Walthall was advertised as 'The image of Poe, a man of the same mould and temperament'. The *Dramatic Mirror* critic agreed, finding that his performance 'ceased to be acting and becomes at times almost uncanny'. Warda Howard

131

played both Virginia Clemm and Helen Whitman, not to mention 'A Spirit' and 'The Lost Lenore'. In this version it is her death in poverty that ultimately inspires Poe to write 'The Raven', after a night of brooding grief and distorted visions. He completes it, dies, and 'is wafted to the heights supernal where he is reunited with his Lenore'. The climax hardly accords to the facts, but it suited the style of 'the most ethereally artistic and soul-stirring drama of the year'.

The imaginative cartoon version of The Tell-Tale Heart'(1953)

(top, above) **Laurence Payne** tormented by the corpse he has buried beneath the floorboards but which still seems alive in *The Tell-Tale Heart* (1960)

The remaining silent films based on Poe's works were closer to the spirit of their subjects. Like the originals, they were all short, and they all tried to substitute visual effects for Poe's verbal imagery. In Germany, Richard Oswald included 'The Black Cat' in his *Unheimliche Geschichten* (1919), the first feature film to be built like an omnibus. Five short stories were visualised, four classics (including Stevenson's *Suicide Club*) and one specially written by Oswald and Richard Liebmann, *Der Spuk*, which caricatured the straight horror of the others. Conrad Veidt, the Sleepwalker of *Caligari*, was listed among the stars. *The Cabinet of Dr Caligari* with its strange, painted sets, influenced many young film-makers. These included Charles F. Klein, who made an experimental *Tell-Tale Heart* in 1927, James Sibley Watson and Melville Webber, who made an abstract *Fall of the House of Usher* in 1928, and Jean Epstein, who did the same film in France as *La Chute de la Maison Usher*, also in 1928.

Epstein and his assistant, a young man called Luis Bunuel, sought to simulate sound with animated objects, while Watson and Webber superimposed cartoon style lettering: B-e-a-t . . . c-r-a-c-k . . . s-c-r-e-a-m . . . But by now there was no need, for *The Jazz Singer* had sung, the Talkies had arrived, and the new whiz-kids of the Sound Department could supply all the beat-crack-screams any Poe picture would ever need. And, of course, they did.

POE'S MURDERS IN THE RUE MORGUE

THE EMPLOYMENT of an orang-outang in the committal of these murders has always seemed to me one of the most original ideas in fiction with which I am acquainted, until now, when I light upon an extract in the 'Chronicle' columns of the *Annual Register*. Poe's story was published in *Graham's Magazine* for April 1841. What took place at Shrewsbury occurred in July or August 1834. At that time certain showmen visited the town with a 'ribbed-faced

Still from 1971 version of 'Murders in the Rue Morgue'

baboon', which, it was afterwards shrewdly suspected, had been taught to burgle, or, as the 'Chronicle' puts it, and I underline, to 'commit robberies by night by climbing up places inaccessible to men, and thereby gaining an entrance through the bedroom windows' – precisely the method of procedure adopted by Poe's anthropoid. In her bedroom one night a Shrewsbury lady found the creature. She raised an alarm, and the baboon 'instantly attacked her, and with so much fury, that the lady's husband, who had come to the rescue, was glad to let it escape by the window'. The orang-outang of the 'Rue Morgue' makes a similar, though more fatal, attack when it is discovered in a lady's bedroom there, and effects its escape by the same means. It is, of course, possible that Poe may never have come across the episode; but it seems something more than probable that he did. Anyhow, the coincidence is singular.

W. F. WALLER
Notes and Queries, 12 May 1894

Karl Malden inspects the handiwork of the ' Phantom of the Rue Morgue' (1954)

Jason Robards in the clutches of the fearsome ape in the latest *Murders in the Rue Morgue* (1971)

Bela Lugosi with his caged orang outang in the 1932 *Murders in the Rue Morgue*

POE, CORMAN AND PRICE: A TALE OF TERRORS

RON HAYDOCK

FROM THE days of the silent Poe films, we jump to what is widely regarded as a remarkable era of pictures based on the master's stories made in the 1960s by the American director, Roger Corman, and starring the redoubtable actor, Vincent Price. Of course, there were films made of Poe's work in the intervening years, but they were in the main undistinguished and those of note are represented by stills on these pages. Perhaps one should just draw attention to the several versions of *The Murders in the Rue Morgue* (to date Poe's most filmed story), of which the best was certainly the 1932 version starring Bela Lugosi; *The Black Cat* made two years later in which Lugosi was teamed up with that other great terror star, Boris Karloff; and the two British efforts, *The Fall of the House of Usher*, starring Kaye Tendeter (1947) and *The Tell-Tale Heart* made in 1960 with Laurence Payne as the haunted murderer. In the article which follows, American screen expert Ron Haydock, recounts the story of the Poe–Corman–Price partnership which has resulted in a group of pictures still widely seen at cinemas and constantly reshown on television.

'And yet in the eyes of foreigners he is the most gifted of all authors of America . . .'

Professor Brander Matthews

133

The Edgar Allan Poe Scrapbook

TALKING ABOUT horror films one afternoon, Vincent Price said, 'They're fun; especially making these Edgar Allan Poe films, because of the medieval and Gothic costumes and settings.'

But writing 'In Defence of Horror Films', which was subsequently published in *Fantastic Monsters Magazine*, Price became more analytical.

Unlike any other type of motion picture, the terror or horror thriller offers the serious actor unique opportunity to fully exercise his craft and critically test his ability to make the unbelievable believable.

I also believe that such films as *The Raven* are additionally important to American culture at a time when method acting, and the sordid stories it usually accompanies, is considered in some quarters as a true reflection of American life. Actually, these 'method dramas' are representative of only a very small segment of our people.

It is in this time that the 'fairy-tale' quality of Poe's writings furnishes a very necessary and healthy entertainment escape-valve for the American public. Let those who condemn the thriller and horror pictures recall, too, that along with Westerns, this type of entertainment was responsible for the original success of our great motion picture industry.

Let's have more imaginative terror stories produced with our top talent and brains, and let's have less time-wasting and corrupting epics of degeneracy.

Overall, Vincent Price did very well with the Edgar

Roger Corman

Welcome – to the House of Usher by courtesy of Vincent Price and company (1960)

Cartoonist's comment on the making of *Tales of Terror* with Corman, Price and Peter Lorre (1962)

Allan Poe films he made for American International Pictures. Totalling them up, the Hollywood-based company produced thirteen Poe titles, and Price starred in all but only two of them. AIP's long, successful series included *The House of Usher* (1960), *The Pit and the Pendulum* (1961), *Poe's Tales of Terror* (1962), *The Premature Burial* (1962; with Ray Milland), *The Raven* (1963), *The Haunted Palace* (1964), *The Masque of the Red Death* (1964), *Tomb of Ligeia* (1965), *War Gods of the Deep* (1965), *The Conqueror Worm* (1968), *The Oblong Box* (1969), *Cry of the Banshee* (1970), and *Murders in the Rue Morgue* (1971; with Jason Robards). American International also released *Spirits of the Dead* (1969), a European vignette film which Price narrated.

Interestingly enough, the AIP-Poe films, while certainly popular and financially profitable in America alone, received even greater acclaim elsewhere in the world, just as had been the case with Poe's original stories. In France, the country that had, in fact, first recognised Poe's genius, the AIP films were so enthusiastically received and praised that entire cults rose up around them and also Roger Corman, who directed the first eight pictures. Particularly noted in the Corman films were 'the dream sequences'; usually bizarre, camera-distorted scenes that actually came the closest in any of the films to capturing the authentic nightmare quality so prevalent in Poe's tales of horror.

Vincent Price was the logical choice to star in the Poe films. At the time of the first film, *The House of Usher*, American International was looking to try and elevate its horror-film production schedule with movies of terror,

THE EDGAR ALLAN POE SCRAPBOOK

The stars of *Tales of Terror* **in a publicity shot: Price, Karloff, Rathbone and Lorre**

back in 1940 when he starred in Universal's *The Invisible Man Returns*, a sequel to that studio's first H. G. Wells thriller, *The Invisible Man*, released in 1933 with Claude Rains as the unseen one. But though Price was hardly much on view in *The Invisible Man Returns*, the film did mark his début in horror movies even if it did not immediately make him famous for such roles, as had *Frankenstein* for Boris Karloff, *Dracula* for Bela Lugosi, or *The Wolf Man* for Lon Chaney. It wasn't until eight years and many other kinds of movie roles later, in fact, that Price again took part in a horror film. At that, it was a horror-comedy,

Boris Karloff with his victims, including Vincent Price, in *The Raven* **(1963)**

suspense and monstrous doings on a larger budget than before; films that were also going to be made in colour now. Previously the studio had been building a very successful reputation as the leading producer of teenage horror films like *I Was a Teen Age Frankenstein*, *Invasion of the Saucer Men*, and *Ghost of Dragstrip Hollow* – black and white films that in the 1950s actually spawned an entire new cycle of horror movie type – but in 1960 AIP was looking to new and other kinds of fantastic-movie worlds to conquer. And Roger Corman, their star producer and director, thought he had the answer for them.

For a long time then, Corman once told me, he'd been wanting to make films based on the stories and poems of Edgar Allan Poe. For years he'd been grinding out science fiction, horror and action quickies which, although very successful productions, never quite seemed to satisfy his own, personal artistic aims. He believed he could produce and direct quality Poe films, and had brought this subject up a few times with James H. Nicholson and Samuel Z. Arkoff, the owners of American International, where he did most of his work. Nothing much came of it, though, until 1960, when Nicholson and Arkoff were sensing changing film trends and realising that, for the most part, the kinds of films they had been making were pretty much on their way out. They had to shoot for something else now; and what they aimed at was Corman's idea about making a Poe film. So they selected *The House of Usher*, and decided also to cast a major horror star in the lead role.

They decided on Vincent Price, who was extremely agreeable to the idea, and whose own ever-increasing fame as a newer star of shock films had begun seven years earlier with the big hit three dimension thriller, *The House of Wax*, and then continued on through the years with *The Mad Magician* (1954), William Castle's *The House on Haunted Hill* and *The Fly* (both 1958), and Castle's *The Tingler*, *The Return of the Fly*, and *The Bat* (all 1959).

Actually, Price first entered the worlds of screen horror

Abbott and Costello Meet Frankenstein, and in it Price again had the role of *The Invisible Man*. He 'appeared' in only the final few moments of the picture, however: his invisible hand lighting a cigarette, and his voice heard on the soundtrack taunting Bud Abbott and Lou Costello. This little bit, was more than enough to throw such a scare into the two comedians that they immediately jumped from their rowing-boat and frantically started swimming through a swampy lagoon for shore and safety.

'It must have taken me all of a minute or two to do that part,' Price said. 'They simply gave me a script, and I stepped up to a recording microphone at the studio. I read the few lines of dialogue a couple of times, laughed menacingly a couple of times, and that was it. No camera-work, no make-up, or anything.'

The later successes of *The House of Wax*, *The Tingler*, *The Return of the Fly* and the other 1950s films where Price was visibly active on screen certainly helped to make his name a household scareword, but starring in the Edgar Allan Poe films was where he gained for himself a solid and lasting recognition as a star of horror films. The Poe roles awarded Price much the same identification with movie terror as had the Frankenstein Monster for Karloff, or the vampire Dracula for Lugosi. In fact, it's difficult anymore *not* to think of Vincent Price whenever anybody, for whatever reason, even mentions the name of Edgar Allan Poe.

In the beginning, however, Nicholson and Arkoff of American International – much less Price himself – really had no idea that eventually they were going to be making an entire series of Edgar Allan Poe films. Their first picture, *The House of Usher*, was a sizeable financial gamble for them, they knew, and they only hoped the film would at least return them a reasonable profit. But after its release, *The House of Usher*, which co-starred Mark Damon and Myrna Fahey, chalked up such a healthy profit that they realised they had a very big hit on their corporative hands. So they decided to try another Poe film, *The Pit and the*

135

THE EDGAR ALLAN POE SCRAPBOOK

Pendulum, again with Price and Corman. Previous to this AIP film, Price had starred in a 1957 radio version of the classic tale, on CBS's famous *Suspense* programme, and unlike the AIP film, Price's radio script was extremely faithful to Poe's story, and was particularly memorable for the sequence in which Price has to ward off hordes of ravenous rats way down in the infamous black pit of horror, while the menacing, giant pendulum slowly, but persistently begins its well-calculated arc towards him.

But AIP's *The Pit and the Pendulum*, with John Kerr and Barbara Steele, proved itself even more successful than *The House of Usher*, and the following year Nicholson and Arkoff released two more Gothic and gloom-ridden Poe films: *Poe's Tales of Terror* and *The Premature Burial*.

Poe's Tales of Terror was another gamble for the studio. A vignette picture comprising four stories, *Poe's Tales of Terror* featured segments based on 'Morella', 'The Facts in the Case of M Valdemar', and 'The Black Cat' (which also incorporated the story 'The Cask of Amontillado'); and the gamble lay in the fact that in 1962 there still existed a strong, industry-wide prejudice against the making of just such an anthology film. Exhibitors, particularly, contended that audiences didn't want to see that kind of film; that what their customers wanted was a film with *one* story, not several; that such a vignette picture would only be a box office, disaster. But feeling that they had Edgar Allan Poe, Vincent Price, Roger Corman, and the success of their earlier Poe films on their side, Nicholson and Arkoff went ahead and made *Poe's Tales of Terror* anyway. To add more

Advertisement for *The Masque of the Red Death* (1964)

Vincent Price and Lon Chaney in *The Haunted Palace* (1964)

weight to their production, however, they decided to sign a larger-name cast than had ever before appeared in the Poe films.

They signed both Basil Rathbone and Peter Lorre, no little names to mystery and fantasy, besides Debra Paget, Joyce Jameson, and Leona Gage, a recent Miss America.

Ironically, for all the prejudice in the industry against making anthology horror films then, many of the classic horror stories in literature are short stories, with certainly those of Edgar Allan Poe the first and foremost. Novels like *Frankenstein, Dracula, Dr Jekyll and Mr Hyde*, or *The Werewolf of Paris* are exceptions rather than the rule. At that, one of the very best of all horror films is still *Dead of Night*, a British vignette film made in 1945 with Mervyn Johns, Michael Redgrave, Sally Ann Howes, and Anthony Baird. Today, of course, vignette films are not only very popular, but they've also helped build a whole new production company: Amicus Films, a British-based concern headed by Milton Subotsky and Max J. Rosenberg, who have produced very successful anthology screamers like *Dr Terror's House of Horrors, Tales from the Crypt*, and *The Vault of Horror*. Amicus have also produced entire films comprised of stories by Robert Bloch, who scripted the Amicus film versions himself: *The House That Dripped Blood, Asylum*, and *Torture Garden*, which featured Peter Cushing and Jack Palance in one story based on Bloch's famous tale 'The Man Who Collected Poe'.

The success of American International's *Poe's Tales of Terror* in 1962 helped set the precedent for the acceptability of making vignette horror films.

Because of other picture commitments, Price was not available to star in AIP's next Poe film, *The Premature Burial*, and for a time Christopher Lee was considered for the lead role of medical student Guy Carrell, who had a great fear of someday being buried alive. But finally Roger Corman, acting as both producer and director of the Poe films, signed Ray Milland, and *The Premature Burial* proved every bit as successful as any of the other films in what had by now become known as 'The Poe series'.

But Price returned strongly to Poe the next year in *The Raven*, a comic version of the poem co-starring Boris Karloff, Hazel Court, Jack Nicholson, and Peter Lorre, who played the Raven in human form, complete with bird feathers. *The Raven* hadn't actually started out as a comedy – it was only after looking at the daily takes, and seeing how humorous Lorre looked as a human raven, that Roger Corman decided they'd best start playing the rest of the film for laughs too. That way the audience would be laughing *with* a film that wasn't taking itself very seriously, rather than laughing *at* a film that was.

Following up on their casting of famous, long-established horror stars like Karloff, Rathbone, and Lorre in their Poe films, American International cast Lon Chaney in their next picture, *The Haunted Palace*, which turned out to be a combination of Poe's poem and the H. P. Lovecraft novel, *The Strange Case of Charles Dexter Ward*. In studio advertising, however, Lovecraft went uncredited as a source for the film.

A tale of necromantic revenge in medieval days, *The Haunted Palace* also turned out to be the last Poe film AIP made in Hollywood, where at Producers Studio art director Daniel Haller (later to become a director of horror films himself) had so magnificently created a time-thrashed, Poesque castle and all the other appropriately gloom-ridden sets that in no little way had been contributing so much to the appeal and success of the studio's Poe films. Starting with *The Masque of the Red Death* later that year – a *Masque* that was quite a lavish and colourfully macabre production with Price and Hazel Court – American International began making all their Poe films in England, and then Italy and Spain, and never again did they return Poe to his home country.

It was actually swiftly rising, unconquerable production costs that ended up driving AIP out of America with Poe. After making the eighth film, *Tomb of Ligeia*, about a man (Price) whose dead wife Ligeia (Elizabeth Shepherd) still exerts a horrible influence over him from the grave, Roger Corman dropped out of the series. At that, Corman practically halted his movie-directing activities altogether, no matter what kind of film, and turned more and more to trying to build his own film distribution company. In the late fifties he'd formed Filmgroup, but this first attempt at distribution was not successful. In the late sixties, however, and continuing through today, Corman's second try, New World Pictures, has more than proved its success. Besides releasing very many profitable 'bread and butter' exploitation films like *Private Duty Nurses*, *Lady Frankenstein*, *Caged Heat*, and *The Velvet Vampire*, Corman has also released in America Ingmar Bergman's *Cries and Whispers*, and other quality films of an artistic nature from around the world, films that have made him doubly important as a distributor and also given him a major recognition within the industry.

Jacques Tourneur directed the next Poe film, *War Gods of the Deep*, starring Price, Tab Hunter, and Susan Hart, and based on Poe's poem 'City in the Sea'. More nearly a Jules Verne adventure, with underwater citadels and deep sea horrors, *War Gods of the Deep* (appropriately enough, actually) didn't even carry the standard, and expected, advertising herald-line proclaiming the picture to be yet another tale of terror and suspense from the immortal pen of Edgar Allan Poe. Jacques Tourneur, though, had earlier directed Price, Karloff, Rathbone and Lorre in AIP's *Comedy of Terrors*, released after *The Raven* in 1963, and had come to AIP's horror and science fiction production line with frankly excellent credits.

In the 1940s, for producer Val Lewton, Tourneur had directed both the legendary *The Cat People*, with Simone Simon and Tom Conway, and *I Walked with a Zombie*, with James Ellison and Frances Dee. Then in 1958 Tourneur directed still another popular, famous and well-executed horror thriller: *Curse of the Demon*, with Dana Andrews and Peggy Cummins.

AIP's version of *The Conqueror Worm* followed. Directed by Michael Reeves, *The Conqueror Worm* was highlighted by Price reading Poe's poem on the sound-track, but the film itself, while one of the best shock *films* in the entire series, was hardly Poe. *The Conqueror Worm* enabled Price to give one of his better performances as a Witchfinder General in the days of the Inquisition, and the film was

Price and mourners at the Tomb of Ligeia (1965)

Witchfinder Price in *The Conqueror Worm* **made in 1968**

simply a good excuse to make a rather unnerving, and violent picture about all the terrible atrocities and persecutions that had been committed during that dark period of mankind's history.

Gordon Hessler directed the remaining three titles: *The Oblong Box*, *Cry of the Banshee*, and *Murders in the Rue Morgue*.

Vincent Price – Lord of the *City under the Sea* **(1965)**

Vincent Price's last Poe film, *Cry of the Banshee* **(1970)**

THE EDGAR ALLAN POE SCRAPBOOK

Christopher Lee finds more than he bargained for in *The Oblong Box* **(1969)**

The Oblong Box starred Price and Christopher Lee in a period thriller that looked as if it had leaped straight out of the pages of Alexandre Dumas, rather than Poe. Actually a very entertaining film, once you realised you were not supposed to be frightened or scared by the events in the story but thrilled by them, *The Oblong Box* played well and told the tale of a man hiding for most of his life behind a crimson mask, and of the earlier circumstances in Africa that had led him to become a prisoner in his own home in England.

The Oblong Box was the kind of film where the audience is always supposed to know more about what's going on than any character in the story, and director Hessler took good advantage of this aspect for building audience-suspense and anticipation of what was going to happen next, or what might likely happen next in the picture.

American International's next Poe release was exactly that: a release. In Europe, directors Roger Vadim, Louis Malle, and Federico Fellini had got together to film a vignette Poe movie, *Spirits of the Dead*, and AIP picked up distribution rights in America. The film, therefore, was not actually one of their own productions, although in America they did hire Price to narrate the opening and closing sequences on the sound-track. The various tales in *Spirits of the Dead* included 'Metzengerstein' (Vadim), with Peter Fonda and Jane Fonda; 'William Wilson' (Malle), with Brigitte Bardot and Alain Delon; and 'Never Bet the Devil Your Head' (Fellini), with Terence Stamp, Salvo Randone, and Anna Tonietti.

Despite the combined talents of Vadim, Malle and Fellini, though, *Spirits of the Dead* was something of a disaster, and vanished quickly from sight.

Vincent Price's last Poe film was *Cry of the Banshee*, a sometimes terrifying tale about a medieval castle and its wailing spectre that foretold doom. Then Gordon Hessler directed *Murders in the Rue Morgue* with Jason Robards, Lilli Palmer, and Herbert Lom to close out the AIP series. Like nearly all the Poe films, *Murders in the Rue Morgue* was also a very original screenplay only vaguely based on its original source, here spotlighting a theatre of the macabre on the rue Morgue in Paris, and telling of the horrible, recurring dreams about an axeman and an ape that are suffered by the theatre owner's wife, played by Christine Kaufman.

All the AIP-Poe films were financially successful ventures, though some were more so than others; but throughout the long run of the series many avid Poe devotees were heard to complain that the films were actually hardly Poe; that most of the screenplays really were much too original and free-wheeling with Poe's stories, and that in most cases the films didn't even capture, or try very much to capture, the true essence of despairing horror and terror and fear that is uniquely Poe.

Most of these arguments are, in fact, valid. Many of the films did simply, for example, use only a title or a line or two from Poe for their screen basis, and really owe very little to Poe. Richard Matheson's script for *The Pit and the Pendulum*, for one – although it does star an infamous pit of horrors, with its diabolical swinging pendulum – takes place some time after the days of the Spanish Inquisition Poe had written about, and also features a cast of characters and situations unknown to Poe's original story. Matheson's script for *The Raven*, too, is hardly anywhere near the 'Raven' Poe had in mind.

But, overall, the films were generally entertaining exercises in Gothic film horror; and it would be, I think, much more reasonable and fair to stop all argument about the debatable authenticity of the screen versions by saying that American International's series of Edgar Allan Poe films were not so much adapted from Poe's tales of mystery, horror and imagination as they were inspired, or *suggested*, by his timeless works.

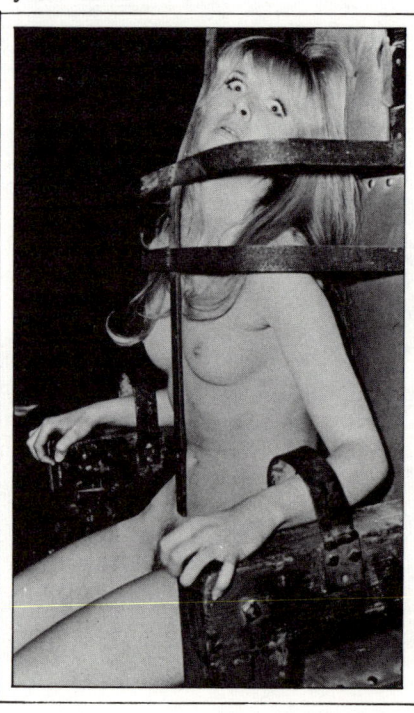

Jane Fonda, the beautiful star of *Spirits of the Dead* **(1969)**

The 'sexploitation' of Poe – a publicity shot for *Cry of the Banshee* **(1970)**

138

THE SPECTRES OF EDGAR ALLAN POE

STARTLINGLY UNIQUE among mystery writers because (for one thing) he actually invented the detective story, Edgar Allan Poe has also become quite an unusual literary giant because he's the only mystery writer ever to have been prominently featured in motion pictures. In 1954 Mickey Spillane became the first mystery writer who ever played himself in movies, in Warner Bros' *Ring of Fear*, but Poe's mythic figure has risen time and again in films that over the years have purported to show his life, his loves, and even how he came to write many of his most famous stories and poems.

One of the more recent examples of this interesting and generally speculative kind of Poe film fiction was Cinerama's *The Spectre of Edgar Allan Poe*, released in 1974. Starring Robert Walker Jr, who was made up to look amazingly like Poe, and directed by Mohy Quandor, who also wrote the screenplay, *The Spectre of Edgar Allan Poe* was blurbed by the studio with provocative advertising catchlines like 'What Drove Him Down Into A Bizarre World of Madness and Murder?' and opened by showing a young, carefree Poe romping happily through a Maryland countryside with his great love, the fragile Lenore (Mary Grover). At this point in his life, the film explained, Poe had not yet written a single horror or mystery story. He was still a cheerful, though struggling, romantic poet. Incredible tragedy, however, was swiftly coming his way.

First, Lenore died; apparently overcome by sheer exhilaration at running through the fields with Poe and then breathing deeply of the intoxicating scent of some wild flowers. Poe, however, did not believe she was dead. He thought she was only the victim of catalepsy, and at the last moment at the cemetery he flung open her coffin to find she was indeed still alive. Alive, yes, but existing now in only a catatonic trance, the result of her terrifying reactions to waking up and finding herself being buried alive in a coffin. This incident, presumably, later inspired Poe to write 'The Premature Burial'. But, before that, there were going to be many more horrors for Poe; horrors that he mostly, in fact, encountered at an insane asylum where he and his friend Dr Forrest (Tom Drake) shortly took Lenore for care and treatment.

The asylum was run by a Dr Grimaldi (Cesar Romero), whose own wife Lisa (Carol Ohmart) was only slightly more deranged than the doctor himself. Outwardly, they both seemed sane, and their characters suggested to audiences Poe's inspiration for 'The System of Dr Tarr and Professor Fether'. But it was while taking up residence at Grimaldi's institution that Poe in the film came into contact with horrors and terrors he would recall later when he started writing his macabre tales. Horrors like pits of poisonous, writhing snakes; unexplained, brutal murders; and horrendous tortures. It wasn't until Poe had witnessed the ultimate horror – the insane murder of his own helpless and beloved Lenore – that he finally 'cracked' and plunged headlong into the famous life of alcoholism and horror story-telling that was going to make him a world-renowned legend.

When Cinerama released this sometime frightening, but mostly long, drawn out and tediously evoked Poe drama in America, they coupled it with another film that, in part, also drew its inspiration from Poe: *Seizure*, starring Johnathan Frid of *Dark Shadows* fame as Edmund Blackstone, a prominent American writer of fantastic terror tales who was being hailed as this century's Poe. A nightmarish tale about Blackstone's own nightmares coming to life to haunt and threaten him at a week-end party at his secluded home, *Seizure* was, according to director-writer Oliver Stone, itself born of nightmares Stone himself had experienced.

Joseph Cotton as *The Man with a Cloak* **(1951)**

John Shepperd as Poe and Virgina Gilmore in *The Loves of Edgar Allan Poe* **(1924)**

Robert Walker Jnr as Poe in *The Spectre of Edgar Allan Poe* **(1974)**

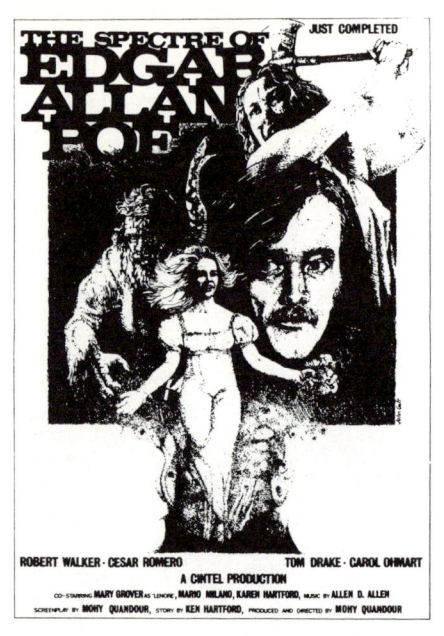

Poster for *The Spectre of Edgar Allan Poe* (1974)

'I woke up in the early dark hours of the morning terrified by images of death,' Stone said. 'I immediately noted them down', and over the period of a few months 'these notes became the basis for my screenplay about a man who experiences a nightmare and its consequences.'

There was a real Poe nightmare in Amicus's *Torture Garden*, directed by Freddie Francis in 1968. A vignette horror film based on stories by Robert Bloch, who also wrote the script, *Torture Garden* featured Peter Cushing as 'The Man who Collected Poe', literally. Besides owning various first editions of Poe's works, even original manuscripts, Cushing showed fellow Poe-enthusiast Jack Palance a never-before-seen Poe tale, written in Poe's own hand. The startling explanation behind this real collectors' item Poe manuscript was that in a secret room behind a wall at his house, Cushing had Poe's own corpse – which was kept alive (and writing new stories) through necromantic powers.

In 1964, Vulsina-Woolner's Italian production of *Castle of Terror* starring Barbara Steele and George Riviera proved itself an interesting Poe-influenced film about three young men (one of them Poe, played by Henry Kruger) who make a bet with Riviera that he doesn't have the nerve to stay the night in a nearby haunted castle. A period thriller directed by Anthony Dawson, *Castle of Terror* showed Riviera taking the bet, meeting vampiress Barbara Steele at the castle, and eventually being killed by Steele and her vampiric brood. When Poe and his two friends discover Riviera's blood-drained corpse the next day, Poe thinks it might make an interesting story to write about sometime.

The actual identity of Edgar Allan Poe, however, wasn't known to audiences until this final moment. It was something of a surprise finish. All along, Poe had been introduced as simply an American writer in Europe looking for interesting stories. MGM's *The Man with a Cloak*, released in 1951, was another surprise Poe film.

Directed by Fletcher Markle from John Dickson Carr's story, 'The Gentleman from Paris', *The Man with a Cloak* starred Joseph Cotten as Poe. The tale took place in New York City in 1849 and involved a certain, rather inexplicable young man named 'Thaddeus Perley' solving a locked-room murder mystery and also, in the film, falling under the amours of the female lead, Barbara Stanwyck. 'Thaddeus Perley' eventually being disclosed as none other than Poe himself was one of the main elements of *The Man with a Cloak*, and in the Whodunit tradition of playing fair with the reader or audience, MGM's film version gave theatre audiences as many as fourteen different clues throughout the picture as to who exactly was the mysterious Man with a Cloak.

Fox's *The Loves of Edgar Allan Poe* in 1942 was more traditional Poe film fiction. Ostensibly a 'biography' of Poe, it was directed by Harry Lachman and focused on Poe's life and tragic loves, with the interesting addition here to Poe's life of no less a personage than Charles Dickens (Morton Lowry), who befriends Poe in the film. Another 'biography' of Poe was Essanay's *The Raven* in 1915. Directed and written by Charles J. Brabin from a novel and stageplay by George C. Heyetta, *The Raven* starred Henry B. Walthall as Poe, with Warda Howard as one of the many women in his life.

Like the later *Loves of Edgar Allan Poe*, 1915's *The Raven* also came to its climax with Poe's tragic and untimely death in Baltimore.

Ironically, unlike films based on actual Poe stories – films like *The Pit and the Pendulum*, *The House of Usher*, *Masque of the Red Death*, *The Mystery of Marie Rogêt*, and *The Black Cat*, among so many more – films *about* Edgar Allan Poe have never been particularly successful with audiences. Perhaps this is because while a Poe horror story is, or can be, sheer escape, a story about the writer himself can hardly ever be that. No matter how much licence or plain distortion or manufacturing of facts about his life there are in the film, Poe as a living figure is always, inevitably, shown as a quite tragic figure *not* redeemed by the final fade-out.

Any story about Poe's life and times is invariably a glimpse behind the scenes at the reality behind all the great horror, mystery and suspense tales Poe wrought – and reality, of course, is a commodity most people prefer to leave outside when they go to the movies.

RON HAYDOCK

Poe restored to life and literary activity in *Torture Garden* (1967)

THE EDGAR ALLAN POE SCRAPBOOK

The Poe House, Philadelphia (SERGEI TROUBETZKOY, POE FOUNDATION INC)

The Poe House, Baltimore (SERGEI TROUBETZKOY, POE FOUNDATION INC)

THE POE INDUSTRY

POE, A sad, rejected soul during his liftime, has, in the century and a quarter since his death, become both an international figure and the centre of a flourishing 'industry'. Perhaps he would find some comfort in the fact that thousands of writers who were born and died after him and enjoyed fame while they lived – something denied to him – are now forgotten, while his work is accorded the stature of immortality. There is scarcely a country in the world where his essays, poems and stories are not continually in print and his name is as familiar to the lovers of literature as those of Chaucer, Balzac and Shakespeare.

As has been shown in the pages of this book, Poe's work has been a source of entertainment and excitement to readers everywhere, not to mention the inspiration of poets, writers and film-makers. From one corner of the globe to another, men of words have drawn on his style and themes to develop the genres he created and in doing so give honour to his memory. Studies of his life and work now fill a library and show no signs of abating; interpretations of his purpose and motives absorb scholars in one controversy after another.

Such is the fascination with the man and his legend that, for instance, in Japan, the leading writer of crime and fantasy stories has even adopted a variation of his mentor's name for his own – Edogawa Rampo. Many others, such as Julian Hawthorne (son of the famous Nathaniel), Walter de la Mare, John Dickson Carr, *et al*, have featured Poe as a central figure in some of their best work.

Poe has, not surprisingly, inspired creativity in media other than stories and films. Plays have been made from his tales, and as recently as 1975, The London Theatre Group were performing a version of 'The Fall of the House of Usher' of which the magazine *Time Out* reported 'The tension is kept up not by the progress of the narrative or by any consistent individual line, but by very carefully orchestrated movement, sound and light – it is a visual feast.' The master has himself been the subject of plays, perhaps none

News clipping from *Monster Times*, June 1974

Edgar Allan Poe Museum, Richmond (POE FOUNDATION INC)

141

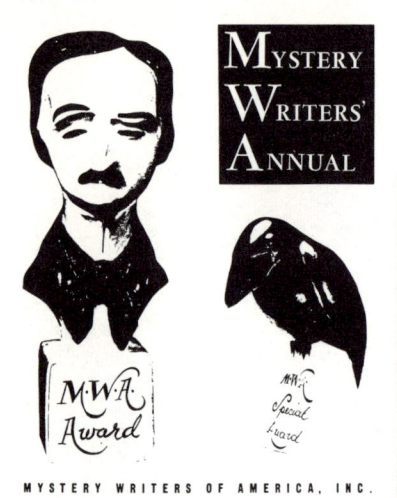

THE EDGAR ALLAN POE SCRAPBOOK

Above left: The coveted 'Edgar' and 'Raven' awards

Above right: One of many records based on Poe material

Below: The 'Enchanted Garden' of the Edgar Allan Poe Museum, Richmond (POE FOUNDATION INC)

On a more serious note, Poe has given his name to several literary awards, the most important being the 'Edgar' presented annually by the Mystery Writers of America Inc. 'The Edgar Allan Poe Award', to give it its full title, consists of a little statuette of Poe and carries the same distinction in the world of mystery writing as the 'Oscar' in films and 'Tony' in television.

Among the categories for which the award is given are the best novel and fact crime book of the year; the Grand Master Award for outstanding contributions to the art of mystery-suspense writing (Graham Greene and Jorge Luis Borges were two recent recipients); and 'Ravens' for the best hardcover and paperback cover designs.

In America, too, there is the annual $5,000 Edgar Allan Poe Poetry Award which 'recognises a younger poet's continuing development on the occasion of a new book of poems' (something Poe would surely have approved), while in Europe the top E.A.P. prize is probably that awarded in Denmark which has done much to promote excellent mystery writing throughout Scandinavia.

His memory is also kept fresh in a number of American universities and museums where materials – including letters, manuscripts and early editions of his books – and also souvenirs of his life and work are made available to students and interested parties. In this context one should particularly mention the University of Virginia (which Poe, of course, briefly attended), the J. K. Lilly Collection at Indiana University, and the Poe Memorabilia in the University of Texas.

more distinguished than *Edgar Allan Poe: A Drama in Five Acts and Seven Scenes* written by the Russian, Valentin Bulgakov, and – demonstrating the universal appeal of Poe – first published in Tientsin, China, in 1940!

On both sides of the Atlantic Poe's work is seen regularly on television, and the highly acclaimed CBS *Mystery Theatre Show* on radio devoted an entire week to dramas based on his stories to celebrate its first year of broadcasting.

Long-playing records have also been released with actors reading some of Poe's most gripping tales, and particularly outstanding are the narrations by Nelson Olmstead, Basil Rathbone and – inevitably – Vincent Price.

Of late Poe has become a 'star' of posters, T-shirts and advertising copy, not forgetting comic books where his stories have provided staple material for the talented artists of the Marvel Comics Group and individual publications such as *Scream*, *Nightmare* (see page oo), *Eerie* and *Psycho*. The Warren Publications magazine *Creepy* went so far as to devote an entire issue to six Poe stories! (During the sixties, Dell Publications brought out a series of one-shot comics, which are now collector's items, based on the Roger Corman-Vincent Price films.)

Some of the souvenirs sold at the Edgar Allan Poe Museum in Richmond

THE EDGAR ALLAN POE SCRAPBOOK

Poe – perennial favourite subject of the horror comics: this feature appeared in *Nightmare*, 1971

Right: 'The Pit and the Pendulum' from a recent issue of *Creepy* (1975) entirely devoted to Poe – and in comparison the first known illustration of the same story (1852) with an almost miniature pendulum!

Stan Lee's *Marvel Comics* update a Poe tale 'Day of the Red Death' in 1971

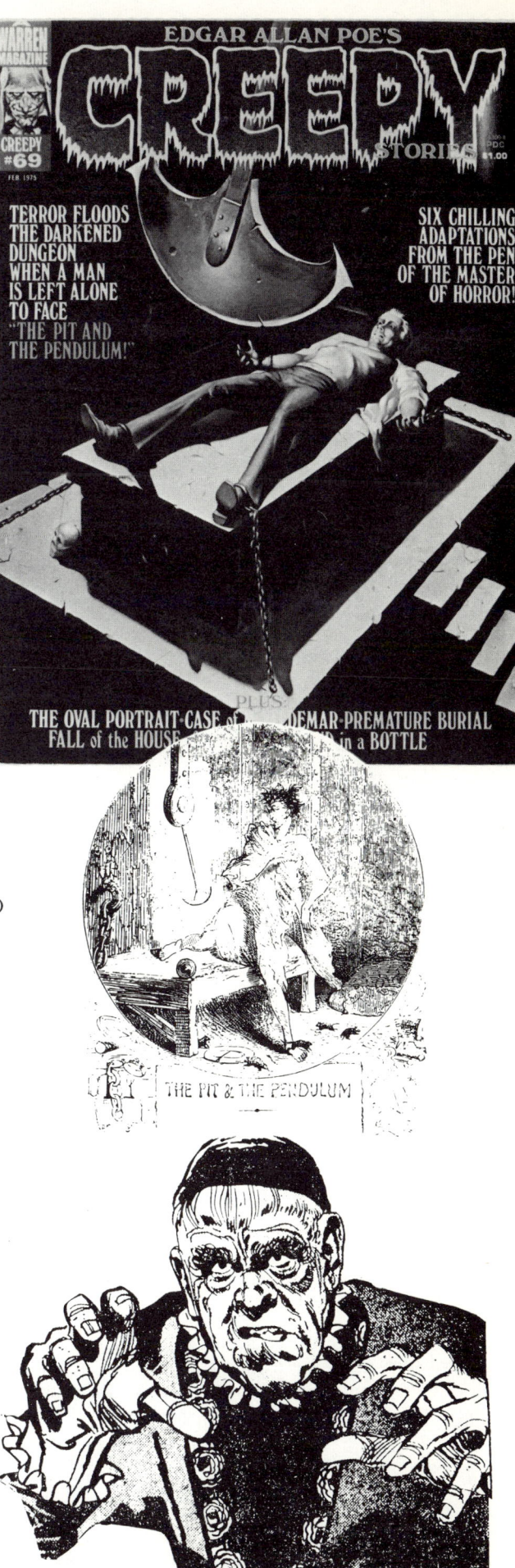

A menacing Boris Karloff from the *Dell Comics* version of 'The Raven' (1963) – now a much sought-after collectors' item

143

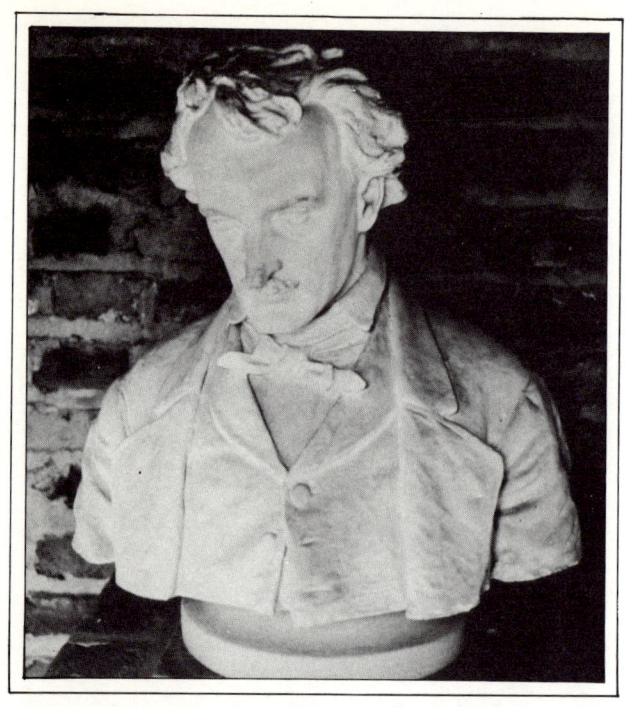

The bronze bust of Edgar Allan Poe by Edmund Quinn at the Fordham Cottage in New York

OUT OF DICKINSON BY POE
or
THE ONLY BEGOTTEN SON OF EDGAR & EMILY

Strange tryst was that from which stillborn
I still knew life midsummer morn,
And son of Emily/Edgar both
Did suck dry teat and swill sour broth;
And midnight know when noon was there,
And every summer breeze foreswear.
Gone blind from stars and dark of moon
This boychild grew from wry cocoon;
For I was spun from spider hands
And misconceived in Usher Lands,
And all of Edgar's nightmares mine
And Em's dust-heart my valentine.
Thus mute old maid and maniac
Then birthed me forth to cataract -
That whirlpool sucked to darkest star
Where all the unborn children are.
So I was torn from maelstrom flesh
And saw in x-ray warp and mesh
A sigh of polar-region breath
That whispered skull-and-socket death.
Em could not stop for Death, so Poe
Meandered graveyards to and fro
And laid his tombstone marble bride
as Jekyll copulated Hyde
And birthed a panic-terror son.
And thus was I, mid-night, begun.
— Ray Bradbury

Anniversary tribute by Ray Bradbury from *Magazine of Fantasy and Science Fiction,* **October 1976**

The Poe Cottage at Fordham is still preserved – though somewhat in need of attention as the cutting reproduced here shows – and there are Poe houses in Baltimore and Philadelphia. A plaque marks the spot near his birthplace in Boston, and his tomb still stands on view in Baltimore. Perhaps of most interest to the general reader is the Edgar Allan Poe Museum in Richmond, Virginia, a shrine to his memory and a focal point for students of his legend. (The museum's brochure is reproduced here, as are a number of photographs and souvenirs all supplied by courtesy of the Poe Foundation Inc and its dedicated and efficient curator, Denise B. Bethel.)

When Poe died in the early hours of the morning of Sunday, 7 October 1849, his last uttered words were reported to be, 'God help my poor soul'. Little could he realise as he went to seek his rest that time was already at work establishing his genius and creating his legend. Today there is no question as to his greatness, as his biographer Arthur Hobson Quinn has so succinctly put it in his work, *Edgar Allan Poe* (1941):

His fame is now secure. The America in which he could find no adequate reward treasures every word he wrote, and in every city in which he lived stands a lasting memorial to him. He has become a world artist and through the translation of his writings he speaks today to every civilised country. He has won this wide recognition by no persistent clamour of a cult, but by the royal right of pre-eminence. For today, over a hundred years since his death, he remains not only the one American, but also the one writer in the English language, who was at once foremost in criticism, supreme in fiction, and in poetry destined to be immortal.

PETER HAINING

POE DESCENDANT KEEPS THE HORROR TRADITION ALIVE!

I HAVE tried all the other horror magazines and I came back to *Nightmare*. Your last issue was great – the story that grabbed me as the best of the issue was 'Greed', it was well written and the art was exciting and unusual.

I am related to Edgar Allan Poe and I'm glad to see one publishing corporation doing a lot of his stories . . .

CHRIS ROOSE
Merritt Island, Florida

Just about all the Poe stories are currently being illustrated by artists, and will be presented soon . . . not only is it our pleasure to adapt and illustrate the works of Entombed Edgar – it's our privilege! Editor.

Nightmare, April 1974

A supernatural reason for Poe's genius? From *Ghosts,* **1975**